The Idea of EQUALITY

The
Idea
of
EQUALITY

An Anthology
by George L. Abernethy

JOHN KNOX PRESS
Richmond, Virginia

TO HELEN

Preface

The idea of equality lies embedded in the very foundation of western civilization, in the amalgamation of Greek, Roman, and Hebraic-Christian ideas and institutions. In part, it is based upon conceptions of natural right and natural law, which are essential elements of a sound philosophy of man and nature and God. Thus it possesses a considerable history before it receives characteristic statement in the great legal and political documents of the eighteenth century. Since the history of the idea of equality has received much less attention than the history of liberty, this anthology seeks to bring together a wide variety of characteristic statements which reveal the historical development of the idea of equality. There is of course a certain violence done to a man's thought when specific passages from his writings are selected which may contradict what he has written elsewhere or about which he may have later changed his mind. No claim is intended here that the selections are always completely representative of a man's work. The purpose is rather to reveal something of the range and complexity of the development of the idea of equality in western thought. The basic pattern of the development and operation of the idea of equality can be discovered only by a historical study of its empirical data.

The question of what equality should mean in practical terms in our contemporary urban and technological civilization characterized by cultural heterogeneity and uncertainty about the value and purpose of an individual's life is indeed a difficult and pressing problem. This anthology does not offer the systematic analysis which this question requires. Its modest hope is that it may give some historical perspective which may illumine and restrain the less flexible analyses of this question.

G. L. A.

Davidson College
Davidson, North Carolina

Contents

Introduction

The idea of equality is one of the great seminal ideas in our political, social, economic, and religious history. Its primitive origins are lost in the unrecorded history of a dim past. Fortunately, something of the record of its role in the development of Hebraic-Christian, Greek, Roman, and modern democratic ideas, which have shaped our civilization, has been preserved. This anthology seeks to bring together in a convenient form some of the typical statements in which thinkers of the West have formulated their various conceptions of equality.

Liberty, equality, and fraternity are rightly held to be the operative ideals of democratic thought. The roots of modern democratic thought are to be found in the seventeenth and eighteenth centuries. The idea of equality, however, antedates modern democratic theory. Some of its roots are found in ancient communities which were aristocratic and slave-owning. Some modern developments in equalitarianism have occurred independently of the framework of democratic ideas. As important and subtle as is the relation of equality to liberty and fraternity, it would be unhistorical to limit the consideration of equality to its role in the democratic trinity. It may be reassuring to many to discover how old and persistent the idea of equality is. It has grown out of common ways of life and out of the criticism of them. Its growth, like that of any other fundamental idea or ideal, was not always even, orderly, or consistent. But the reality and significance of its development invite our understanding and appreciation.

Undoubtedly one of the roots of the idea of equality lies in the experience of the ancient Hebrews in their Covenant with God. The Book of the Covenant was the earliest instance of the social contract, in idea and to a considerable extent in actual practice. Under the Covenant, God governed through His Law which was binding on all and thus a moral guarantee to all of equal justice. It is obvious that men are born with different capacities and talents, but such inequalities have no particular relevance to God's concern with His creatures. In relation to God all men are equal, possessing no rights but only duties. Man has come on earth simply to fulfill his Creator's purposes and to perform His will. God is no respecter of persons. Every man owes his existence to God, who requires infinite dedication and absolute obe-

15

dience. Thus all men are equally dependent upon God for the continuance of their lives, and all equally owe Him infinite service in return for infinite mercy. It was the Hebrew prophets who taught for all generations the ideal of the reign of equity which God had instituted for all His equal children. In the light of that system of divine equity all earthly governments are unjust. It is, therefore, not surprising that many American and British movements in the direction of social and political equality have sought sanction and inspiration in the teachings of the Old Testament prophets.

It is clear that there are important differences between the problems and institutions of ancient Greek city-states and those of contemporary urban and industrialized, democratic societies. To the Athenians of the fifth century B.C., however, equality had much of the meaning which it possesses for us today. Within the limits of the free citizenry all men were equal. They shared equally in making public decisions, and under normal circumstances in Athens one in six could hope to hold public office during his lifetime. Early expressions of the notion of human equality are found in the writings of Herodotus, Thucydides, Plato, and Aristotle. In Book II of his *History*, Herodotus represents three Persians—Otanes, Megabyzus, and Darius—as discussing the relative merits of monarchy, aristocracy, and democracy. Otanes, the defender of democracy, after commenting on the behavior of kings, says: "As for the rule of the multitude, first its very name is so beautiful —equality before the law: then it settles offices by lot, it makes officials responsible to scrutiny, it brings all deliberation to the community."

In Thucydides' *History*, in the speech of Pericles democracy receives one of its noblest and most eloquent defenses. Pericles makes explicit references to the equal freedom of speech and political action possessed by Athenian citizens and to the equality of opportunity which they enjoyed. Obviously such equality does not imply economic equality, nor does it assume the fundamental identity of human nature. Plato was critical of the Periclean ideal that citizens could share equally in the public business and make contributions to, as well as receive benefits from, the commonwealth. In fact, it never occurred to Plato and Aristotle that all men everywhere are equal. They did recognize that citizens were equal in their participation in the common decisions of the city-state. But the consequences and quality of these decisions came in for very sharp and persistent criticism by Plato. Beyond a belief that all individuals had an equal chance to carry on their functions in the state, however humble, and the belief that the relative equality of the sexes made advisable co-education, it cannot be said that Plato possessed much interest in equality.

Aristotle, the great advocate of the golden mean, advanced as the most practicable form of government a moderate democracy. He believed that a city ought to be composed, "as far as possible, of equals and similars; and these are generally the middle classes. Wherefore the city which is composed of middle-class citizens is necessarily best constituted." No one should infer from this that Aristotle is an apostle of equalitarian democracy. It is true that he believed that all citizens alike should take their turn of governing and being governed and that equality consists in the same treatment of similar persons. But Aristotle did not think it undemocratic to exclude from the body of the citizens, not only the slaves, resident aliens, and women, but the mechanics, tradesmen, and husbandmen. From the perspective of our own century, Aristotle seems perverse in regarding a majority of men as by nature slaves and unfit to participate in political life, thereby throwing away one of the main advantages of the small size of the city-state which he had realistically observed makes it possible for all of its inhabitants to share fully in its life. It should be noted that in his numerous comments on equality Aristotle is usually discussing not arithmetic equality, but proportionate equality—to each according to his deserts or virtue. This kind of equality is, for Aristotle, just and necessary for the good life. The absence of proportionate equality, of a fair deal, is what splits the city-state into factions and destroys the essential sense of community. Aristotle reveals his standard when he states: "If the persons be not equal, their shares will not be equal; and this is the source of disputes and accusations, when persons who are not equal receive equal shares."

Fragments from the provocative and often contradictory teachings of the Greek Sophists have survived. Among them are vigorous denials of the absolute distinction between freemen and slaves. Alcidamas, the student of Gorgias, is reported to have said, "God set all men free. Nature has made none a slave." Not only did Antiphon the Sophist disapprove of the custom of honoring his fellow Greeks on the mere ground of ancestry, he also argued that since in the physical process of growth all men are alike, keeping alive by means of breathing and eating, Greeks and Barbarians do not differ and should be treated alike. Lycophron advanced the view that the weak naturally become strong if they keep together, and that the power of the nobles was a figment of the imagination since there was no difference between the well-born and the low-born. All of these ancient assertions anticipate later doctrines.

These early Greeks never really achieved the ideals of universal citizenship and of universal law. These contributions we owe to the developments that stemmed from the Stoic notion of rational justice and from the Hebraic-Christian prophetic insistence on the Fatherhood of God and the brotherhood of man. During the troubled times of the second and third centuries B.C. which followed Alexander's conquests and early death, the gradual disintegration of the independent city-states, and the collapse of various dynasties, the Stoic school formulated its philosophy. Its teachings were fundamentally an effort to provide peace of mind and fortitude during a period of cultural disorganization and to fashion wider loyalties and deeper perspectives to replace those that had crumbled. Its teachers were speculative thinkers and rational mystics rather than the architects of a new social order.

To the Stoics the entire universe was the creation of reason and man could understand it if he used his own reason. Everything in the universe partook of this reason. They identified reason with God and thus attributed to each man a spark of divinity. This universe was seen to be the product of a divine purpose, revealing itself throughout nature in a rational plan. God is not transcendent or external to the universe. God is immanent or all-pervading, since wherever there is reason there is God. From these metaphysical doctrines the Stoics drew conclusions which had a profound social relevance. Reason embodied itself throughout the universe as law or laws. Any rational creature had, therefore, a share of these laws and was bound by them. The Stoics uncompromisingly affirmed the equality of all human beings. This was in sharp contrast to the teaching of Plato and Aristotle. To the Stoics the differences between human beings were less important than their resemblances. Thus the Stoics rejected the institution of slavery as an unnatural institution. They also emphasized the fact that individual differences in the reasoning ability of men are less important than the fact that everyone alike possesses some ability to reason. This accounts for the unity of mankind and at the same time differentiates man from the animals. Consequently, for the Stoic, the quality of being human does not admit of degree. As human beings, all are equal. When one denies that any human being is a full member of the human race or that he is entitled to equal consideration, he denies or rejects a fragment of divinity. The Stoics taught that there were laws universally operative to which we humans must conform. They readily admitted the differences between the various positive human systems of law. But they pointed out that positive human law is really binding only to the extent that it conforms to the higher universal law. The Stoics were not democrats although these ideas did reappear in the seventeenth and eighteenth centuries when equalitarian and other democratic ideas were being hammered out in political controversy.

It was left to the Romans to give full practical expression to the ideas of the Stoics. Although the Romans were the most successful governmental administrators of the ancient world, they had to import Greek philosophy to justify and interpret their political activities. The century that marked the importation of Stoicism coincided with the great expansion of Roman military power over the countries that surrounded the Mediterranean. As legal disputes arose involving these subject peoples, with different cultural and legal traditions, the Romans established a special court to hear the cases of foreigners. If the presiding judge could find common legal principles in the territories of both parties to the dispute, he would render a decision in terms of them. If not, he would attempt to settle the case as equitably as he could. Over a period of time these decisions established a body of precedents out of which developed the "law of the peoples" or *jus gentium*. Although the Roman jurists had been working pragmatically and inductively with particular cases, they evolved a coherent system of general principles which included principles of law and right common to or observed by all peoples. The philosophers with their Stoic inheritance concluded that the common legal concepts which the Roman jurists had formulated and applied by the use of reason were really the workings of the same immanent reason the Stoics had taught was the law of the universe. Although *jus gentium* came to terms with the institution of slavery, the Stoic conception of natural law and *jus gentium* tended to converge in a belief in the equality and unity of mankind.

The Romans went even further in demonstrating their practical support of the principle of equality in the extension of Roman citizenship. In building up their empire the Romans had the military problem of maintaining the loyalty of conquered peoples. Often the Romans were very brutal in the early stages of their conquests. When a new generation grew up the Romans frequently softened their policy and granted some rights and privileges to the conquered. Gradually a few leaders were made citizens and then finally all inhabitants of the conquered territory were granted citizenship. Roman citizenship was of course not like the citizenship of Athens which involved direct democratic participation in the governing of the city-state. In A.D. 212 the Emperor Caracalla granted full citizenship to all free (non-slave) inhabitants of the empire. This was a momentous achievement even though a motivating factor was the desire of the imperial treasury to extend the application of inheritance taxes. It should be viewed in the light of the failure of the Greeks to grant citizenship to conquered peoples.

The Christian contributions to the idea of equality were important and far-reaching. They both reinforced and changed some of the emphases of the Greek philosophers and the Roman jurists. St. Paul wrote to the Galatians: "There is neither Jew nor Greek, there is neither bond nor free, there is neither male nor female: for ye are all one in Christ Jesus." This teaching united Stoic, Roman, and Christian emphases. In the light of it Paul has sometimes been criticized for his acceptance of slavery; he did send Onesimus back to his master. Slavery was of course lawful, but for Paul the slave was not a slave by nature. The circumstances of war induced by the corrupt nature of man had enslaved him. But the slave was a child of God, had reason and was capable of virtue. Paul and the later Church Fathers may have "accepted" the fact of slavery in the temporal world, but they did not agree with Aristotle that some men were slaves by nature nor consider that the distinction between bond and free was of any significance within the fellowship of the Christian Church.

It should be noted that the Christian doctrine of equality found its institutional expression in the establishment of a Church where the inequalities of the political order were often annulled or reversed. "Ye see your calling, brethren," the Apostle Paul reminds the Corinthian Christians, "how that not many wise men after the flesh, not many mighty, not many noble, are called: but God hath chosen the foolish things of the world to confound the wise; and God hath chosen the weak things of the world to confound the things which are mighty; and base things of the world, and things which are despised, hath God chosen, yea, and things which are not, to bring to nought things that are." Human society might display the great contrasts of power and weakness, luxury and poverty, elevated status and lowliness. Yet the value of the individual soul was to be judged not by mere man, but by God whose universal Fatherhood made all men brothers and who was no respecter of persons. Even in the most corrupt phases of its later history when inequalities and distinctions became important, the Christian Church did not mirror exactly the inequalities of the secular world. Christianity taught that it was in terms of their souls, which could be either saved or lost, that men stood on level ground in the sight of God. The purity of heart, humility, and chastity which the Church taught were important in establishing the proper communion of the individual soul with God. The rich and powerful were the ones handicapped in the struggle for salvation, since their earthly position made them vulnerable to greater temptation and thus more likely to fall into sin. Christianity made the distinction between social and moral superiority sharper than it had been made previously in antiquity.

In the primitive Church there was undoubtedly something like a communistic equality of goods. Yet even here the stress was not on a this-worldly sharing of production or goods, but on a generous and spontaneous outpouring of love among spiritual equals. Their special talents or positions are simply incidental. Fellowship with God is something that completely transcends any human distinction between more or less. In the writings of Church Fathers in the fourth century there is an obvious strain of Stoic rationalist ideas of the equality of man. This comes to an end with the triumph of Augustinian concepts of predestination which established the orthodox view that worldly inequality is a necessary part of the divine scheme of things. Inequality is stressed as a consequence of a fall willed by God and thus completely different from the Stoic law of nature.

The medieval Church reflected the feudal organization of society and the organic theory of the state. One cannot characterize its inner life as democratic and equalitarian. It demanded strict obedience in the ecclesiastical hierarchy, and it permitted some priests to live in splendor while others lived in bare poverty. However, the priestly office was always in theory, and often in practice, open to all men on equal terms. This provided a kind of "equality of opportunity" in medieval society. Medieval theologians and philosophers, however, were not interested in deducing from their premises any conclusion to the effect that political institutions should seek for every individual an equal opportunity to share in the supreme values for which those institutions were established. In general, they fell back on Aristotle's notion of the division of labor for the common good and on Augustinian predestination. It was easy, then, to interpret the unequal sufferings of men and worldly inequalities as punishment for original sin. Medieval thinkers readily accepted social stratification, inequality of political rights, and the concentration of a paternalistic authority in the hands of the few without the consent of the governed.

There were some efforts made to introduce democratic ideas into the medieval system. Nicholas of Cusa used the doctrine of the original freedom and equality of men to support the idea that government must be based on popular consent. Marsilius argued that good government was more likely to be achieved through the inclusion of all citizens in the base of authority. Also, the idea that "what touches all must be approved by all" had great appeal to many writers and legal minds as a basic premise whenever the public good seemed to require the invasion of the area of private rights by the ruler. But the logical and historical conclusions of such ideas had to await the development of profound social and economic changes for effective implementation in modern times. The fate of the Hussites and Lollards, who mixed medieval heresy with something like the demand for social and political equality, underlines this point.

The contribution of the Protestant Reformers to the development of the idea of equality is complex and difficult to assess. For example, one may search the writings of John Calvin without discovering much that would support equalitarianism, democracy, or a favorable estimate of the common man. There is no question that Calvin and Calvinism strengthened the doctrines of predestination, of the sinfulness of man, and of the incommensurability of God's plan and man's. Calvinism reinforced the notion that human inequalities cannot be remedied. Yet Calvin in a very real sense stressed equality. He rejected the idea of the necessity of the clergy as mediators between God and the laity. He denied the whole hierarchy of offices. In fact, among the elect, the saved, there is no distinction of persons. They are all equal in the sight of God—a classical Christian doctrine. For Calvin the constitution of the Church was democratic: lay elders are to be elected by the community because there is "a common right and liberty" in the Church in the election of ministers. Calvinism applied its rigorous moral code to all without distinction of rank or wealth. The explosion of Calvinism in the English Revolution gave dramatic expression to equalitarianism and democratic ideas.

The period from 1640 to 1789 is the period in which the modern democratic state emerged as shaped, in part, by the English, American, and French Revolutions. In the spate of ideas from which these revolutions developed and which they extended we single out the idea of equality as it functioned in the English Revolution among the Levellers, farmers, artisans, and small tradesmen with Puritan or Calvinist backgrounds serving in Cromwell's army. These Levellers, or political democrats, were led by John Lilburne, who in 1638 was just out of his apprenticeship in the wool trade. As the civil war progressed he became increasingly the spokesman of the rank and file in the Parliamentary army. He protested against certain oppressive features of church order, and he urged constitutional reform in the political order. He denounced, as violations of English law and God's plan for man, certain existing conditions of society which denied equality of opportunity to men of his class. Although Lilburne's ideas and specific proposals were rejected by his contemporaries, they became the working principles of British and American democracy in the nineteenth century.

The Leveller ideas owed much to the Hebraic-Christian tradition of a spiritual equality among men. From believing that all Christians are reborn free and equal, the Levellers proceeded to the claim first that all Englishmen and finally that all men are born free and equal. They went on to argue that the authority of the state should rest upon a basic law, an Agreement of the People, stated in written form for all to understand and obey, governors and governed alike. Under such an agreement the authority of the state would be vested in a representative assembly chosen by the equal vote of all citizens. Such a state would maintain the equal right of each citizen to worship in whatever Christian form his conscience dictated, to think and speak freely, to have equality before the law, and to have opportunity to hold property and engage in trade.

The Levellers insisted that it was in the people that the sovereignty lay, and that it was only by their consent that Parliament governed. It has never been put more vividly than by Colonel Rainborough, a Leveller spokesman in the Putney Debates in Cromwell's army: "For I really think that the poorest he that is in England hath a life to live, as the greatest he; and therefore truly, sir, I think it's clear, that every man that is to live under a government ought first by his own consent to put himself under that government . . ." The Levellers furnish us with the first important example of the insistence upon the rights of persons as against the rights of property and vested interests. We need to remember the circumstances which made possible the development whereby John Lilburne and his followers were able to participate on more nearly equal terms than ever before with their social and political superiors in the life of the community. One was the experience of leadership and confidence which they drew from their own participation as equals in the self-governing Christian congregations. The other was the development of printing and the book trade. The circulation of the Bible among the people after 1560 undoubtedly stimulated the publication of books and tracts. It has been determined that (during the course of the English Civil War) more than twenty thousand tracts were published which must have been the first great mass experiment in adult education. Undeniably this had a profound effect upon popular thinking about the Church and society.

Although their writings frequently refer to the economic distress which the English Civil War brought to the lower middle class, the Levellers, as radical democrats, looked for relief primarily through a program of more radical political equality and the removal of such legal discriminations as monopoly. There was, however, a small left-wing group known as "True Levellers" or Diggers who saw the political revolution as an opportunity to extend economic equality and to remove the burden of poverty from the masses. These utopian socialists or agrarian communists received their name, Diggers, from the ill-fated attempt of a small group under the leadership of Gerrard Winstanley to seize and cultivate unenclosed common land, with the aim of giving the produce to the poor. Their effort was quickly defeated by violent means. The Diggers shared with the Levellers the sanction of the law of nature, but they interpreted it as a communal right to the means of subsistence which gave the individual merely the right to share in the produce of the common land and the common labor. "None ought to be lords or landlords over another, but the earth is free for every son and daughter of mankind to live free upon." Undoubtedly the Diggers have affinities with the Peasant Revolt in Germany and the Anabaptist movement. The principle upon which these movements were based was the Christian belief, common in the Middle Ages, that common possession was a more perfect way of life than private ownership. As among other utopians, there was a strong pacifist tradition among the Diggers. Just as the Levellers anticipated further developments in political equality, the Diggers were prophetic of the thought of Marx, Bellamy, Henry George, and others who were to stress the dependence of political liberty and equality upon the control of economic causes.

Locke's "Second Treatise on Civil Government" was primarily a justification of the Whig Revolution of 1688. His political philosophy inspired both Voltaire and the founders of American democratic ideas and practices. Voltaire, Rousseau, Jefferson, and Paine, following the example of Locke, organized their political philosophy in terms of a theory of social contract and a law of nature and the effort to establish the rights of the individual to liberty and equality. The state of nature was interpreted as involving equality of conditions and equality of rights. Glaring inequalities and other deviations from the idealized state of nature which were found in actual societies were held to be artificial creations in contravention of nature itself. It was obvious then that men ought to bring political arrangements into conformity with nature. Influenced by Locke, the Virginia Declaration of Rights states: "That all men are by nature equally free and independent, and have certain inherent rights, of which, when they enter into a state of society, they cannot, by any compact, deprive or divest their posterity; namely, the enjoyment of life and liberty, with the means of acquiring and possessing property, and pursuing and obtaining happiness and safety. . . . all men are equally entitled to the free exercise of religion, according to the dictates of conscience . . ." In similar fashion the Declaration of Independence announces: "We hold these truths to be self-evident, that all men are created equal, that they are endowed by their Creator with certain unalienable Rights, that among these are Life, Liberty and the pursuit of Happiness. That to secure these rights, Governments are instituted among Men, deriving their just powers from the consent of the governed. That whenever any Form of Government becomes destructive of these ends, it is the Right of the People to alter or to abolish it, and to institute new Government, laying its foundation on such principles and organizing its powers in such form, as to them shall seem most likely to effect their Safety and Happiness." Echoing similar doctrines the French Declaration of the Rights of Man and of the Citizen declared that governments are instituted to guarantee to men the enjoyment of their natural and imprescriptible rights. These rights are equality, liberty, security, and property. By nature and before the law, all men are equal. The interesting thing about these declarations which stress equality as a fundamental principle is that they were adopted by public bodies and were not merely the utterances of solitary thinkers. This type of secular thinking, like that of the Christian radicals of the seventeenth-century English Revolution, was strongly tinctured with utopianism. The story of how it was combined with other doctrines and effectively related to specific social and economic movements is one that is too complex to be summarized here, but it invited the attention and brilliant comment of de Tocqueville. Suffice it to say that we have been able to develop a remarkably equalitarian and "open" society in America partly because we have enjoyed the resources of a virgin continent, an advancing frontier, and a continually expanding economy, and we have had a somewhat more realistic appraisal of the perfectibility of man than that possessed by the French philosophers. The failure to assess properly these factors is probably responsible for the extravagant hopes which Americans occasionally reveal for the application of equalitarian and democratic ideas in other parts of the world.

Throughout the nineteenth and the twentieth centuries the idea of equality remained in the background of a wide variety of social movements which have pushed into an increasing number of areas of human experience. To review them would be to trace the intellectual and social history of the last 150 years. It is much simpler instead to point to the types of equality which men have sought and still seek. Men seek political equality, in the sense of demanding an effective share in the policy decisions that shape the basic life of the community. One of the classical means employed to achieve this from the time of the ancient Greek city-states to contemporary emergent nationalisms has been the equality of suffrage. In America the equalization of the franchise has been achieved by attacks on the barriers of wealth, sex, and color. Men also seek civil or legal equality, in the sense of enjoying equal power and right to control the conditions under which they participate in group life—their choice of religion, their expression of opinions, their right of assembly and petition, their right to belong to associations of their own choosing, their right to serve on juries, etc. They seek economic equality, in the sense of the equality of opportunity to provide for the minimum needs of their families and to secure the good things of life. The trade union movement, social security, minimum wage legislation, and the typical American wage-earner's desire that his son shall have a better job than he has are only a few of the countless expressions of the search for economic equality. Americans, in general, seem to be more interested in achieving very specific improvements in their economic status as steps toward greater equalization than they are in exploring the questions of what constitutes economic equality and what the costs of greater economic equalization are. Men also seek social equality, in the sense of the absence or removal of discrimination. Colored people, women, linguistic and national minorities, and various religious groups resent social discriminations which they feel are irrelevant and irrational in terms of the differences to which they are applied. Hence, they more and more seek constitutional and international prohibitions which put the continuing practice of discrimination at a moral and practical disadvantage. Men, in addition, seek equality of opportunity for personal development. This includes most of the preceding types of equality but it goes beyond them in ways which are not easy to define or to describe. Men increasingly seek equality for the groups and associations of which they are members. All over the world we see minorities within nations pressing more firmly for equality of status and opportunity. Undoubtedly the rapidity of communication has accelerated this process. In the forum provided by the United Nations smaller nations have been able to co-operate and to influence world opinion in ways that have resulted in greater equality between them and the larger nations. This is likely to be an increasingly lively development in the future.

The preceding attempt to classify simply the major types of equality reveals that it is not possible to separate them clearly and sharply. Any social movement which works in the direction of greater equality usually involves several, or possibly all, of these major types of equality. This is clearly seen in the movement for greater racial equality, which in the last fifteen years has become the most significant and complex of all the drives toward equalitarianism. It is obviously related to the drive to secure greater and more effective equalization of the franchise and to achieve full civil or legal equality. Partial success in achieving these equalities not only whets the appetite for greater achievement, but actually makes possible the achievement of other types of equality. This is particularly true of equality of opportunity and the equality of personal development which greater educational opportunity makes possible. Negro leadership in the drive for greater equality is the product, in part, of increased educational opportunity. In so far as it presses for still greater equalization of educational opportunity it ensures the existence of continuing pressures in the future for greater equalization of opportunity in economic, educational, political, religious, and social life. There is no way of avoiding these dynamic, reciprocal interrelationships. That is, there is no way of stopping them without giving up an "open" society and the American Dream.

There is little debate today over the abstract idea of equality. As a nation we are too committed to the centrality of equality in the American Dream. We can, however, look forward to continuing controversy about equality within the democratic process. Some types of equality conflict with other types of equality. Often the equality of opportunity depends upon and encourages inequalities, such as the inequalities of talent and character. Both greater equality and less equality have specific social and economic costs. We can be certain that the efforts to reach and to re-examine policy decisions with reference to these matters will provoke lively controversies for which we shall need all the resources of education, the social sciences, ethics, religion, and communication. Although it will not resolve automatically the conflicts, a knowledge of the history of the idea of equality may be helpful in establishing a perspective within which partial solutions may be achieved a little more easily.

The Old Testament

1. The idea of equality before God and therefore of equity and justice in human relations is found throughout the literature of the Old Testament. The period from Moses to Malachi is approximately a thousand years (1400-400 B.C.).

from The Book of Genesis

In the beginning God created the heaven and the earth. (1:1.)

And God said, Let us make man in our image, after our likeness: and let them have dominion over the fish of the sea, and over the fowl of the air, and over the cattle, and over all the earth, and over every creeping thing that creepeth upon the earth. So God created man in his own image, in the image of God created he him; male and female created he them. (1:26-27.)

from The Book of Deuteronomy

At the end of every seven years thou shalt make a release. And this is the manner of the release: Every creditor that lendeth ought unto his neighbour shall release it; he shall not exact it of his neighbour, or of his brother; because it is called the Lord's release. (15:1-2.)

If there be among you a poor man of one of thy brethren within any of thy gates in thy land which the Lord thy God giveth thee, thou shalt not harden thine heart, nor shut thine hand from thy poor brother: but thou shalt open thine hand wide unto him, and shalt surely lend him sufficient for his need, in that which he wanteth. Beware that there be not a thought in thy wicked heart, saying, The seventh year, the year of release, is at hand; and thine eye be evil against thy poor brother, and thou givest him nought; and he cry unto the Lord against thee, and it be sin unto thee. Thou shalt surely give him, and thine heart shall not be grieved when thou givest unto him: because that for this thing the Lord thy God shall bless thee in all thy works, and in all that thou puttest thine hand unto. For the poor shall never cease out of the land: therefore I command thee, saying, Thou shalt open thine hand wide unto thy brother, to thy poor, and to thy needy, in thy land. (15:7-11.)

Thou shalt not abhor an Edomite; for he is thy brother: thou shalt not abhor an Egyptian; because thou wast a stranger in his land. The children that are begotten of them shall enter into the congregation of the Lord in their third generation. (23:7-8.)

Thou shalt not oppress an hired servant that is poor and needy, whether he be of thy brethren, or of thy strangers that are in thy land within thy gates: at his day thou shalt give him his hire, neither shall the sun go down upon it; for he is poor, and setteth his heart upon it: lest he cry against thee unto the Lord, and it be sin unto thee. (24:14-15.)

Thou shalt not have in thy bag divers weights, a great and a small. Thou shalt not have in thine house divers measures, a great and a small. But thou shalt have a perfect and just weight, a perfect and just measure shalt thou have: that thy days may be lengthened in the land which the Lord thy God giveth thee. (25:13-15.)

from The Book of Job

If I did despise the cause of my manservant or of my maidservant, when they contended with me; what then shall I do when God riseth up? and when he visiteth, what shall I answer him? Did not he that made me in the womb make him? and did not one fashion us in the womb? (31:13-15.)

from The Book of Proverbs

The rich and poor meet together: the Lord is the maker of them all. (22:2.)

from The Book of Isaiah

Also the sons of the stranger, that join themselves to the Lord, to serve him, and to love the name of the Lord, to be his servants, every one that keepeth the sabbath from polluting it, and taketh hold of my covenant; even them will I bring to my holy mountain, and make them joyful in my house of prayer: their burnt offerings and their sacrifices shall be accepted upon mine altar; for mine house shall be called an house of prayer for all people. (56:6-7.)

Cry aloud, spare not, lift up thy voice like a trumpet, and shew my people their transgression, and the house of Jacob their sins. Yet they seek me daily, and delight to know my ways, as a nation that did righteousness, and forsook not the ordinance of their God: they ask of me the ordinances of justice; they take delight in approaching to God.

Wherefore have we fasted, say they, and thou seest not? wherefore have we afflicted our soul, and thou takest no knowledge? Behold, in the day of your fast ye find pleasure, and exact all your labours. Behold, ye fast for strife and debate, and to smite with the fist of wickedness: ye shall not fast as ye do this day, to make your voice to be heard on high. Is it such a fast that I have chosen? a day for a man to afflict his soul? is it to bow down his head as a bulrush, and to spread sackcloth and ashes under him? wilt thou call this a fast, and an acceptable day to the Lord? Is not this the fast that I have chosen? to loose the bands of wickedness, to undo the heavy burdens, and to let the oppressed go free, and that ye break every yoke? Is it not to deal thy bread to the hungry, and that thou bring the poor that are cast out to thy house? when thou seest the naked, that thou cover him; and that thou hide not thyself from thine own flesh?

Then shall thy light break forth as the morning, and thine health shall spring forth speedily: and thy righteousness shall go before thee; the glory of the Lord shall be thy rereward. Then shalt thou call, and the Lord shall answer; thou shalt cry, and he shall say, Here I am. If thou take away from the midst of thee the yoke, the putting forth of the finger, and speaking vanity; and if thou draw out thy soul to the hungry, and satisfy the afflicted soul; then shall thy light rise in obscurity, and thy darkness be as the noon day: and the Lord shall guide thee continually, and satisfy thy soul in drought, and make fat thy bones: and thou shalt be like a watered garden, and like a spring of water, whose waters fail not. And they that shall be of thee shall build the old waste places: thou shalt raise up the foundations of many generations; and thou shalt be called, The repairer of the breach, The restorer of paths to dwell in. (58:1-12.)

But now, O Lord, thou art our father; we are the clay, and thou our potter; and we all are the work of thy hand.

Be not wroth very sore, O Lord, neither remember iniquity for ever: behold, see, we beseech thee, we are all thy people. (64:8-9.)

from The Book of Jeremiah

Behold, the days come, saith the Lord, that I will make a new covenant with the house of Israel, and with the house of Judah . . . But this shall be the covenant that I will make with the house of Israel; After those days, saith the Lord, I will put my law in their inward parts, and write it in their hearts; and will be their God, and they shall be my people. And they shall teach no more every man his neighbour, and every man his brother, saying, Know the Lord: for they shall all know me, from the least of them unto the greatest of them, saith the Lord: for I will forgive their iniquity, and I will remember their sin no more. (31:31,33-34.)

Therefore the word of the Lord came to Jeremiah from the Lord, saying, Thus saith the Lord, the God of Israel; I made a covenant with your fathers in the day that I brought them forth out of the land of Egypt, out of the house of bondmen, saying, At the end of seven years let ye go every man his brother an Hebrew, which hath been sold unto thee; and when he hath served thee six years, thou shalt let him go free from thee: but your fathers hearkened not unto me, neither inclined their ear. And ye were now turned, and had done right in my sight, in proclaiming liberty every man to his neighbour; and ye had made a covenant before me in the house which is called by my name: but ye turned and polluted my name, and caused every man his servant, and every man his handmaid, whom he had set at liberty at their pleasure, to return, and brought them into subjection, to be unto you for servants and for handmaids. Therefore thus saith the Lord; Ye have not hearkened unto me, in proclaiming liberty, every one to his brother, and every man to his neighbour: behold, I proclaim a liberty for you, saith the Lord, to the sword, to the pestilence, and to the famine; and I will make you to be removed into all the kingdoms of the earth. (34:12-17.)

from The Book of Amos

Though ye offer me burnt offerings and your meat offerings, I will not accept them: neither will I regard the peace offerings of your fat beasts. Take thou away from me the noise of thy songs; for I will not hear the melody of thy viols. But let judgment run down as waters, and righteousness as a mighty stream. (5:22-24.)

Are ye not as children of the Ethiopians unto me, O children of Israel? saith the Lord. Have not I brought up Israel out of the land of Egypt? and the Philistines from Caphtor, and the Syrians from Kir? (9:7.)

from The Book of Micah

Wherewith shall I come before the Lord, and bow myself before the high God? shall I come before him with burnt offerings, with calves of a year old? will the Lord be pleased with thousands of rams, or with ten thousands of rivers of oil? shall I give my firstborn for my transgression, the fruit of my body for the sin of my soul? He hath shewed thee, O man, what is good; and what doth the Lord require of thee, but to do justly, and to love mercy, and to walk humbly with thy God? (6:6-8.)

from The Book of Malachi

Have we not all one father? hath not one God created us? why do we deal treacherously every man against his brother, by profaning the covenant of our fathers? (2:10.)

Herodotus

(c. 484-425 B.C.)

2.

Herodotus, the Greek historian often called the "father of history," reports the speech of Otanes, one of the leaders of the revolt against the Magi, rulers of the Persians.

from The History

80. When the tumult was abated, and five days had passed, the rebels against the Magians held a council on the whole state of affairs, at which words were uttered which to some Greeks seem incredible; but there is no doubt that they were spoken. Otanes was for giving the government to the whole body of the Persian people. "I hold," he said, "that we must make an end of monarchy; there is no pleasure or advantage in it. You have seen to what lengths went the insolence of Cambyses, and you have borne your share of the insolence of the Magian. What right order is there to be found in monarchy, when the ruler can do what he will, nor be held to account for it? Give this power to the best man on earth, and his wonted mind must leave him. The advantage which he holds breeds insolence, and nature makes all men jealous. This double cause is the root of all evil in him; he will do many wicked deeds, some from the insolence which is born of satiety, some from jealousy. For whereas an absolute ruler, as having all that heart can desire, should rightly be jealous of no man, yet it is contrariwise with him in his dealing with his countrymen; he is jealous of the safety of the good, and glad of the safety of the evil; and no man is so ready to believe calumny. Nor is any so hard to please; accord him but just honour, and he is displeased that you make him not your first care; make him such, and he damns you for a flatterer. But I have yet worse to say of him than that; he turns the laws of the land upside down, he rapes women, he puts high and low to death. But the virtue of a multitude's rule lies first in its excellent name, which signifies equality before the law; and secondly, in that its acts are not the acts of the monarch. All offices are assigned by lot, and the holders are accountable for what they do therein; and the general assembly arbitrates on all counsels. Therefore I declare my opinion, that we make an end of monarchy and increase the power of the multitude, seeing that all good lies in the many."

· · · · · · ·

78. Thus grew the power of Athens; and it is proved not by one but by many instances that equality is a good thing; seeing **that** while they were under despotic rulers the Athenians were no better in war than any of their neighbours, yet once they got quit of despots they were far and away the first of all. This, then, shows that while they were oppressed they willed to be cravens, as men working for a master, but when they were freed each one was zealous to achieve for himself.

Euripides

3.

(c. 484-407 B.C.)

Euripides, Greek tragic poet, reveals his realistic interest in contemporary problems in these excerpts from two of his plays.

from The Phoenician Maidens

JOCASTA:
My son Eteocles, evil unalloyed
Cleaves not to old age: nay, experience
Can plead more wisely than the lips of youth.
Why at Ambition, worst of deities,
Son, graspest thou? Do not: she is Queen of Wrong.
Homes many and happy cities enters she,
Nor leaves till ruined are her votaries.
Thou art mad for her!—better to honour, son,
Equality, which knitteth friends to friends,
Cities to cities, allies unto allies.
Nature gave men the law of equal rights,
And the less, ever marshalled foe against
The greater, ushers in the dawn of hate.
Measures for men Equality ordained,
Meting of weights and number she assigned.
The sightless face of night, and the sun's beam
Equally pace along their yearly round,
Nor either envieth that it must give place.
Sun, then, and night are servants unto men:
Shalt thou not brook to halve your heritage
And share with him? . . . Ah, where is justice then
Why overmuch dost thou prize Sovranty—
Injustice throned!—and count it some great thing?
Is worship precious? Nay, 'tis vanity.
Wouldst have, with great wealth in thine halls, great travail?
What is thy profit?—profit but in name;
Seeing enough sufficeth for the wise.
Mortals hold their possessions not in fee:
We are but stewards of the gifts of God:
Whene'er he will, he claims his own again.
And wealth abides not, 'tis but for a day.

from The Suppliants

THESEUS:
An eloquent herald this, a speech-crammed babbler!
But, since thou hast plunged into this strife, hear me:—
'Twas thou flung'st down this challenge unto parley:—
No worse foe than the despot hath a state,
Under whom, first, can be no common laws,
But one rules, keeping in his private hands
The law: so is equality no more.
But when the laws are written, then the weak
And wealthy have alike but equal right.
Yea, even the weaker may fling back the scoff
Against the prosperous, if he be reviled;
And, armed with right, the less o'ercomes the great.
Thus Freedom speaks:—"What man desires to bring
Good counsel for his country to the people?"
Who chooseth this, is famous: who will not,
Keeps silence. Can equality further go?
More—when the people piloteth the land,
She joyeth in young champions native-born:
But in a king's eyes this is hatefullest;
Yea, the land's best, whose wisdom he discerns,
He slayeth, fearing lest they shake his throne.
How can a state be stablished then in strength,
When, even as sweeps the scythe o'er springtide mead,
One lops the brave young hearts like flower-blooms?
What boots it to win wealth and store for sons,
When all one's toil but swells a despot's hoard?
Or to rear maiden daughters virtuously
To be a king's sweet morsels at his will,
And tears to them that dressed this dish for him?
May I die ere I see my daughters ravished!

Thucydides

(C. 460-C. 400 B.C.)

4.

Thucydides, an Athenian, writing in his *History of the Pelopon-nesian War* reports the famous Funeral Oration of Pericles, which is perhaps the noblest expression of the ideals of Athenian culture.

---

from "Funeral Oration" of Pericles

Our constitution does not copy the laws of neighboring states; we are rather a pattern to others than imitators ourselves. Its administration favors the many instead of the few; this is why it is called a democracy. If we look to the laws, they afford equal justice to all in their private differences; if to social standing, advancement in public life falls to reputation for capacity, class consideration not being allowed to interfere with merit; nor again does poverty bar the way—if a man is able to serve the state, he is not hindered by the obscurity of his condition. The freedom which we enjoy in our government extends also to our ordinary life. There, far from exercising a jealous surveillance over each other, we do not feel called upon to be angry with our neighbor for doing what he likes, or even to indulge in those injurious looks which cannot fail to be offensive, although they inflict no positive penalty. But all this ease in our private relations does not make us lawless as citizens. Against this fear is our chief safeguard, teaching us to obey the magistrates and the laws, particularly such as regard the protection of the injured, whether they are actually on the statute book, or belong to that code which, although unwritten, yet cannot be broken without acknowledged disgrace.

Further, we provide plenty of means for the mind to refresh itself from business. We celebrate games and sacrifices all the year round, and the elegance of our private establishments forms a daily source of pleasure and helps to banish the spleen; while the magnitude of our city draws the produce of the world into our harbor, so that to the Athenian the fruits of other countries are as familiar a luxury as those of his own.

If we turn to our military policy, there also we differ from our antagonists. We throw open our city to the world, and never by alien acts exclude foreigners from any opportunity of learning or observing, although the eyes of any enemy may occasionally profit by our liberality; trusting less in system and policy than to the native spirit of our citizens; while in education, where our rivals from their very cradles by a painful discipline seek after manliness, at Athens we live exactly as we please, and yet are just as ready to encounter every legitimate danger. . . .

5.

Isocrates
(436-338 B.C.)

Isocrates, a Greek orator, was a pupil of Socrates and a celebrated teacher, who recognized the significance of equality.

from Areopagiticus

For those who directed the state in the time of Solon and Cleisthenes did not establish a polity which in name merely was hailed as the most impartial and the mildest of governments, while in practice showing itself the opposite to those who lived under it, nor one which trained the citizens in such fashion that they looked upon insolence as democracy, lawlessness as liberty, impudence of speech as equality, and licence to do what they pleased as happiness, but rather a polity which detested and punished such men and by so doing made all the citizens better and wiser.

But what contributed most to their good government of the state was that of the two recognized kinds of equality—that which makes the same award to all alike and that which gives to each man his due—they did not fail to grasp which was the more serviceable; but, rejecting as unjust that which holds that the good and the bad are worthy of the same honours, and preferring rather that which rewards and punishes every man according to his deserts, they governed the city on this principle, not filling the offices by lot from all the citizens, but selecting the best and the ablest for each function of the state; for they believed that the rest of the people would reflect the character of those who were placed in charge of their affairs.

. . . Furthermore, it is easy to judge of my purpose from the fact that in most of the discourses which I have written, you will find that I condemn oligarchies and special privileges, while I commend equal rights and democratic governments—not all of them, but those which are well-ordered, praising them not indiscriminately, but on just and reasonable grounds. For I know that under this constitution our ancestors were far superior to the rest of the world, and that the Lacedaemonians are the best governed of peoples because they are the most democratic; for in their selection of magistrates, in their daily life, and in their habits in general, we may see that the principles of equity and equality have greater influence than elsewhere in the world—principles to which oligarchies are hostile, while well-ordered democracies practise them continually.

Plato

(c. 428-c. 348 B.C.)

6.

Plato, Greek philosopher who was one of the most influential thinkers of all time, discussed equality in a number of contexts. His classic discussion of the equality of the sexes is reprinted from *The Republic*.

from The Republic

Well, I replied, I suppose that I must retrace my steps and say what I perhaps ought to have said before in the proper place. The part of the men has been played out, and now properly enough comes the turn of the women. Of them I will proceed to speak, and the more readily since I am invited by you.

For men born and educated like our citizens, the only way, in my opinion, of arriving at a right conclusion about the possession and use of women and children is to follow the path on which we originally started, when we said that the men were to be the guardians and watchdogs of the herd.

True.

Let us further suppose the birth and education of our women to be subject to similar or nearly similar regulations; then we shall see whether the result accords with our design.

What do you mean?

What I mean may be put into the form of a question, I said: Are dogs divided into hes and shes, or do they both share equally in hunting and in keeping watch and in the other duties of dogs? or do we entrust to the males the entire and exclusive care of the flocks, while we leave the females at home, under the idea that the bearing and suckling their puppies is labour enough for them?

No, he said, they share alike; the only difference between them is that the males are stronger and the females weaker.

But can you use different animals for the same purpose, unless they are bred and fed in the same way?

You cannot.

Then, if women are to have the same duties as men, they must have the same nurture and education?

Yes.

The education which was assigned to the men was music and gymnastic.

41

Yes.

Then women must be taught music and gymnastic and also the art of war, which they must practise like the men?

That is the inference, I suppose.

I should rather expect, I said, that several of our proposals, if they are carried out, being unusual, may appear ridiculous.

No doubt of it.

Yes, and the most ridiculous thing of all will be the sight of women naked in the palaestra, exercising with the men, especially when they are no longer young; they certainly will not be a vision of beauty, any more than the enthusiastic old men who in spite of wrinkles and ugliness continue to frequent the gymnasia.

Yes, indeed, he said: according to present notions the proposal would be thought ridiculous.

But then, I said, as we have determined to speak our minds, we must not fear the jests of the wits which will be directed against this sort of innovation; how they will talk of women's attainments both in music and gymnastic, and above all about their wearing armour and riding upon horseback!

Very true, he replied.

Yet having begun we must go forward to the rough places of the law; at the same time begging of these gentlemen for once in their life to be serious. Not long ago, as we shall remind them, the Hellenes were of the opinion, which is still generally received among the barbarians, that the sight of a naked man was ridiculous and improper; and when first the Cretans and then the Lacedaemonians introduced the custom, the wits of that day might equally have ridiculed the innovation.

No doubt.

But when experience showed that to let all things be uncovered was far better than to cover them up, and the ludicrous effect to the outward eye vanished before the better principle which reason asserted, then the man was perceived to be a fool who directs the shafts of his ridicule at any other sight but that of folly and vice, or seriously inclines to weigh the beautiful by any other standard but that of the good.

Very true, he replied.

First, then, whether the question is to be put in jest or in earnest, let us come to an understanding about the nature of woman: Is she capable of sharing either wholly or partially in the actions of men, or not at all? And is the art of war one of those arts in which she can or can not share? That will be the best way of commencing the enquiry, and will probably lead to the fairest conclusion.

That will be much the best way.

Shall we take the other side first and begin by arguing against ourselves; in this manner the adversary's position will not be undefended.

Why not? he said.

Then let us put a speech into the mouths of our opponents. They will say: 'Socrates and Glaucon, no adversary need convict you, for you yourselves, at the first foundation of the State, admitted the principle that everybody was to do the one work suited to his own nature.' And certainly, if I am not mistaken, such an admission was made by us. 'And do not the natures of men and women differ very much indeed?' And we shall reply: Of course they do. Then we shall be asked, 'Whether the tasks assigned to men and to women should not be different, and such as are agreeable to their different natures?' Certainly they should. 'But if so, have you not fallen into a serious inconsistency in saying that men and women, whose natures are so entirely different, ought to perform the same actions?'—What defence will you make for us, my good Sir, against any one who offers these objections?

That is not an easy question to answer when asked suddenly; and I shall and I do beg of you to draw out the case on our side.

These are the objections, Glaucon, and there are many others of a like kind, which I foresaw long ago; they made me afraid and reluctant to take in hand any law about the possession and nurture of women and children.

By Zeus, he said, the problem to be solved is anything but easy.

Why yes, I said, but the fact is that when a man is out of his depth, whether he has fallen into a little swimming bath or into mid ocean, he has to swim all the same.

Very true.

And must not we swim and try to reach the shore: we will hope that Arion's dolphin or some other miraculous help may save us?

I suppose so, he said.

Well then, let us see if any way of escape can be found. We acknowledged—did we not? that different natures ought to have different pursuits, and that men's and women's natures are different. And now what are we saying?—that different natures ought to have the same pursuits, —this is the inconsistency which is charged upon us.

Precisely.

Verily, Glaucon, I said, glorious is the power of the art of contradiction!

Why do you say so?

Because I think that many a man falls into the practice against his will. When he thinks that he is reasoning he is really disputing, just because he cannot define and divide, and so know that of which he is speaking; and he will pursue a merely verbal opposition in the spirit of contention and not of fair discussion.

Yes, he replied, such is very often the case; but what has that to do with us and our argument?

A great deal; for there is certainly a danger of our getting unintentionally into a verbal opposition.

In what way?

Why we valiantly and pugnaciously insist upon the verbal truth, that different natures ought to have different pursuits, but we never considered at all what was the meaning of sameness or difference of nature, or why we distinguished them when we assigned different pursuits to different natures and the same to the same natures.

Why, no, he said, that was never considered by us.

I said: Suppose that by way of illustration we were to ask the question whether there is not an opposition in nature between bald men and hairy men; and if this is admitted by us, then, if bald men are cobblers, we should forbid the hairy men to be cobblers, and conversely?

That would be a jest, he said.

Yes, I said, a jest; and why? because we never meant when we constructed the State, that the opposition of natures should extend to every difference, but only to those differences which affected the pursuit in which the individual is engaged; we should have argued, for example, that a physician and one who is in mind a physician may be said to have the same nature.

True.

Whereas the physician and the carpenter have different natures?
Certainly.

And if, I said, the male and female sex appear to differ in their fitness for any art or pursuit, we should say that such pursuit or art ought to be assigned to one or the other of them; but if the difference consists only in women bearing and men begetting children, this does not amount to a proof that a woman differs from a man in respect of the sort of education she should receive; and we shall therefore continue to maintain that our guardians and their wives ought to have the same pursuits.

Very true, he said.

Next, we shall ask our opponent how, in reference to any of the pursuits or arts of civic life, the nature of a woman differs from that of a man?

That will be quite fair.

And perhaps he, like yourself, will reply that to give a sufficient answer on the instant is not easy; but after a little reflection there is no difficulty.

Yes, perhaps.

Suppose then that we invite him to accompany us in the argument, and then we may hope to show him that there is nothing peculiar in the constitution of women which would affect them in the administration of the State.

By all means.

Let us say to him: Come now, and we will ask you a question:— when you spoke of a nature gifted or not gifted in any respect, did you mean to say that one man will acquire a thing easily, another with difficulty; a little learning will lead the one to discover a great deal; whereas the other, after much study and application, no sooner learns than he forgets; or again, did you mean, that the one has a body which is a good servant to his mind, while the body of the other is a hindrance to him?—would not these be the sort of differences which distinguish the man gifted by nature from the one who is ungifted?

No one will deny that.

And can you mention any pursuit of mankind in which the male sex has not all these gifts and qualities in a higher degree than the female? Need I waste time in speaking of the art of weaving, and the management of pancakes and preserves, in which womankind does really appear to be great, and in which for her to be beaten by a man is of all things the most absurd?

You are quite right, he replied, in maintaining the general inferiority of the female sex: although many women are in many things superior to many men, yet on the whole what you say is true.

And if so, my friend, I said, there is no special faculty of administration in a state which a woman has because she is a woman, or which a man has by virtue of his sex, but the gifts of nature are alike diffused in both; all the pursuits of men are the pursuits of women also, but in all of them a woman is inferior to a man.

Very true.

Then are we to impose all our enactments on men and none of them on women?

That will never do.

One woman has a gift of healing, another not; one is a musician, and another has no music in her nature?

Very true.

And one woman has a turn for gymnastic and military exercises, and another is unwarlike and hates gymnastics?

Certainly.

And one woman is a philosopher, and another is an enemy of philosophy; one has spirit, and another is without spirit?

That is also true.

Then one woman will have the temper of a guardian, and another not. Was not the selection of the male guardians determined by differences of this sort?

Yes.

Men and women alike possess the qualities which make a guardian; they differ only in their comparative strength or weakness.

Obviously.

And those women who have such qualities are to be selected as the companions and colleagues of men who have similar qualities and whom they resemble in capacity and in character?

Very true.

And ought not the same natures to have the same pursuits?

They ought.

Then, as we were saying before, there is nothing unnatural in assigning music and gymnastic to the wives of the guardians—to that point we come round again.

Certainly not.

The law which we then enacted was agreeable to nature, and therefore not an impossibility or mere aspiration; and the contrary practice, which prevails at present, is in reality a violation of nature.

That appears to be true.

We had to consider, first, whether our proposals were possible, and secondly whether they were the most beneficial?

Yes.

And the possibility has been acknowledged?

Yes.

The very great benefit has next to be established?

Quite so.

You will admit that the same education which makes a man a good guardian will make a woman a good guardian; for their original nature is the same?

Yes.

I should like to ask you a question.

What is it?

Would you say that all men are equal in excellence, or is one man better than another?

The latter.

And in the commonwealth which we were founding do you conceive the guardians who have been brought up on our model system to be more perfect men, or the cobblers whose education has been cobbling?

What a ridiculous question!

You have answered me, I replied: Well, and may we not further say that our guardians are the best of our citizens?

By far the best.

And will not their wives be the best women?

Yes, by far the best.

And can there be anything better for the interests of the State than that the men and women of a State should be as good as possible?

There can be nothing better.

And this is what the arts of music and gymnastic, when present in such manner as we have described, will accomplish?

Certainly.

Then we have made an enactment not only possible but in the highest degree beneficial to the State?

True.

Then let the wives of our guardians strip, for their virtue will be their robe, and let them share in the toils of war and the defence of their country; only in the distribution of labours the lighter are to be assigned to the women, who are the weaker natures, but in other respects their duties are to be the same. And as for the man who laughs at naked women exercising their bodies from the best of motives, in his laughter he is plucking

'A fruit of unripe wisdom,'

and he himself is ignorant of what he is laughing at, or what he is about;—for that is, and ever will be, the best of sayings, *That the useful is the noble and the hurtful is the base.*

Very true.

Here, then, is one difficulty in our law about women, which we may say that we have now escaped; the wave has not swallowed us up alive for enacting that the guardians of either sex should have all their pursuits in common; to the utility and also to the possibility of this arrangement the consistency of the argument with itself bears witness.

Yes, that was a mighty wave which you have escaped.

Aristotle

(384-322 B.C.)

7.

Aristotle, Greek philosopher, in the course of many ethical and political discussions offered critical comments on the concept of equality. A few of them from Books V, VI, VII of *The Politics* are presented here.

from The Politics

In the first place we must assume as our starting-point that in the many forms of government which have sprung up there has always been an acknowledgement of justice and proportionate equality, although mankind fail in attaining them, as indeed I have already explained. Democracy, for example, arises out of the notion that those who are equal in any respect are equal in all respects; because men are equally free, they claim to be absolutely equal. Oligarchy is based on the notion that those who are unequal in one respect are in all respects unequal; being unequal, that is, in property, they suppose themselves to be unequal absolutely. The democrats think that as they are equal they ought to be equal in all things; while the oligarchs, under the idea that they are unequal, claim too much, which is one form of inequality. All these forms of government have a kind of justice, but, tried by an absolute standard, they are faulty; and, therefore, both parties, whenever their share in the government does not accord with their preconceived ideas, stir up revolution. Those who excel in virtue have the best right of all to rebel (for they alone can with reason be deemed absolutely unequal), but then they are of all men the least inclined to do so. There is also a superiority which is claimed by men of rank; for they are thought noble because they spring from wealthy and virtuous ancestors. Here then, so to speak, are opened the very springs and fountains of revolution; and hence arise two sorts of changes in governments; the one affecting the constitution, when men seek to change from an existing form into some other, for example, from democracy into oligarchy, and from oligarchy into democracy, or from either of them into constitutional government or aristocracy, and conversely; the other not affecting the constitution, when, without disturbing the form of government, whether oligarchy, or monarchy, or any other, they try to get the administration into their own hands. . . . Everywhere inequality is a cause of revolution, but an inequality in which there is no proportion—for instance, a perpetual monarchy among equals; and always it is the desire of equality which rises in rebellion.

Now equality is of two kinds, numerical and proportional; by the first I mean sameness or equality in number or size; by the second, equality of ratios. For example, the excess of three over two is numerically equal to the excess of two over one; whereas four exceeds two in the same ratio in which two exceeds one, for two is the same part of four that one is of two, namely, the half. As I was saying before, men agree that justice in the abstract is proportion, but they differ in that some think that if they are equal in any respect they are equal absolutely, others that if they are unequal in any respect they should be unequal in all. Hence there are two principal forms of government, democracy and oligarchy; for good birth and virtue are rare, but wealth and numbers are more common. In what city shall we find a hundred persons of good birth and of virtue? whereas the rich everywhere abound. That a state should be ordered, simply and wholly, according to either kind of equality, is not a good thing; the proof is the fact that such forms of government never last. They are originally based on a mistake, and, as they begin badly, cannot fail to end badly. The inference is that both kinds of equality should be employed; numerical in some cases, and proportionate in others.

Still democracy appears to be safer and less liable to revolution than oligarchy. For in oligarchies there is the double danger of the oligarchs falling out among themselves and also with the people; but in democracies there is only the danger of a quarrel with the oligarchs. No dissension worth mentioning arises among the people themselves. And we may further remark that a government which is composed of the middle class more nearly approximates to democracy than to oligarchy, and is the safest of the imperfect forms of government. . . .

The basis of a democratic state is liberty; which, according to the common opinion of men, can only be enjoyed in such a state;—this they affirm to be the great end of every democracy. One principle of liberty is for all to rule and be ruled in turn, and indeed democratic justice is the application of numerical not proportionate equality; whence it follows that the majority must be supreme, and that whatever the majority approve must be the end and the just. Every citizen, it is said, must have equality, and therefore in a democracy the poor have more power than the rich, because there are more of them, and the will of the majority is supreme. This, then, is one note of liberty which all democrats affirm to be the principle of their state. Another is that a man should live as he likes. This, they say, is the privilege of a freeman, since, on the other hand, not to live as a man likes is the mark of a slave. This is the second characteristic of democracy, whence has arisen the claim of men to be ruled by none, if possible, or, if this is impossible, to rule and be ruled in turns; and so it contributes to the freedom based upon equality.

Such being our foundation and such the principle from which we start, the characteristics of democracy are as follows:—the election of officers by all out of all; and that all should rule over each, and each in his turn over all; that the appointment to all offices, or to all but those which require experience and skill, should be made by lot; that no property qualifications should be required for offices, or only a very low one; that a man should not hold the same office twice, or not often, or in the case of few except military offices: that the tenure of all offices, or of as many as possible, should be brief; that all men should sit in judgment, or that judges selected out of all should judge, in all matters, or in most and in the greatest and most important—such as the scrutiny of accounts, the constitution, and private contracts; that the assembly should be supreme over all causes, or at any rate over the most important, and the magistrates over none or only over a very few. Of all magistracies, a council is the most democratic when there is not the means of paying all the citizens, but when they are paid even this is robbed of its power; for the people then draw all cases to themselves, as I said in the previous discussion. The next characteristic of democracy is payment for services; assembly, law-courts, magistrates, everybody receives pay, when it is to be had; or when it is not to be had for all, then it is given to the law-courts and to the stated assemblies, to the council and to the magistrates, or at least to any of them who are compelled to have their meals together. And whereas oligarchy is characterized by birth, wealth, and education, the notes of democracy appear to be the opposite of these—low birth, poverty, mean employment. Another note is that no magistracy is perpetual, but if any such have survived some ancient change in the constitution it should be stripped of its power, and the holders should be elected by lot and no longer by vote. These are the points common to all democracies; but democracy and demos in their truest form are based upon the recognized principle of democratic justice, that all should count equally; for equality implies that the poor should have no more share in the government than the rich, and should not be the only rulers, but that all should rule equally according to their numbers. And in this way men think that they will secure equality and freedom in their state.

Next comes the question, how is this equality to be obtained? Are we to assign to a thousand poor men the property qualifications of five hundred rich men? and shall we give the thousand a power equal to that of the five hundred? or, if this is not to be the mode, ought we, still retaining the same ratio, to take equal numbers from each and give them control of the elections and of the courts?—Which, according to the democratical notion, is the juster form of the constitution—this or one based on numbers only? Democrats say that justice is that to which the majority agree, oligarchs that to which the wealthier class; in their opinion the decision should be given according to the amount of property. In both principles there is some inequality and injustice. For if justice is the will of the few, any one person who has more wealth than all the rest of the rich put together, ought, upon the oligarchical principle, to have the sole power—but this would be tyranny; or if justice is the will of the majority, as I was before saying, they will unjustly confiscate the property of the wealthy minority. To find a principle of equality in which they both agree we must inquire into their respective ideas of justice.

Now they agree in saying that whatever is decided by the majority of the citizens is to be deemed law. Granted:—but not without some reserve; since there are two classes out of which a state is composed—the poor and the rich—that is to be deemed law, on which both or the greater part of both agree; and if they disagree, that which is approved by the greater number, and by those who have the higher qualification. For example, suppose that there are ten rich and twenty poor, and some measure is approved by six of the rich and is disapproved by fifteen of the poor, and the remaining four of the rich join with the party of the poor, and the remaining five of the poor with that of the rich; in such a case the will of those whose qualifications, when both sides are added up, are the greatest, should prevail. If they turn out to be equal, there is no greater difficulty than at present, when, if the assembly or the courts are divided, recourse is had to the lot, or to some similar expedient. But, although it may be difficult in theory to know what is just and equal, the practical difficulty of inducing those to forbear who can, if they like, encroach, is far greater, for the weaker are always asking for equality and justice, but the stronger care for none of these things. . . .

. . . Equality consists in the same treatment of similar persons, and no government can stand which is not founded upon justice. For if the government be unjust every one in the country unites with the governed in the desire to have a revolution, and it is an impossibility that the members of the government can be so numerous as to be stronger than all their enemies put together. . . .

We conclude that from one point of view governors and governed are identical, and from another different. And therefore their education must be the same and also different. For he who would learn to command well must, as men say, first of all learn to obey. As I observed in the first part of this treatise, there is one rule which is for the sake of the rulers and another rule which is for the sake of the ruled; the former is a despotic, the latter a free government. Some commands differ not in the thing commanded, but in the intention with which they are imposed. Wherefore, many apparently menial offices are an honour to the free youth by whom they are performed; for actions do not differ as honourable or dishonourable in themselves so much as in the end and intention of them. But since we say that the virtue of the citizen and ruler is the same as that of the good man, and that the same person must first be a subject and then a ruler, the legislator has to see that they become good men, and by what means this may be accomplished, and what is the end of the perfect life.

Cicero

(106-43 B.C.)

8.

Cicero, Roman orator, politician, and philosopher, restates the Stoic doctrine of the equality of all men by nature in these excerpts from two of his dialogues.

from On the Laws

M. The points which are now being briefly touched upon are certainly important; but out of all the material of the philosophers' discussions, surely there comes nothing more valuable than the full realization that we are born for Justice, and that right is based, not upon men's opinions, but upon Nature. This fact will immediately be plain if you once get a clear conception of man's fellowship and union with his fellow-men. For no single thing is so like another, so exactly its counterpart, as all of us are to one another. Nay, if bad habits and false beliefs did not twist the weaker minds and turn them in whatever direction they are inclined, no one would be so like his own self as all men would be like all others. And so, however we may define man, a single definition will apply to all. This is a sufficient proof that there is no difference in kind between man and man; for if there were, one definition could not be applicable to all men; and indeed reason, which alone raises us above the level of the beasts and enables us to draw inferences, to prove and disprove, to discuss and solve problems, and to come to conclusions, is certainly common to us all, and, though varying in what it learns, at least in the capacity to learn it is invariable. For the same things are invariably perceived by the senses, and those things which stimulate the senses, stimulate them in the same way in all men; and those rudimentary beginnings of intelligence to which I have referred, which are imprinted on our minds, are imprinted on all minds alike; and speech, the mind's interpreter, though differing in the choice of words, agrees in the sentiments expressed. In fact, there is no human being of any race who, if he finds a guide, cannot attain to virtue.

XI. The similarity of the human race is clearly marked in its evil tendencies as well as in its goodness. For pleasure also attracts all men; and even though it is an enticement to vice, yet it has some likeness to what is naturally good. For it delights us by its lightness and agreeableness; and for this reason, by an error of thought, it is embraced as

53

something wholesome. It is through a similar misconception that we shun death as though it were a dissolution of nature, and cling to life because it keeps us in the sphere in which we were born; and that we look upon pain as one of the greatest of evils, not only because of its cruelty, but also because it seems to lead to the destruction of nature. In the same way, on account of the similarity between moral worth and renown, those who are publicly honoured are considered happy, while those who do not attain fame are thought miserable. Troubles, joys, desires, and fears haunt the minds of all men without distinction, and even if different men have different beliefs, that does not prove, for example, that it is not the same quality of superstition that besets those races which worship dogs and cats as gods, as that which torments other races. But what nation does not love courtesy, kindliness, gratitude, and remembrance of favours bestowed? What people does not hate and despise the haughty, the wicked, the cruel, and the ungrateful? Inasmuch as these considerations prove to us that the whole human race is bound together in unity, it follows, finally, that knowledge of the principles of right living is what makes men better . . .

XII. M. The next point, then, is that we are so constituted by Nature as to share the sense of Justice with one another and to pass it on to all men. And in this whole discussion I want it understood that what I shall call Nature is [that which is implanted in us by Nature]; that, however, the corruption caused by bad habits is so great that the sparks of fire, so to speak, which Nature has kindled in us are extinguished by this corruption, and the vices which are their opposites spring up and are established. But if the judgments of men were in agreement with Nature, so that, as the poet says, they considered "nothing alien to them which concerns mankind," then Justice would be equally observed by all. For those creatures who have received the gift of reason from Nature have also received right reason, and therefore they have also received the gift of Law, which is right reason applied to command and prohibition. And if they have received Law, they have received Justice also. Now all men have received reason; therefore all men have received Justice. Consequently Socrates was right when he cursed, as he often did, the man who first separated utility from Justice; for this separation, he complained, is the source of all mischief. . . . From this it is clear that, when a wise man shows toward another endowed with equal virtue the kind of benevolence which is so widely diffused among men, that will then have come to pass which, unbelievable as it seems to some, is after all the inevitable result—namely, that he loves himself no whit more than he loves another. For what difference can there be among things which are all equal? But if the least distinction should be made in friendship, then the very name of friendship would perish forthwith; for its essence is such that, as soon as either friend prefers anything for himself, friendship ceases to exist.

Now all this is really a preface to what remains to be said in our discussion, and its purpose is to make it more easily understood that Justice is inherent in Nature. After I have said a few words more on this topic, I shall go on to the civil law, the subject which gives rise to all this discourse.

XIII. Q. You certainly need to say very little more on that head, for from what you have already said, Atticus is convinced, and certainly I am, that Nature is the source of Justice.

A. How can I help being convinced, when it has just been proved to us, first, that we have been provided and equipped with what we may call the gifts of the gods; next, that there is only one principle by which men may live with one another, and that this is the same for all, and possessed equally by all; and, finally, that all men are bound together by a certain natural feeling of kindliness and good-will, and also by a partnership in Justice? Now that we have admitted the truth of these conclusions, and rightly, I think, how can we separate Law and Justice from Nature?

from The Republic

XXII. . . . True law is right reason in agreement with nature; it is of universal application, unchanging and everlasting; it summons to duty by its commands, and averts from wrongdoing by its prohibitions. And it does not lay its commands or prohibitions upon good men in vain, though neither have any effect on the wicked. It is a sin to try to alter this law, nor is it allowable to attempt to repeal any part of it, and it is impossible to abolish it entirely. We cannot be freed from its obligations by senate or people, and we need not look outside ourselves for an expounder or interpreter of it. And there will not be different laws at Rome and at Athens, or different laws now and in the future, but one eternal and unchangeable law will be valid for all nations and all times, and there will be one master and ruler, that is, God, over us all, for he is the author of this law, its promulgator, and its enforcing judge. Whoever is disobedient is fleeing from himself and denying his human nature, and by reason of this very fact he will suffer the worst penalties, even if he escapes what is commonly considered punishment. . . .

Seneca

(C. 4 B.C.-A.D. 65)

9.

Seneca, Roman philosopher, dramatist, and statesman, relates typical Stoic ethical teaching to the situation of the slave.

from On Benefits

18. . . . He who denies that a slave can sometimes give a benefit to his master is ignorant of the rights of man; for, not the status, but the intention, of the one who bestows is what counts. Virtue closes the door to no man; it is open to all, admits all, invites all, the freeborn and the freedman, the slave and the king, and the exile; neither family nor fortune determines its choice—it is satisfied with the naked human being. For what protection would it find against sudden events, what great assurance would the human mind be able to hold out to itself if Fortune could rob it of unchangeable virtue? . . .

· · · · · ·

20. It is a mistake for anyone to believe that the condition of slavery penetrates into the whole being of a man. The better part of him is exempt. Only the body is at the mercy and disposition of a master; but the mind is its own master, and is so free and unshackled that not even this prison of the body, in which it is confined, can restrain it from using its own powers, following mighty aims, and escaping into the infinite to keep company with the stars. It is, therefore, the body that Fortune hands over to a master; it is this that he buys, it is this that he sells; that inner part cannot be delivered into bondage. All that issues from this is free; nor, indeed, are we able to command all things from slaves, nor are they compelled to obey us in all things; they will not carry out orders that are hostile to the state, and they will not lend their hands to any crime.

· · · · · ·

28. After so many instances, can there be any doubt that a master may sometimes receive a benefit from a slave? Why should a man's condition lessen the value of a service, and the very value of the service not exalt the man's condition? We all spring from the same source, have the same origin; no man is more noble than another except in so far as the nature of one man is more upright and more capable of good

actions. Those who display ancestral busts in their halls, and place in the entrance of their houses the names of their family, arranged in a long row and entwined in the multiple ramifications of a genealogical tree—are these not notable rather than noble? Heaven is the one parent of us all, whether from his earliest origin each one arrives at his present degree by an illustrious or obscure line of ancestors. You must not be duped by those who, in making a review of their ancestors, wherever they find an illustrious name lacking, foist in the name of a god. Do not despise any man, even if he belongs with those whose names are forgotten, and have had too little favour from Fortune. Whether your line before you holds freedmen or slaves or persons of foreign extraction, boldly lift up your head, and leap over the obscure names in your pedigree; great nobility awaits you at its source. Why are we raised by our pride to such a pitch of vanity that we scorn to receive benefits from slaves, and, forgetting their services, look only upon their lot? You who are a slave of lust, of gluttony, of a harlot—nay, who are the common property of harlots—do you call any other man a slave? *You* call any other man a slave? Whither, pray, are you being rushed by those bearers who carry around your cushioned litter? Whither are those fellows in cloaks, tricked out in remarkable livery to look like soldiers—whither, I say, are these conveying you? To some door-keeper's door, to the gardens of some slave whose duties are not even fixed; and then you deny that your own slave is capable of giving you a benefit, when in your eyes it is a benefit to have from another man's slave a kiss? What great inconsistency is this? At the same time you both despise slaves and court them—inside your threshold you are imperious and violent, outside abject, and scorned as greatly as ever you scorn. For none are more prone to abase themselves than those who are presumptuously puffed up, and none are more ready to trample upon others than those who from receiving insults have learned how to give them.

The New Testament

10. Jesus of Nazareth (4 B.C.-A.D. 29) added a new dimension to the idea of equality. In the literature of the Christian Church the standard of life became *agapé* love based on His teaching and example.

from The Gospel According to Matthew

Let your light so shine before men, that they may see your good works, and glorify your Father which is in heaven.

Think not that I am come to destroy the law, or the prophets: I am not come to destroy, but to fulfil. For verily I say unto you, Till heaven and earth pass, one jot or one tittle shall in no wise pass from the law, till all be fulfilled. Whosoever therefore shall break one of these least commandments, and shall teach men so, he shall be called the least in the kingdom of heaven: but whosoever shall do and teach them, the same shall be called great in the kingdom of heaven. For I say unto you, That except your righteousness shall exceed the righteousness of the scribes and Pharisees, ye shall in no case enter into the kingdom of heaven.

Ye have heard that it was said by them of old time, Thou shalt not kill; and whosoever shall kill shall be in danger of the judgment: but I say unto you, That whosoever is angry with his brother without a cause shall be in danger of the judgment: and whosoever shall say to his brother, Raca, shall be in danger of the council: but whosoever shall say, Thou fool, shall be in danger of hell fire. Therefore if thou bring thy gift to the altar, and there rememberest that thy brother hath ought against thee; leave there thy gift before the altar, and go thy way; first be reconciled to thy brother, and then come and offer thy gift. (5:16-24.)

Ye have heard that it hath been said, An eye for an eye, and a tooth for a tooth: but I say unto you, That ye resist not evil: but whosoever shall smite thee on thy right cheek, turn to him the other also. And if any man will sue thee at the law, and take away thy coat, let him have thy cloke also. And whosoever shall compel thee to go a mile, go with him twain. Give to him that asketh thee, and from him that would borrow of thee turn not thou away.

Ye have heard that it hath been said, Thou shalt love thy neighbour, and hate thine enemy. But I say unto you, Love your enemies, bless them that curse you, do good to them that hate you, and pray for them which despitefully use you, and persecute you; that ye may be the children of your Father which is in heaven: for he maketh his sun to rise on the evil and on the good, and sendeth rain on the just and on the unjust. For if ye love them which love you, what reward have ye? do not even the publicans the same? And if ye salute your brethren only, what do ye more than others? do not even the publicans so? Be ye therefore perfect, even as your Father which is in heaven is perfect. (5:38-48.)

Then spake Jesus to the multitude, and to his disciples, saying, The scribes and the Pharisees sit in Moses' seat: all therefore whatsoever they bid you observe, that observe and do; but do not ye after their works: for they say, and do not. For they bind heavy burdens and grievous to be borne, and lay them on men's shoulders; but they themselves will not move them with one of their fingers. But all their works they do for to be seen of men: they make broad their phylacteries, and enlarge the borders of their garments, and love the uppermost rooms at feasts, and the chief seats in the synagogues, and greetings in the markets, and to be called of men, Rabbi, Rabbi. But be not ye called Rabbi: for one is your Master, even Christ; and all ye are brethren. And call no man your father upon the earth: for one is your Father, which is in heaven. Neither be ye called masters: for one is your Master, even Christ. But he that is greatest among you shall be your servant. And whosoever shall exalt himself shall be abased; and he that shall humble himself shall be exalted. (23:1-12.)

When the Son of man shall come in his glory, and all the holy angels with him, then shall he sit upon the throne of his glory: and before him shall be gathered all nations: and he shall separate them one from another, as a shepherd divideth his sheep from the goats: and he shall set the sheep on his right hand, but the goats on the left. Then shall the King say unto them on his right hand, Come, ye blessed of my Father, inherit the kingdom prepared for you from the foundation of the world: for I was an hungred, and ye gave me meat: I was thirsty, and ye gave me drink: I was a stranger, and ye took me in: naked, and ye clothed me: I was sick, and ye visited me: I was in prison, and ye came unto me. Then shall the righteous answer him, saying, Lord, when saw we thee an hungred, and fed thee? or thirsty, and gave thee drink? When saw we thee a stranger, and took thee in? or naked, and clothed thee? Or when saw we thee sick, or in prison, and came unto thee? And the King shall answer and say unto them, Verily I say unto you, Inasmuch as ye have done it unto one of the least of these my brethren, ye have done it unto me. Then shall he say also unto them on the left hand, Depart from me, ye cursed, into everlasting fire, prepared for the devil and his angels: for I was an hungred, and ye gave me no meat: I was thirsty, and ye gave me no drink: I was a stranger, and ye took me not in: naked, and ye clothed me not: sick, and in prison, and ye visited me not. Then shall they also answer him, saying, Lord, when saw we thee an hungred, or athirst, or a stranger, or naked, or sick, or in prison, and did not minister unto thee? Then shall he answer them, saying, Verily I say unto you, Inasmuch as ye did it not to one of the least of these, ye did it not to me. And these shall go away into everlasting punishment: but the righteous into life eternal. (25:31-46.)

from The Acts of the Apostles

Then they that gladly received his word were baptized: and the same day there were added unto them about three thousand souls. And they continued stedfastly in the apostles' doctrine and fellowship, and in breaking of bread, and in prayers. And fear came upon every soul: and many wonders and signs were done by the apostles. And all that believed were together, and had all things common; and sold their possessions and goods, and parted them to all men, as every man had need. (2:41-45.)

And the multitude of them that believed were of one heart and of one soul: neither said any of them that ought of the things which he possessed was his own; but they had all things common. And with great power gave the apostles witness of the resurrection of the Lord Jesus: and great grace was upon them all. Neither was there any among them that lacked: for as many as were possessors of lands or houses sold them, and brought the prices of the things that were sold, and laid them down at the apostles' feet: and distribution was made unto every man according as he had need. (4:32-35.)

Then Peter opened his mouth, and said, Of a truth I perceive that God is no respecter of persons: but in every nation he that feareth him, and worketh righteousness, is accepted with him. (10:34-35.)

Then Paul stood in the midst of Mars' hill, and said, Ye men of Athens, I perceive that in all things ye are too superstitious. For as I passed by, and beheld your devotions, I found an altar with this inscription, TO THE UNKNOWN GOD. Whom therefore ye ignorantly worship, him declare I unto you. God that made the world and all things therein, seeing that he is Lord of heaven and earth, dwelleth not in temples made with hands; neither is worshipped with men's hands, as though he needed any thing, seeing he giveth to all life, and breath, and all things; and hath made of one blood all nations of men for to dwell on all the face of the earth, and hath determined the times before appointed, and the bounds of their habitation; that they should seek the Lord, if haply they might feel after him, and find him, though he be not far from every one of us: for in him we live, and move, and have our being; as certain also of your own poets have said, For we are also his offspring. Forasmuch then as we are the offspring of God, we ought not to think that the Godhead is like unto gold, or silver, or stone, graven by art and man's device. And the times of this ignorance God winked at; but now commandeth all men every where to repent: because he hath appointed a day, in the which he will judge the world in righteousness by that man whom he hath ordained; whereof he hath given assurance unto all men, in that he hath raised him from the dead.

And when they heard of the resurrection of the dead, some mocked: and others said, We will hear thee again of this matter. So Paul departed from among them. (17:22-33.)

from The Epistle to the Romans

[God] will render to every man according to his deeds: to them who by patient continuance in well doing seek for glory and honour and immortality, eternal life: but unto them that are contentious, and do not obey the truth, but obey unrighteousness, indignation and wrath, tribulation and anguish, upon every soul of man that doeth evil, of the Jew first, and also of the Gentile; but glory, honour, and peace, to every man that worketh good, to the Jew first, and also to the Gentile: for there is no respect of persons with God. (2:6-11.)

The word is nigh thee, even in thy mouth, and in thy heart: that is, the word of faith, which we preach; that if thou shalt confess with thy mouth the Lord Jesus, and shalt believe in thine heart that God hath raised him from the dead, thou shalt be saved. For with the heart man believeth unto righteousness; and with the mouth confession is made unto salvation. For the scripture saith, Whosoever believeth on him shall not be ashamed. For there is no difference between the Jew and the Greek: for the same Lord over all is rich unto all that call upon him. For whosoever shall call upon the name of the Lord shall be saved. (10:8b-13.)

Him that is weak in the faith receive ye, but not to doubtful disputations. For one believeth that he may eat all things: another, who is weak, eateth herbs. Let not him that eateth despise him that eateth not; and let not him which eateth not judge him that eateth: for God hath received him. Who art thou that judgest another man's servant? to his own master he standeth or falleth. Yea, he shall be holden up: for God is able to make him stand. One man esteemeth one day above another: another esteemeth every day alike. Let every man be fully persuaded in his own mind. He that regardeth the day, regardeth it unto the Lord; and he that regardeth not the day, to the Lord he doth not regard it. He that eateth, eateth to the Lord, for he giveth God thanks; and he that eateth not, to the Lord he eateth not, and giveth God thanks. For none of us liveth to himself, and no man dieth to himself. For whether we live, we live unto the Lord; and whether we die, we die unto the Lord: whether we live therefore, or die, we are the Lord's. For to this end Christ both died, and rose, and revived, that he might be Lord both of the dead and living. But why dost thou judge thy brother? or why dost thou set at nought thy brother? for we shall all stand before the judgment seat of Christ. For it is written, As I live, saith the Lord, every knee shall bow to me, and every tongue shall confess to God. So then every one of us shall give account of himself to God. Let us not therefore judge one another any more: but judge this rather, that no man put a stumblingblock or an occasion to fall in his brother's way. (14:1-13.)

from The First Epistle to the Corinthians

For the body is not one member, but many. If the foot shall say, Because I am not the hand, I am not of the body; is it therefore not of the body? And if the ear shall say, Because I am not the eye, I am not of the body; is it therefore not of the body? If the whole body were an eye, where were the hearing? If the whole were hearing, where were the smelling? But now hath God set the members every one of them in the body, as it hath pleased him. And if they were all one member, where were the body? But now are they many members, yet but one body. And the eye cannot say unto the hand, I have no need of thee: nor again the head to the feet, I have no need of you. Nay, much more those members of the body, which seem to be more feeble, are necessary: and those members of the body, which we think to be less honourable, upon these we bestow more abundant honour; and our uncomely parts have more abundant comeliness. For our comely parts have no need: but God hath tempered the body together, having given more abundant honour to that part which lacked: that there should be no schism in the body; but that the members should have the same care one for another. And whether one member suffer, all the members suffer with it; or one member be honoured, all the members rejoice with it. (12:14-26.)

from The Epistle to the Galatians

Is the law then against the promises of God? God forbid: for if there had been a law given which could have given life, verily righteousness should have been by the law. But the scripture hath concluded all under sin, that the promise by faith of Jesus Christ might be given to them that believe. But before faith came, we were kept under the law, shut up unto the faith which should afterwards be revealed. Wherefore the law was our schoolmaster to bring us unto Christ, that we might be justified by faith. But after that faith is come, we are no longer under a schoolmaster. For ye are all the children of God by faith in Christ Jesus. For as many of you as have been baptized into Christ have put on Christ. There is neither Jew nor Greek, there is neither bond nor free, there is neither male nor female: for ye are all one in Christ Jesus. And if ye be Christ's, then are ye Abraham's seed, and heirs according to the promise. (3:21-29.)

from The Epistle to the Colossians

Masters, give unto your servants that which is just and equal; knowing that ye also have a Master in heaven. (4:1.)

from The Epistle of James

Let the brother of low degree rejoice in that he is exalted: but the rich, in that he is made low: because as the flower of the grass he shall pass away. For the sun is no sooner risen with a burning heat, but it withereth the grass, and the flower thereof falleth, and the grace of the fashion of it perisheth: so also shall the rich man fade away in his ways. (1:9-11.)

My brethren, show no partiality as you hold the faith of our Lord Jesus Christ, the Lord of glory. For if a man with gold rings and in fine clothing comes into your assembly, and a poor man in shabby clothing also comes in, and you pay attention to the one who wears the fine clothing and say, "Have a seat here, please," while you say to the poor man, "Stand there," or, "Sit at my feet," have you not made distinctions among yourselves, and become judges with evil thoughts? Listen, my beloved brethren. Has not God chosen those who are poor in the world to be rich in faith and heirs of the kingdom which he has promised to those who love him? But you have dishonored the poor man. Is it not the rich who oppress you, is it not they who drag you into court? Is it not they who blaspheme that honorable name by which you are called? If you really fulfil the royal law, according to the scripture, "You shall love your neighbor as yourself," you do well. But if you show partiality, you commit sin, and are convicted by the law as transgressors. (2:1-9, Revised Standard Version.)

from The First Epistle of John

We love him, because he first loved us. If a man say, I love God, and hateth his brother, he is a liar: for he that loveth not his brother whom he hath seen, how can he love God whom he hath not seen? And this commandment have we from him, That he who loveth God love his brother also. (4:19-21.)

Wisdom from the Gemara

11.

(3rd century)

These excerpts are from the discussions by Rabbinic scholars on the Mishna, the code of Jewish law, developed by Rabbi Judah I the Patriarch and his colleagues.

WISDOM FROM THE GEMARA

One man alone was brought forth at the time of Creation in order that thereafter none should have the right to say to another, "My father was greater than your father."

—Talmud Jerushalmi Sanhedrin, 4:5

Why was man created a solitary human being, without a companion? So that it might not be said that some races are better than others.

—Sanhedrin, 37a

The life of one man may not be sacrificed to save the life of another man.

—Ahalot, 7b

Formerly the deceased of the wealthy were buried in fancy caskets, and those of the poor in cheap coffins. The Rabbis have decreed, however, that now all who die, whether rich or poor, should be buried in inexpensive caskets.

—Moed Katon, 27a

A man came to Raba and said, "The prefect of my town has ordered me to kill so and so, or he will kill me." Raba replied, "Let him kill you; do you commit no murder. Why should you think that your blood is redder than his? Perhaps his is redder than yours."

—Pesachim, 25b

It was a favorite saying of the Rabbis of Jabneh: I am a creature [of God], and my neighbor is also His creature; my work is in the city, and his in the field; I rise early to my work, and he rises early to his. As he cannot excel in my work, so I cannot excel in his work. But perhaps you say, I do great things, and he does small things. We have learnt that [it matters not whether] a man does much or little, if only he direct his heart to Heaven.

—Berakot, 17a

Cyprian
(c. 200-258)

12.

Cyprian, a Father of the Church and Bishop of Carthage, in his
exposition of Christian teaching takes note of the problem of
equality.

from On Works and Alms

25. Let us consider, beloved brethren, what the congregation of believers did in the time of the apostles, when at the first beginnings the
mind flourished with greater virtues, when the faith of believers
burned with a warmth of faith as yet new. Then they sold houses and
farms, and gladly and liberally presented to the apostles the proceeds
to be dispensed to the poor; selling and alienating their earthly estate,
they transferred their lands thither where they might receive the fruits
of an eternal possession, and there prepared homes where they might
begin an eternal habitation. Such, then, was the abundance in labours,
as was the agreement in love, as we read in the Acts of the Apostles:
"And the multitude of them that believed acted with one heart and
one soul; neither was there any distinction among them, nor did they
esteem anything their own of the goods which belonged to them, but
they had all things common." (Acts iv. 32.) This is truly to become sons
of God by spiritual birth; this is to imitate by the heavenly law the
equity of God the Father. For whatever is of God is common in our
use; nor is any one excluded from His benefits and His gifts, so as to
prevent the whole human race from enjoying equally the divine goodness and liberality. Thus the day equally enlightens, the sun gives
radiance, the rain moistens, the wind blows, and the sleep is one to
those that sleep, and the splendour of the stars and of the moon is common. In which example of equality, he who, as a possessor in the earth,
shares his returns and his fruits with the fraternity, while he is common
and just in his gratuitous bounties, is an imitator of God the Father.

from Ad Demetrianum

You yourself exact servitude from your slave and, yourself a man,
compel a man to obey you, though you share in the same lot of birth,
the same condition of death, like bodily substance, the same mental
frame, and by equal right and the same rule come into this world and

later leave it. Yet unless he serves you according to your will, unless he is subservient to your whim, you act the imperious and over-exacting master, afflicting and torturing him often with stripes, lashes, hunger, thirst, nakedness and the sword, with chains and imprisonment. And do you not recognize your God and master, who yourself exercise mastery in this fashion?

Lactantius

13.

Lactantius

(c. 260-c. 340)

Lactantius, a Christian apologist who became a member of Constantine's household, was sometimes called the "Christian Cicero" since his exposition of Christian doctrine reveals the influence of Stoicism.

from The Divine Institutes, Book V

CHAPTER XV—*Of folly, wisdom, piety, equity, and justice*

. . . . .

The other part of justice, therefore, is equity; and it is plain that I am not speaking of the equity of judging well, though this also is praiseworthy in a just man, but of making himself equal to others, which Cicero calls equability. For God, who produces and gives breath to men, willed that all should be equal, that is, equally matched. He has imposed on all the same condition of living; He has produced all to wisdom; He has promised immortality to all; no one is cut off from His heavenly benefits. For as He distributes to all alike His one light, sends forth His fountains to all, supplies food, and gives the most pleasant rest of sleep; so He bestows on all equity and virtue. In His sight no one is a slave, no one a master; for if all have the same Father, by an equal right we are all children. No one is poor in the sight of God, but he who is without justice; no one is rich, but he who is full of virtues; no one, in short, is excellent, but he who has been good and innocent; no one is most renowned, but he who has abundantly performed works of mercy; no one is most perfect, but he who has filled all the steps of virtue. Therefore neither the Romans nor the Greeks could possess justice, because they had men differing from one another by many degrees, from the poor to the rich, from the humble to the powerful; in short, from private persons to the highest authorities of kings. For where all are not equally matched, there is not equity; and inequality of itself excludes justice, the whole force of which consists in this, that it makes those equal who have by an equal lot arrived at the condition of this life.

68

CHAPTER XVI—*Of the duties of the just man, and the equity of Christians*

Therefore, since those two fountains of justice are changed, all virtue and all truth are taken away, and justice itself returns to heaven. And on this account the true good was not discovered by philosophers, because they were ignorant both of its origin and effects: which has been revealed to no others but to our people. Some one will say, Are there not among you some poor, and others rich; some servants, and others masters? Is there not some difference between individuals? There is none; nor is there any other cause why we mutually bestow upon each other the name of brethren, except that we believe ourselves to be equal. For since we measure all human things not by the body, but by the spirit, although the condition of bodies is different, yet we have no servants, but we both regard and speak of them as brothers in spirit, in religion as fellow-servants. Riches also do not render men illustrious, except that they are able to make them more conspicuous by good works. For men are rich, not because they possess riches, but because they employ them on works of justice; and they who seem to be poor, on this account are rich, because they are not in want, and desire nothing.

Though, therefore, in lowliness of mind we are on an equality, the free with slaves, and the rich with the poor, nevertheless in the sight of God we are distinguished by virtue. And everyone is more elevated in proportion to his greater justice. For if it is justice for a man to put himself on a level even with those of lower rank, although he excels in this very thing, that he made himself equal to his inferiors; yet if he has conducted himself not only as an equal, but even as an inferior, he will plainly obtain a much higher rank of dignity in the judgment of God. For assuredly, since all things in this temporal life are frail and liable to decay, men both prefer themselves to others, and contend about dignity; than which nothing is more foul, nothing more arrogant, nothing more removed from the conduct of a wise man: for these earthly things are altogether opposed to heavenly things. For as the wisdom of men is the greatest foolishness with God, and foolishness is (as I have shown) the greatest wisdom; so he is low and abject in the sight of God who shall have been conspicuous and elevated on earth. For, not to mention that these present earthly goods to which great honour is paid are contrary to virtue, and enervate the vigour of the mind, what nobility, I pray, can be so firm, what resources, what power, since God is able to make kings themselves even lower than the lowest?

And therefore God has consulted our interest in placing this in particular among the divine precepts: "He that exalteth himself shall be abased; and he that humbleth himself shall be exalted." And the wholesomeness of this precept teaches that he who shall [simply] place himself on a level with [other] men, and carry himself with humility, is esteemed excellent and illustrious in the sight of God. For the sentiment is not false which is brought forward in Euripides to this effect: —"The things which are here considered evil are esteemed good in heaven."

St. Benedict of Nursia

14.

(c. 480-543)

St. Benedict, an Italian monk, founded the first Benedictine monastery and created the Rule of St. Benedict, the chief rule of Western monasticism.

from The Rule of St. Benedict

XXXIII. *Whether the Monks Should Have Anything of Their Own.* —More than anything else is this vice of property to be cut off root and branch from the monastery. Let no one presume to give or receive anything without the leave of the abbot, or to retain anything as his own. He should have nothing at all: neither a book, nor tablets, nor a pen—nothing at all. For indeed it is not allowed to the monks to have bodies or wills in their own power. But for all things necessary they must look to the Father of the monastery; nor is it allowable to have anything which the abbot has not given or permitted. All things shall be common to all, as it is written: 'Let not any man presume or call anything his own' [Acts iv. 32]. But if anyone is found delighting in this most evil vice: being warned once and again, if he do not amend, let him be subjected to punishment.

XXXIV. *Whether All Ought to Receive Necessaries Equally.*—As it is written: 'It was divided among them singly, according as each had need' [Acts iv. 35]: whereby we do not say—far from it—that there should be respect of persons, but a consideration for infirmities. Wherefore he who needs less, let him thank God and not be grieved; but he who needs more, let him be humiliated on account of his weakness, and not made proud on account of the indulgence that is shown him. And thus all members will be in peace. Above all, let not the evil of grumbling appear, on any account, by the least word or sign whatever. But, if such a grumbler is discovered, he shall be subjected to stricter discipline.

St. Gregory the Great

15.

(c. 540-604)

St. Gregory the Great, Pope and Doctor of the Church, states a characteristic teaching of the Church with respect to equality.

---

from The Book of Pastoral Rule

How servants and masters are to be admonished (Admonition 6). Differently to be admonished are servants and masters. Servants, to wit, that they ever keep in view the humility of their condition; but masters, that they lose not recollection of their nature, in which they are constituted on an equality with servants. Servants are to be admonished that they despise not their masters, lest they offend God, if by behaving themselves proudly they gainsay His ordinance: masters, too, are to be admonished, that they are proud against God with respect to His gift, if they acknowledge not those whom they hold in subjection by reason of their condition to be their equals by reason of their community of nature. The former are to be admonished to know themselves to be servants of masters; the latter are to be admonished to acknowledge themselves to be fellow-servants of servants. For to those it is said, *Servants, obey your masters according to the flesh* (Coloss. iii. 22); and again, *Let as many servants as are under the yoke count their masters worthy of all honour* (I Tim. vi. 1); but to these it is said, *And ye, masters, do the same things unto them, forbearing threatening, knowing that both their and your Master is in heaven* (Ephes. vi. 9).

St. Thomas Aquinas

16. (1225?-1274)

St. Thomas, theologian, philosopher, and Dominican monk, attempted to synthesize Aristotelian philosophy and Christian doctrine. His work marks the highest point of the development of scholasticism.

from The Summa Contra Gentiles

THAT WE ARE DIRECTED BY THE DIVINE LAW TO THE LOVE OF OUR NEIGHBOUR

1. From this it follows that the divine law aims at the love of our neighbour.

For there should be union of affection between those who have one common end. Now, men have one common last end, namely happiness, to which they are directed by God. Therefore men should be united together by mutual love.

Again. Whosoever loves a man, loves those whom he loves, and those who are his kindred. Now, men are loved by God, since He prepared for them a last end consisting in the enjoyment of Himself. Therefore as a man is a lover of God, so must he be a lover of his neighbour.

Moreover. Since man by nature is a *social animal,* he needs assistance from other men in order to obtain his own end. Now this is most suitably done if men love one another mutually. Hence the law of God, which directs men to their last end, commands us to love one another.

Again. In order to apply himself to divine things, man needs calm and peace. Now mutual love, more than aught else, removes the obstacles to peace. Seeing then that the divine law directs men to apply themselves to divine things, we must conclude that this same law leads men to love one another.

Further. The divine law is offered to man in aid of the natural law. Now it is natural to all men to love one another: a proof of which is that a man, by a kind of natural instinct, comes to the assistance of anyone even unknown that is in need, for instance by warning him, should he have taken the wrong road, by helping him to rise, should he have fallen, and so forth: *as though every man were intimate and friendly with his fellow-man.* Therefore mutual love is prescribed to man by the divine law. Wherefore it is said (Jo. xv. 12): *This is My commandment that you love one another:* and (I Jo. iv. 21): *This commandment we have from God, that he who loveth God, love also his brother:* and (Matth. xxii. 39) that the second commandment is, *Thou shalt love thy neighbour.*

17.

Walther von der Vogelweide

(13th century)

The minnesinger and most gifted lyric poet of medieval Germany reflects on the meaning of equality.

MY BROTHER MAN

Who fears not, God, Thy gifts to take,
And then Thy ten commandments break,
Lacks that true love which should be his salvation.
For many call Thee Father, who
Will not own me as brother too:
They speak deep words from shallow meditation.
Mankind arises from one origin;
We are alike both outward and within;
Our mouths are sated with the selfsame fare.
And when their bones into confusion fall,
Say ye, who knew the living man by sight,
Which is the villein now and which the knight,
That worms have gnawed their carcasses so bare?
Christians, Jews, and heathens serve Him all,
And God has all creation in His care.

William Langland

(c. 1332-c. 1400)

18.

The supposed author of *Piers Plowman* was born probably at Ledbury, near Welsh Marshes; lived in London. He took minor orders, but because of marriage never became a priest. This allegorical poem, of which only a portion is reprinted here, preaches a dedicated Christianity.

from Piers Plowman's Protest

Therefore I warn you rich, who are able in this world
On trust of your treasure to have triennials and pardons,
Be never the bolder to break the ten commandments;
And most of all you masters, mayors and judges,
Who have the wealth of this world, and are held wise by your
 neighbours,
You who purchase your pardons and papal charters:
At the dread doom, when the dead shall rise
And all come before Christ, and give full accounting,
When the doom will decide what day by day you practised,
How you led your life and were lawful before him,
Though you have pocketfuls of pardons there or provincial letters,
Though you be found in the fraternity of all the four orders,
Though you have double indulgences—unless Do Well help you
I set your patents and your pardons at the worth of a peascod!
Therefore I counsel all Christians to cry God mercy,
And Mary His Mother be our mean between Him,
That God may give us grace, ere we go hence,
To work with such a will, while we are here,
That after our death day, and at the Day of Doom,
Do Well may declare that we did as He commanded.

*   *   *

The poor may plead and pray in the doorway;
They may quake for cold and thirst and hunger;
None receives them rightfully and relieves their suffering.
They are hooted at like hounds and ordered off.
Little does he love the Lord, who lent him all these favours,
And who so parts his portion with the poor who are in trouble.
If there were no more mercy among poor than among rich men,

Mendicants might go meatless to slumber.
God is often in the gorge of these great masters,
But among lowly men are His mercy and His works;
And so says the psalter, as I have seen it often:
Ecce audivimus eam in Effrata, invenimus eam in campis silvae.
Clerics and other conditions converse of God readily,
And have Him much in the mouth, but mean men in their hearts.

* * *

The wealth of this world is evil to its keeper,
Howsoever it may be won, unless it be well expended.
If he is far from it, he fears often
That false men or felons will fetch away his treasure.
Moreover wealth makes men on many occasions
To sin, and to seek out subtlety and treason
Or from coveting of goods to kill the keepers.
Thus many have been murdered for their money or riches,
And those who did the deed damned forever,
And he himself, perhaps, in hell for his hard holding;
And greed for goods was the encumbrance of all together.
Pence have often purchased both palaces and terror;
Riches are the root of robbery and of murder;
He who so gathers his goods prizes God at little.

Ah! well may it be with poverty, for he may pass untroubled,
And in peace among the pillagers if patience follow him!
Our Prince Jesus and His Apostles chose poverty together,
And the longer they lived the less wealth they mastered.

* * *

"If priesthood were perfect all the people would be converted
Who are contrary to Christ's law and who hold Christendom in dis-
     honour.
All pagans pray and believe rightly
In the great and holy God, and ask His grace to aid them.
Their mediator is Mohammed to move their petition.
Thus the folk live in a faith but with a false advocate,
Which is rueful for righteous men in the realms of Christendom,
And a peril to the pope and to the prelates of his creation
Who bear the names of the bishops of Bethlehem and Babylon."

* * *

"And would that you, Conscience, were in the court of the king always,
That Grace, whom you commend so, were the guide of all clergy,
And that Piers with his plows, the newer and the older,
Were emperor of all the world, and all men Christian!
He is but a poor pope who should be the peoples' helper
And who sends men to slay the souls that they should rescue.
But well be it with Piers the Plowman who pursues his duty!
Qui pluit super justos et injustos equally,
Sends forth the sun to shine on the villein's tillage
As brightly as on the best man's and on the best woman's.
So Piers the Plowman is at pains to harrow
As well for a waster and for wenches in the brothels
As for himself and his servants, though he is served sooner.
He toils and tills for a traitor as earnestly
As for an honest husbandman, and at all times equally.
May he be worshipped who wrought all, both the good and the wicked,
And suffers the sinful till the season of their repentance!
God amend the pope, who pillages Holy Church,
Who claims that before the king he is the keeper of Christians,
Who accounts it nothing that Christians are killed and beaten,
Who leads the people to battle and spills the blood of Christians,
Against the Old Law and the New Law, as Luke witnesses. . . .
Surely it seems that if himself has his wishes
He recks nothing of the right nor of the rest of the people.
But may Christ in His Kindness save the cardinals and prelates
And turn their wit into wisdom and to welfare of the spirit!"

*   *   *

"Charity is God's champion, like a child that is gentle,
And the merriest of mouth at meat and at table.
For the love that lies in his heart makes him lightsome in language,
And he is companionable and cheerful as Christ bids him.
Nolite fieri sicut hypocritae tristes, etc.
I have seen him in silk and sometimes in russet,
In grey and in furred gowns and in gilt armour;
And he gave them as gladly to any creature who needed them.
Edmund and Edward were each kings
And considered saints when Charity followed them.
I have seen Charity also singing and reading,
Riding, and running in ragged clothing;
But among bidders and beggars I beheld him never.

In rich robes he is most rarely witnessed,
With a cap or a crown glistening and shaven,
Or in cleanly clothes of gauze or Tartary.
In a friar's frock he was found once,
But that was afar back in Saint Francis' lifetime;
In that sect since he has been too seldom witnessed.
He receives the robes of the rich, and praises
All who lead their lives without deception.
Beatus est dives qui, etc.
He comes often in the king's court where the council is honest,
But if Covetousness is of the council he will not come into it.
He comes but seldom in court with jesters,
Because of brawling and backbiting and bearing false witness.
He comes but rarely in the consistory where the commissary is seated,
For their lawsuits are overlong unless they are lifted by silver,
And they make and unmake matrimony for money.
Whom Conscience and Christ have combined firmly
They undo unworthily, these Doctors of Justice.
His ways were once among the clergy,
With archbishops and bishops and prelates of Holy Church,
To apportion Christ's patrimony to the poor and needy.
But now Avarice keeps the keys and gives to his kinsmen,
To his executors and his servants and sometimes to his children.

"I blame no man living; but Lord amend us
And give us all grace, good God, to follow Charity!
Though he mistrusts such manners in all men who meet him,
He neither blames nor bans nor boasts nor praises,
Nor lowers nor lauds nor looks sternly
Nor craves nor covets nor cries after more.
In pace in idipsum dormiam, etc.
The chief livelihood that he lives by is love in God's passion.
He neither bids nor begs nor borrows to render.
He misuses no man and his mouth hurts no one."

Marsilius of Padua

19.

Marsilius was an Italian political theorist, influenced by Aristotle and William of Ockham, who developed the position that the power of the state and the power of the Church derive equally from the people.

from The Defender of Peace

6. . . . The authority to make the law belongs only to those men whose making of it will cause the law to be better observed or observed at all. Only the whole body of the citizens are such men. To them, therefore, belongs the authority to make the law. The first proposition of this demonstration is very close to self-evident, for a law would be useless unless it were observed. Hence Aristotle said in the *Politics*, Book IV, Chapter 6: "Laws are not well ordered when they are well made but not obeyed." He also said in Book VI, Chapter 5: "Nothing is accomplished by forming opinions about justice and not carrying them out." The second proposition I prove as follows. That law is better observed by every citizen which each one seems to have imposed upon himself. But such is the law which is made through the hearing and command of the entire multitude of the citizens. The first proposition of this prosyllogism is almost self-evident; for since "the state is a community of free men," as is written in the *Politics*, Book III, Chapter 4, every citizen must be free, and not undergo another's despotism, that is, slavish dominion. But this would not be the case if one or a few of the citizens by their own authority made the law over the whole body of citizens. For those who thus made the law would be despots over the others, and hence such a law, however good it was, would be endured only with reluctance, or not at all, by the rest of the citizens, the more ample part. Having suffered contempt, they would protest against it, and not having been called upon to make it, they would not observe it. On the other hand, a law made by the hearing or consent of the whole multitude, even though it were less useful, would be readily observed and endured by every one of the citizens, because then each would seem to have set the law upon himself, and hence would have no protest against it, but would rather tolerate it with equanimity. The second proposition of the first syllogism I also prove in another way, as follows. The power to cause the laws to be observed belongs

only to those men to whom belongs coercive force over the transgressors of the laws. But these men are the whole body of citizens or the
weightier part thereof. Therefore, to them alone belongs the authority
to make the laws.

7. . . . For men came together to the civil community in order to
attain what was beneficial for sufficiency of life, and to avoid the opposite. Those matters, therefore, which can affect the benefit and harm of
all ought to be known and heard by all, in order that they may be able
to attain the beneficial and to avoid the opposite. Such matters are the
laws, as was assumed in the minor premise. For in the laws being
rightly made consists a large part of the whole common sufficiency of
men, while under bad laws there arise unbearable slavery, oppression,
and misery of the citizens, the final result of which is that the polity
is destroyed.

Nicholas of Cusa

20.

(1401?-1464)

Nicholas, German Cardinal, humanist and mystic who tried to reform monasteries, was an independent thinker in the fifteenth century.

from De Concordantia Catholica

Every decree is rooted in natural law, and if a decree contradicts it it cannot be valid *(Decretum,* di. 9, *Dicta Gratiani, 'cum ergo'* and *'constitutiones').* Whence, since natural law is naturally in the reason, every law is known to man in its root. The wiser and more eminent are chosen rulers of others for this reason: that they, being endowed with their natural clear reason, wisdom, and foresight, may discover just laws and through them rule others and settle disputes, that peace may be preserved (c.5, di. 2). Whence it follows that those who are vigorous in reason are naturally lords and rulers of others, but not through coercive law or judgment rendered against the unwilling. Whence, since by nature all are free, every government—whether it consists in written law or in a living law in the prince—through which the subjects are coerced from evil deeds and their liberty is regulated to good by fear of punishment is based on agreement alone and the consent of the subjects. For if by nature men are equally powerful and equally free, the valid and ordained authority of one man naturally equal in power with the others cannot be established except by the choice and consent of the others, even as law also is established by consent (c. 1, di. 2; c. 2, di. 8, where it is said that 'there is a general compact of human society to obey its kings'). Now, since by a general compact human society has agreed to obey its kings, it follows that in a true order of government there should be an election to choose the ruler himself, through which election he is constituted ruler and judge of those who elect him; thus ordained and righteous lordships and presidencies are constituted through election.

21. Desiderius Erasmus

(1466?-1536)

Erasmus, Dutch humanist, Catholic priest and teacher, had great influence in the sixteenth century.

from The Education of a Christian Prince

Nature created all men equal, and slavery was superimposed on nature, which fact the laws of even the pagans recognized. Now stop and think how out of proportion it is for a Christian to usurp full power over other Christians, whom the laws did not design to be slaves, and whom Christ redeemed from all slavery. Recall the instance when Paul called Onesimus (who was born a slave) the brother of his former master Philemon, from the time of his baptism. How incongruous it is to consider them slaves whom Christ redeemed with the same blood [as He did you]; whom He declared free along with all others; whom He fostered with the same sacraments as He did you; whom He calls to the same heritage of immortality! And over them, who have the same Master as you, the Prince, Jesus Christ, will you impose the yoke of slavery?

There is only one Master of Christian men. Why, then, do those who assume His functions, prefer to take their pattern of government from anyone except Him, who alone is in all ways to be imitated? It is proper enough to gather from others whatever virtues they have; but in Him is the perfect example of all virtue and wisdom. This seems the [essence of] foolishness to those outside the faith, but to us, if we are really faithful, He is the goodness of God and the wisdom of God. Now I do not want you to think that this means that you should be a slave, not a ruler. On the contrary, it illustrates the finest way to rule, unless, of course, you think God is only a bondsman because He governs the whole universe without recompense, because everyone and everything has felt His kindness, although they give Him nothing in return, and unless the mind seems a slave because it looks out so zealously for the welfare of the body, which it does not need, or unless you think the eye is a slave to all the other parts of the body because it sees for them all. You may well consider this: if someone should turn all these men whom you call your own into swine and asses by the art of Circe, would you not say your ruling power had been reduced to a lower level? I think you would. And yet you may exercise more authority over swine and asses than over men. You may treat them as you please, divide them off as you will, and even kill them. Surely he who has reduced his free subjects to slaves has put his power on a meaner level. The loftier the ideal to which you fashion your authority, the more magnificently and splendidly will you rule. Whoever protects the liberty and standing of your subjects is the one that helps your sovereign power. God gave the angels and men free will so that He would not be ruling over bondsmen, and so that He might glorify and add further grandeur to His kingdom. And who, now, would swell with pride because he rules over men cowed down by fear, like so many cattle?

Martin Luther

(1483-1546)

22.

The German leader of the Protestant Reformation wrote this treatise as one of a series of four which appeared in the latter half of the year 1519. It was Luther's first extended statement of his interpretation of the Lord's Supper. The portion reprinted here reveals Luther's conception of spiritual equality as it is found in common brotherhood of saints.

from A Treatise Concerning the Blessed Sacrament

4. The significance or purpose of this sacrament is the fellowship of all saints, whence it derives its common name *synaxis* or *communio*, that is, fellowship; and *communicare* means to take part in this fellowship, or as we say, to go to the sacrament, because Christ and all saints are one spiritual body, just as the inhabitants of a city are one community and body, each citizen being a member of the other and a member of the entire city. All the saints, therefore, are members of Christ and of the Church, which is a spiritual and eternal city of God, and whoever is taken into this city is said to be received into the community of saints, and to be incorporated into Christ's spiritual body and made a member of Him. On the other hand, *excommunicare* means to put out of the community and to sever a member from this body, and that is called in our language "putting one under the ban"; yet there is a difference, as I shall show in the following treatise, concerning the ban.

To receive the bread and wine of this sacrament, then, is nothing else than to receive a sure sign of this fellowship and incorporation with Christ and all saints. As though a citizen were given a sign, a document, or some other token as a proof that he is a citizen of the city, a member of the community. Even so St. Paul says: "We are all one bread and one body, for we are all partakers of one bread and of one cup."

5. This fellowship is of such a nature that all the spiritual possessions of Christ and His saints are imparted and communicated to him who receives this sacrament; again, all his sufferings and sins are communicated to them, and thus love engenders love and unites all. To carry out our homely figure: it is like a city where every citizen shares with all the others the name, honor, freedom, trade, customs, usages,

help, support, protection and the like, of that city, and on the other hand shares all the danger of fire and flood, enemies and death, losses, imposts and the like. For he who would have part in the common profits must also share in the losses, and ever recompense love with love. Here we see that whoever wrongs a citizen wrongs the entire city and all the citizens; whoever benefits one deserves favor and thanks from all the others. So, too, in our natural body, as St. Paul says in I Corinthians xii, where this sacrament is given a spiritual explanation: the members have a care one for another; whether one member suffer, all the members suffer with it; whether one member be honored, all the members rejoice with it. It is apparent then that if any one's foot hurts him, nay, even the smallest toe, the eye at once looks toward it, the fingers grasp it, the face frowns, the whole body bends to it, and all are concerned with this small member; on the other hand, if it is cared for, all the other members rejoice. This figure must be well weighed if one wishes to understand this sacrament; for the Scriptures employ it for the sake of the unlearned.

6. In this sacrament, therefore, God Himself gives through the priest a sure sign to man, to show that, in like manner, he shall be united with Christ and His saints and have all things in common with them; that Christ's sufferings and life shall be his own, together with the lives and sufferings of all the saints, so that whoever does him an injury does injury to Christ and all the saints, as He says by the prophet, "He that toucheth you toucheth the apple of My eye"; on the other hand, whoever does him a kindness does it to Christ and all His saints, as He says, "What ye have done unto one of the least of My brethren, that ye have done unto Me." Again, he must be willing to share all the burdens and misfortunes of Christ and His saints, their sorrow and joy. . . .

8. If any one be in despair, if he be distressed by his sinful con-science or terrified by death, or have any other burden on his heart, and desire to be rid of them all, let him go joyfully to the sacrament of the altar and lay down his grief in the midst of the congregation and seek help from the entire company of the spiritual body; just as when a citizen whose property has suffered injury or misfortune at the hands of his enemies makes complaint to his town council and fellow citizens and asks them for help. Therefore, the immeasurable grace and mercy of God are given us in this sacrament, that we may there lay down all misery and tribulation and put it on the congregation, and especially on Christ, and may joyfully strengthen and comfort ourselves and say: "Though I am a sinner and have fallen, though this or that misfortune

has befallen me, I will go to the sacrament to receive a sign from God that I have on my side Christ's righteousness, life and sufferings, with all holy angels and all the blessed in heaven, and all pious men on earth. If I die, I am not alone in death; if I suffer, they suffer with me. I have shared all my misfortune with Christ and the saints, since I have a sure sign of their love toward me." Lo, this is the benefit to be derived from this sacrament, this is the use we should make of it; then the heart cannot but rejoice and be comforted.

9. When you have partaken of this sacrament, therefore, or desire to partake of it, you must in turn also share the misfortunes of the congregation, as was said. But what are these? Christ in heaven and the angels together with all the saints have no misfortunes of their own, save when injury is done to the truth and to God's Word; yea, as we said, every bane and blessing of all the saints on earth affects them. There your heart must go out in love and devotion and learn that this sacrament is a sacrament of love, and that love and service are given you and you again must render love and service to Christ and His needy ones. You must feel with sorrow all the dishonor done to Christ in His holy Word, all the misery of Christendom, all the unjust suffering of the innocent, with which the world is everywhere filled to overflowing: you must fight, work, pray, and, if you cannot do more, have heartfelt sympathy. That is bearing in your turn the misfortune and adversity of Christ and His saints. Here the saying of Paul applies, "Bear ye one another's burdens, and so fulfil the law of Christ." Lo, thus you uphold them all, thus they all again in turn uphold you, and all things are in common, both good and evil. Then all things become easy, and the evil spirit cannot prevail against such a community. . . .

12. It is His will, then, that we partake of it frequently, in order that we may remember Him and exercise ourselves in this fellowship according to His example. For if His example were no longer kept before us, the fellowship also would soon be forgotten. So we at present see to our sorrow that many masses are held and yet the Christian fellowship which should be preached, practiced and kept before us by Christ's example has quite perished; so that we hardly know what purpose this sacrament serves, or how it should be used, nay, with our masses we frequently destroy this fellowship and pervert everything. This is the fault of the preachers who do not preach the Gospel nor the sacraments, but their humanly devised fables concerning the many works to be done and the ways to live aright.

But in times past this sacrament was so properly used, and the people were taught to understand this fellowship so well, that they even gathered material food and goods in the church and there distributed them among those who were in need, as St. Paul writes. Of this we have a relic in the word "collect," which still remains in the mass, and means a general collection, just as a common fund is gathered to be given to the poor. That was the time when so many became martyrs and saints. There were fewer masses, but much strength and blessing resulted from the masses; Christians cared for one another, assisted one another, sympathized with one another, bore one another's burden and affliction. This has all disappeared, and there remain only the many masses and the many who receive this sacrament without in the least understanding or practicing what it signifies.

13. There are those, indeed, who would share the benefits but not the cost, that is, who gladly hear in this sacrament that the help, fellowship and assistance of all the saints are promised and given to them, but who, because they fear the world, are unwilling in their turn to contribute to this fellowship, to help the poor, to endure sins, to care for the sick, to suffer with the suffering, to intercede for others, to defend the truth, to seek the reformation of the Church and of all Christians at the risk of life, property and honor. They are unwilling to suffer disfavor, harm, shame or death, although it is God's will that they be driven, for the sake of the truth and their neighbors, to desire the great grace and strength of this sacrament. They are self-seeking persons, whom this sacrament does not benefit. Just as we could not endure a citizen who wanted to be helped, protected and made free by the community, and yet in his turn would do nothing for it nor serve it. No, we on our part must make others' evil our own, if we desire Christ and His saints to make our evil their own; then will the fellowship be complete and justice be done to the sacrament. For the sacrament has no blessing and significance unless love grows daily and so changes a man that he is made one with all others.

Francisco Suarez

23.

(1548-1617)

Spanish Jesuit theologian, last of the old scholastics. His political doctrine that the power of kings is properly derived from the body of men and not by divine right was significant.

from On Laws and God the Lawgiver

Thus there remains to be proved only the assertion regarding the other and third part of justice, which relates to the form, that is, to distributive equity.

As to this factor, it is manifestly essential to the justice of law; since, if a law is imposed upon certain subjects, and not upon others to whom its subject-matter is equally applicable, then it is unjust, unless the exception is the result of some reasonable cause; a point which we have demonstrated above.

Again, the imposition of equal burdens upon all persons, without regard to the strength or capacity of each, is also contrary to reason and to justice, as is self-evident. And as to the fact that such injustice suffices to nullify a law, this is expressly affirmed by St. Thomas [I.-II, qu. 96, art. 4], when he says: '[Precepts] of this sort are manifestations of violence, rather than laws, and therefore they are not binding in conscience.' In my opinion, this statement should be interpreted as referring to cases in which the disproportion and inequality of a law are so great that the latter redounds to the common detriment, and results in a grave and unjust burdening of many members of the community. If it so happens, however, that a law is in itself useful, while some exceptional instance to which it applies involves injustice, the law would not on that account be entirely null, nor would it cease to bind the other subjects. For, strictly speaking, no positive injustice (as it were) is done these subjects in the imposition of such a burden upon them, since the burden would not in itself be wrongful and since there results simply a measure of disproportion as between certain individuals and the community as a whole, a disproportion which would seem insufficient to nullify the law. But if, by an exception in favour of certain persons, others are burdened to a degree that exceeds the bounds of equity, then, to the extent of that excess, the law will fail to bind; while it will nevertheless be able to bind in other ways wherein it is not unjust. An example of this sort may be noted in the case of the laws on taxes . . .

(1612)

Samuel Rutherford

(c. 1600-1661)

24.

Scottish ecclesiastic and political theorist. He served as a commissioner from Scotland to the Westminster Assembly and as professor of divinity in the University of St. Andrews. He was noted for the zeal with which he attacked the absolutist claims of the royalists and with which he defended presbyterianism against Erastians and advocates of episcopacy. At the Restoration his *Lex, Rex* was publicly burned in Edinburgh.

from Lex, Rex

[II] As domestic society is by nature's instinct, so is civil society natural *in radice,* in the root, and voluntary *in modo,* in the manner of coalescing. . . .

We are to distinguish betwixt a power of government, and a power of government by magistracy. That we defend ourselves from violence by violence, is a consequent of unbroken and sinless nature; but that we defend ourselves by devolving our power over in the hands of one or more rulers, seemeth rather positively moral than natural, except that it is natural for the child to expect help against violence, from his father. For which cause I judge . . . that princedom, empire, kingdom, or jurisdiction hath its rise from a positive and secondary law of nations, and not from the law of pure nature. The law saith, there is no law of nature agreeing to all living creatures for superiority; for by no reason in nature hath a boar dominion over a boar, a lion over a lion, a dragon over a dragon, a bull over a bull. And if all men be born equally free (as I hope to prove), there is no reason in nature why one man should be king and lord over another; therefore . . . I conceive all jurisdiction of man over man to be, as it were, artificial and positive, and that it inferreth some servitude whereof nature from the womb hath freed us, if you except that subjection of children to parents, and the wife to the husband. And the law saith, *De jure gentium secundarius est omnis principatus.* This also the scripture proveth, whileas the exalting of Saul or David above their brethren to be kings, and captains of the Lord's people, is ascribed, not to nature (for king and beggar spring of one clay-metal), but to an act of divine bounty and grace above nature. . . .

If we once lay the supposition that God hath immediately by the law of nature appointed there should be a government, and mediately defined, by the dictate of natural light in a community, that there shall be one or many rulers to govern the community; then the scripture's arguments may well be drawn out of the school of nature. . . .

[IV] *Whether the king be only and immediately from God, and not from the people? . . .*

But the question is concerning the designation of the person: whence is that this man rather than this man is crowned king . . . ; is it from God immediately and only . . . or is it from the people also, and their free choice? For the pastor and the doctor's office is from Christ only; but that John rather than Thomas be the doctor or the pastor is from the will and choice of men, the presbyters and people.

The royal power is three ways in the people: (1) Radically and virtually, as in the first subject; (2) *Collative vel communicative*, by way of free donation, they giving it to this man, not to this man, that he may rule over them; (3) *Limitate*, they giving it so as these three acts remain with the people: that they may measure out by ounce weights so much royal power and no more and no less, so as they may limit, moderate, and set banks and marches to the exercise; that they give it out *conditionate*, upon this and this condition, that they may take again to themselves what they gave out upon condition if the condition be violated. The first I conceive is clear: (1) Because if every living creature have radically in them a power of self-preservation to defend themselves from violence (as we see lions have paws, some beasts have horns, some claws), men, being reasonable creatures, united in society, must have power in a more reasonable and honourable way, to put this power of warding off violence in the hands of one or more rulers, to defend themselves by magistrates. (2) If all men be born, as concerning civil power, alike (for no man cometh out of the womb with a diadem on his head, or a sceptre in his hand), and yet men united in a society may give crown and sceptre to this man, and not to this man, then this power was in this united society. But it was not in them formally, for they should then all have been one king. . . . Therefore this power must have been virtually in them, because neither man nor community of men can give that which they neither have formally nor virtually in them. (3) Royalists cannot deny but cities have power to choose and create inferior magistrates. *Ergo* many cities united have power to create a higher ruler; for royal power is but the united and superlative power of inferior judges in one greater judge, whom they call a king. . . .

[XIII] *Whether or no royal dignity have its spring from nature;*

and how that is true, 'Every man is born free'; and how servitude is contrary to nature? . . .

As a man cometh into the world a member of a politic society, he is by consequence born subject to the laws of that society; but this maketh him not from the womb and by nature subject to a king, as by nature he is subject to his father who begat him (no more than by nature a lion is born subject to another king-lion); for it is by accident that he is born of parents under subjection to a monarch, or to either democratical or aristocratical governors, for Cain and Abel were born under none of these forms of government properly; and if he had been born in a new-planted colony in a wilderness where no government were yet established, he should be under no such government.***

Every man by nature is a free man born, that is, by nature no man cometh out of the womb under any civil subjection to king, prince, or judge, to master, captain, conqueror, teacher, etc., because freedom is natural to all, except freedom from subjection to parents; and subjection politic is merely accidental, coming from some positive laws of men as they are in a politic society, whereas they might have been born with all concomitants of nature, though born in a single family, the only natural and first society in the world.*** Man by nature is born free and as free as beasts.*** If any reply that the freedom natural of beasts and birds who never sinned cannot be one with the natural freedom of men who are now under sin, and so under bondage for sin, my answer is: that . . . he who is supposed to be the man born free from subjection politic, even the king born a king, is under the same state of sin, and so by reason of sin, of which he hath a share equally with all other men by nature, he must be by nature born under as great subjection penal for sin . . . as other men; *ergo* he is not born freer by nature than other men.*** For things that agree to men by nature agree to all men equally.*** If men be not by nature free from politic subjection, then must some, by the law of relation, by nature be kings. But none are by nature kings, because none have by nature these things which essentially constitute kings, for they have neither by nature the calling of God, nor gifts for the throne, nor the free election of the people, nor conquest. And if there be none a king by nature, there can be none a subject by nature. And the law saith, *Omnes sumus natura liberi, nullius ditioni subjecti.**** We are all by nature free.*** As domestic society is natural, being grounded upon nature's instinct, so politic society is voluntary, being grounded on the consent of men. And so politic society is natural *in radice,* in the root, and voluntary and free *in modo,* in the manner of their union; and the scripture cleareth to us that a king is made by the free consent of the people (Deut. 17.15), and so not by nature. What is from the womb, and so natural, is eternal, and agreeth to all societies of men; but a monarchy agreeth not to all societies of men; for many hundred years *de facto* there was not a king, till Nimrod's time the world being governed by families, and till Moses his time we find no institution for kings (Gen. 7). And the numerous multiplication of mankind did occasion monarchies. Otherwise fatherly government being the first, and measure of the rest, must be the best.

(1644)

John Lilburne

(c. 1614-1657)

25.

Lilburne was a pamphleteer and leader of the left-wing Puritan sect known as the Levellers during the Puritan Revolution. The Leveller movement aimed at religious and political equality, but it was crushed by Cromwell. Lilburne spent much of his life in prison or exile.

from The Free-man's Freedom Vindicated

A POSTSCRIPT CONTAINING A GENERAL PROPOSITION

God, the absolute sovereign Lord and King of all things in heaven and earth, the original fountain and cause of all causes, who is circumscribed, governed, and limited by no rules, but doth all things merely and only by his sovereign will and unlimited good pleasure, who made the world and all things therein for his own glory, by his own will and pleasure gave man, his mere creature, the sovereignty (under himself) over all the rest of his creatures (Gen. 1. 26, 28, 29) and endued him with a rational soul or understanding, and thereby created him after his own image (Gen. 1. 26-7, and 9. 6). The first of which was Adam, . . . made out of the dust or clay, out of whose side was taken a rib, which by the sovereign and absolute mighty creating power of God was made a female . . . called Eve. Which two are the earthly original fountain . . . of all and every particular and individual man and woman . . . in the world since, who are, and were, by nature all equal and alike in power, dignity, authority, and majesty, none of them having by nature any authority, dominion, or magisterial power one over or above another; neither have they, or can they exercise any, but merely by institution or donation, that is to say, by mutual agreement or consent, given, derived, or assumed by mutual consent and agreement, for the good benefit and comfort each of other, and not for the mischief, hurt, or damage of any; it being unnatural, irrational, . . . wicked, and unjust, for any man or men whatsoever to part with so much of their power as shall enable any of their Parliament-men, commissioners, trustees, deputies, . . . or servants, to destroy and undo them therewith. And unnatural, irrational, sinful, wicked, unjust, devilish, and tyrannical, it is for any man whatsoever, spiritual or temporal, clergyman or layman, to appropriate and assume unto himself a power, authority and jurisdiction, to rule, govern or reign over any sort of men in the world without their free consent, and whosever doth it . . . do thereby, as much as in them lies, endeavour to appropriate and assume unto themselves the office and sovereignty of God (who alone doth, and is to, rule by his will and pleasure), and to be like their Creator, which was the sin of the devils, who, not being content with their first station, would be like God, for which sin they were thrown down into hell, reserved in everlasting chains under darkness, unto the judgment of the great day (Jude, ver. 6). And Adam's sin it was, which brought the curse upon him and all his posterity, that he was not content with the station and condition that God created him in, but did aspire unto a better and more excellent, namely to be like his Creator, which proved his ruin, yea, and indeed had been the everlasting ruin and destruction of him and all his, had not God been the more merciful unto him in the promised Messiah (Gen., chap. 3). . . .

(1646)

An Agreement of the People

(1647)

26.

The *Agreement of the People* was a Leveller document drafted by representatives of the rank and file in Cromwell's Army. It outlined the form of government and of equality of representation which they desired. It was a counter-proposal to the document, "Heads of Proposals," drafted by the council of officers. Although it failed of achievement, it anticipated with great clarity the arguments and appeals which were to be made by revolutionary liberalism in the eighteenth and early nineteenth centuries.

from An Agreement of the People

Having by our late labours and hazards made it appeare to the world at how high a rate wee value our just freedome, and God having so far owned our cause, as to deliver the Enemies thereof into our hands: We do now hold our selves bound in mutual duty to each other, to take the best care we can for the future, to avoid both the danger of returning into a slavish condition, and the chargable remedy of another war: for as it cannot be imagined that so many of our Countrymen would have opposed us in this quarrel, if they had understood their owne good; so may we safely promise to our selves, that when our Common Rights and liberties shall be cleared, their endeavours will be disappointed, that seek to make themselves our Masters: since therefore our former oppressions, and scarce yet ended troubles have beene occasioned, either by want of frequent Nationall meetings in Councell, or by rendring those meetings ineffectuall; We are fully agreed and resolved, to provide that hereafter our Representatives be neither left to an uncertainty for the time, nor made uselesse to the ends for which they are intended: In order whereunto we declare,

I.

That the People of England being at this day very unequally distributed by Counties, Cities, & Burroughs, for the election of their Deputies in Parliament, ought to be more indifferently proportioned, according to the number of the Inhabitants: the circumstances whereof, for number, place, and manner, are to be set down before the end of this present Parliament.

II.

That to prevent the many inconveniences apparently arising from the long continuance of the same persons in authority, this present Parliament be dissolved upon the last day of September, which shall be in the year of our Lord, 1648.

III.

That the People do of course chuse themselves a Parliament once in two yeares, viz. upon the first Thursday in every 2d. March, after the manner as shall be prescribed before the end of this Parliament, to begin to sit upon the first Thursday in Aprill following at Westminster, or such other place as shall bee appointed from time to time by the preceding Representatives; and to continue till the last day of September, then next ensuing, and no longer.

IV.

That the power of this, and all future Representatives of this Nation, is inferiour only to theirs who chuse them, and doth extend, without the consent or concurrence of any other person or persons; to the enacting, altering, and repealing of Lawes; to the erecting and abolishing of Offices and Courts; to the appointing, removing, and calling to account Magistrates, and Officers of all degrees; to the making War and peace, to the treating with forraign States. And generally, to whatsoever is not expresly, or implyedly reserved by the represented to themselves.

Which are as followeth,

1. That matters of Religion, and the wayes of Gods Worship, are not at all intrusted by us to any humane power, because therein wee cannot remit or exceed a tittle of what our Consciences dictate to be the mind of God, without wilfull sinne: neverthelesse the publike way of instructing the Nation (so it be not compulsive) is referred to their discretion.

2. That the matter of impresting and constraining any of us to serve in the warres, is against our freedome; and therefore we do not allow it in our Representatives; the rather, because money (the sinews of war) being alwayes at their disposall, they can never want numbers of men, apt enough to engage in any just cause.

3. That after the dissolution of this present Parliament, no person

be at any time questioned for anything said or done, in reference to the late publike differences, otherwise then in execution of the Judgments of the present Representatives, or House of Commons.

4. That in all Laws made, or to be made, every person may be bound alike, and that no Tenure, Estate, Charter, Degree, Birth, or place, do confer any exemption from the ordinary Course of Legall proceedings, whereunto others are subjected.

5. That as the Laws ought to be equall, so they must be good, and not evidently destructive to the safety and well-being of the people.

These things we declare to be our native Rights, *and therefore are agreed and resolved to maintain them with our utmost possibilities, against all opposition whatsoever, being compelled thereunto, not only by the examples of our Ancestors, whose bloud was often spent in vain for the recovery of their Freedomes, suffering themselves,* through fradulent accommodations, *to be still deluded of the fruit of their Victories, but also by our own wofull experience, who having long expected, & dearly earned the establishment of these certain rules of Government are yet made to depend for the settlement of our Peace and Freedome, upon him that intended our bondage, and brought a cruell Warre upon us.*

(1647)

The Putney Debates
(1647)

27.

The debates in Cromwell's Army between the officers and the representatives of the common soldiers over the *Agreement of the People* raise the most fundamental questions about the nature of representation in democracy and serve to bring equality into sharp focus. A portion of the debates as they have been preserved in the Clarke papers is reprinted here.

from The Putney Debates

... *Major [William] Rainborough:* I desire we may come to that end we all strive after. I humbly desire you will fall upon that which is the engagement of all, which is the rights and freedoms of the people, and let us see how far we have made sure to them a right and freedom, and if anything be tendered as to that [in this paper]. And when that engagement is gone through, then, let us consider of those [things only] that are of greater weight.

(The paper called the Agreement read. Afterwards the first article read by itself.)

Ireton: The exception that lies in it is this. It is said, they are to be distributed according to the number of the inhabitants: 'The people of England,' &c. And this doth make me think that the meaning is, that every man that is an inhabitant is to be equally considered, and to have an equal voice in the election of those representers, the persons that are for the general Representative; and if that be the meaning, then I have something to say against it. But if it be only that those people that by the civil constitution of this kingdom, which is original and fundamental, and beyond which I am sure no memory of record does go—

[Cowling, interrupting]: Not before the Conquest.

[Ireton]: But before the Conquest it was so. If it be intended that those that by that constitution that was before the Conquest, that hath been beyond memory, such persons that have been before [by] that constitution [the electors], should be [still] the electors, I have no more to say against it.

Colonel Rainborough objected: That others might have given their hands to it.

Captain Denne denied that those that were set of their regiment were their hands.

100

Ireton [asked]: Whether those men whose hands are to it, or those that brought it, do know so much of the matter as [to know] whether they mean that all that had a former right of election [are to be electors], or [that] those that had no right before are to come in.

Cowling: In the time before the Conquest. Since the Conquest the greatest part of the kingdom was in vassalage.

Petty: We judge that all inhabitants that have not lost their birthright should have an equal voice in elections.

Rainborough: I desired that those that had engaged in it [might be included]. For really I think that the poorest he that is in England hath a life to live, as the greatest he; and therefore truly, sir, I think it's clear, that every man that is to live under a government ought first by his own consent to put himself under that government; and I do think that the poorest man in England is not at all bound in a strict sense to that government that he hath not had a voice to put himself under; and I am confident that, when I have heard the reasons against it, something will be said to answer those reasons, insomuch that I should doubt whether he was an Englishman or no, that should doubt of these things.

Ireton: That's [the meaning of] this, ['according to the number of the inhabitants']?

Give me leave to tell you, that if you make this the rule I think you must fly for refuge to an absolute natural right, and you must deny all civil right; and I am sure it will come to that in the consequence. This, I perceive, is pressed as that which is so essential and due: the right of the people of this kingdom, and as they are the people of this kingdom, distinct and divided from other people, and that we must for this right lay aside all other considerations; this is so just, this is so due, this is so right to them. And that those that they do thus choose must have such a power of binding all, and loosing all, according to those limitations, this is pressed as so due, and so just, as [it] is argued, that it is an engagement paramount [to] all others . . . For my part, I think it is no right at all. I think that no person hath a right to an interest or share in the disposing of the affairs of the kingdom, and in determining or choosing those that shall determine what laws we shall be ruled by here—no person hath a right to this, that hath not a permanent fixed interest in this kingdom, and those persons together are properly the represented of this kingdom, and consequently are [also] to make up the representers of this kingdom, who taken together do comprehend whatsoever is of real or permanent interest in the kingdom. And I am sure otherwise I cannot tell what any man can say why a foreigner com-

ing in amongst us—or as many as will coming in amongst us, or by
force or otherwise settling themselves here, or at least by our permission
having a being here—why they should not as well lay claim to it as any
other. We talk of birthright. Truly [by] birthright there is thus much
claim. Men may justly have by birthright, by their very being born in
England, that we should not seclude them out of England, that we
should not refuse to give them air and place and ground, and the freedom of the highways and other things, to live amongst us . . . That I
think is due to a man by birth. But that by a man's being born here he
shall have a share in that power that shall dispose of the lands here,
and of all things here, I do not think it a sufficient ground. I am sure
if we look upon that which is the utmost (within [any] man's view) of
what was originally the constitution of this kingdom, upon that which
is most radical and fundamental, and which if you take away, there is
no man hath any land, any goods, [or] any civil interest, that is this:
that those that choose the representers for the making of laws by which
this state and kingdom are to be governed, are the persons who, taken
together, do comprehend the local interest of this kingdom; that is, the
persons in whom all land lies, and those in corporations in whom all
trading lies. This is the most fundamental constitution of this kingdom
and [that] which if you do not allow, you allow none at all. This constitution hath limited and determined it that only those shall have
voices in elections. It is true, as was said by a gentleman near me, the
meanest man in England ought to have [a voice in the election of the
government he lives under—but only if he has some local interest]. I
say this: that those that have the meanest local interest—that man that
hath but forty shillings a year, he *hath* as great voice in the election of
a knight for the shire as he that hath ten thousand a year, or more if
he had never so much; and therefore there is that regard had to it. But
this [local interest], still the constitution of this government hath had
an eye to (and what other government hath not an eye to this?). It doth
not relate to the interest of the kingdom if it do not lay the foundation
of the power that's given to the representers, in those who have a permanent and a local interest in the kingdom, and who taken all together
do comprehend the whole [interest of the kingdom]. There is all the
reason and justice that can be, [in this]: if I will come to live in a
kingdom, being a foreigner to it, or live in a kingdom, having no
permanent interest in it, [and] if I will desire as a stranger, or claim as
one freeborn here, the air, the free passage of highways, the protection
of laws, and all such things—if I will either desire them or claim them,
[then] I (if I have no permanent interest in that kingdom) must sub-

mit to those laws and those rules [which they shall choose], who, taken together, do comprehend the whole interest of the kingdom. And if we shall go to take away this, we shall plainly go to take away all property and interest that any man hath either in land by inheritance, or in estate by possession, or anything else—[I say], if you take away this fundamental part of the civil constitution.

Rainborough: Truly, sir, I am of the same opinion I was, and am resolved to keep it till I know reason why I should not. . . . I do hear nothing at all that can convince me, why any man that is born in England ought not to have his voice in election of burgesses. It is said that if a man have not a permanent interest, he can have no claim; and [that] we must be no freer than the laws will let us be, and that there is no [law in any] chronicle will let us be freer than that we [now] enjoy. Something was said to this yesterday. I do think that the main cause why Almighty God gave men reason, it was that they should make use of that reason, and that they should improve it for that end and purpose that God gave it them. And truly, I think that half a loaf is better than none if a man be anhungry: [this gift of reason without other property may seem a small thing], yet I think there is nothing that God hath given a man that any [one] else can take from him. And therefore I say, that either it must be the Law of God or the law of man that must prohibit the meanest man in the kingdom to have this bene-fit as well as the greatest. I do not find anything in the Law of God, that a lord shall choose twenty burgesses, and a gentleman but two, or a poor man shall choose none: I find no such thing in the Law of Nature, nor in the Law of Nations. But I do find that all Englishmen must be subject to English laws, and I do verily believe that there is no man but will say that the foundation of all law lies in the people, and if [it lie] in the people, I am to seek for this exemption.

And truly I have thought something [else]: in what a miserable distressed condition would many a man that hath fought for the Parliament in this quarrel, be! I will be bound to say that many a man whose zeal and affection to God and this kingdom hath carried him forth in this cause, hath so spent his estate that, in the way the state [and] the Army are going, he shall not hold up his head, if when his estate is lost, and not worth forty shillings a year, a man shall not have any interest. And there are many other ways by which [the] estates men have (if that be the rule which God in his providence does use) do fall to decay. A man, when he hath an estate, hath an interest in mak-ing laws, [but] when he hath none, he hath no power in it; so that a man cannot lose that which he hath for the maintenance of his family but he must [also] lose that which God and nature hath given him! And therefore I do [think], and am still of the same opinion, that every man born in England cannot, ought not, neither by the Law of God nor the Law of Nature, to be exempted from the choice of those who are to make laws for him to live under, and for him, for aught I know, to lose his life under. And therefore I think there can be no great stick in this.

Truly I think that there is not this day reigning in England a greater fruit or effect of tyranny than this very thing would produce. Truly I know nothing free but only the knight of the shire, nor do I know anything in a parliamentary way that is clear from the height and fulness of tyranny, but only [that]. As for this of corporations [which you also mentioned], it is as contrary to freedom as may be. For, sir, what is it? The King he grants a patent under the Broad Seal of England to such a corporation to send burgesses, he grants to [such] a city to send burgesses. When a poor base corporation from the King ['s grant] shall send two burgesses, when five hundred men of estate shall not send one, when those that are to make their laws are called by the King, or cannot act [but] by such a call, truly I think that the people of England have little freedom.

Ireton: I think there was nothing that I said to give you occasion to think that I did contend for this, that such a corporation [as that] should have the electing of a man to the Parliament. I think I agreed to this matter, that all should be equally distributed. But the question is, whether it should be distributed to all persons, or whether the same persons that are the electors [now] should be the electors still, and it [be] equally distributed amongst *them.* . . .

All the main thing that I speak for, is because I would have an eye to property. I hope we do not come to contend for victory—but let every man consider with himself that he do not go that way to take away all property. For here is the case of the most fundamental part of the constitution of the kingdom, which if you take away, you take away all by that. Here men of this and this quality are determined to be the electors of men to the Parliament, and they are all those who have any permanent interest in the kingdom, and who, taken together, do comprehend the whole [permanent, local] interest of the kingdom. I mean by permanent [and] local, that [it] is not [able to be removed] anywhere else. . . . Now I wish we may all consider of what right you will challenge that all the people should have right to elections. Is it by the right of nature? If you will hold forth that as your ground, then I think you must deny all property too, and this is my reason. For thus:

by that same right of nature (whatever it be) that you pretend, by
which you can say, one man hath an equal right with another to the
choosing of him that shall govern him—by the same right of nature, he
hath the same [equal] right in any goods he sees—meat, drink, clothes—
to take and use them for his sustenance. He hath a freedom to the
land, [to take] the ground, to exercise it, till it; he hath the [same] freedom to anything that any one doth account himself to have any propriety in. Why now I say then, if you, against the most fundamental
part of [the] civil constitution (which I have now declared), will plead
the Law of Nature, that a man should (paramount [to] this, and contrary to this) have a power of choosing those men that shall determine
what shall be law in this state, though he himself have no permanent
interest in the state, [but] whatever interest he hath he may carry
about with him—if this be allowed, [because by the right of nature] we
are free, we are equal, one man must have as much voice as another,
then show me what step or difference [there is], why [I may not] by
the same right [take your property, though not] of necessity to sustain
nature. It is for my better being, and [the better settlement of the
kingdom]? Possibly not for it, neither: possibly I may not have so real
a regard to the peace of the kingdom as that man who hath a permanent interest in it. He that is here to-day, and gone to-morrow, I do not
see that he hath such a permanent interest. Since you cannot plead to
it by anything but the Law of Nature, [or for anything] but for the end
of better being, and [since] that better being is not certain, and [what
is] more, destructive to another; upon these grounds, if you do, paramount [to] all constitutions, hold up this Law of Nature, I would fain
have any man show me their bounds, where you will end, and [why
you should not] take away all property.

Rainborough: I shall now be a little more free and open with you
than I was before. I wish we were all true-hearted, and that we did all
carry ourselves with integrity. If I did mistrust you I would [not] use
such asseverations. I think it doth go on mistrust, and things are
thought too [readily] matters of reflection, that were never intended.
For my part, as I think, *you* forgot something that was in *my* speech,
and you do not only yourselves believe that [some] men are inclining
to anarchy, but you would make all men believe that. And, sir, to say
because a man pleads that every man hath a voice [by right of nature],
that therefore it destroys [by] the same [argument all property—this is
to forget the Law of God]. That there's a property, the Law of God
says it; else why [hath] God made that law, *Thou shalt not steal?* I am
a poor man, therefore I must be [op]pressed: if I have no interest in

the kingdom, I must suffer by all their laws be they right or wrong. Nay thus: a gentleman lives in a country and hath three or four lordships, as some men have (God knows how they got them); and when a Parliament is called he must be a Parliament-man; and it may be he sees some poor men, they live near this man, he can crush them—I have known an invasion to make sure he hath turned the poor men out of doors; and I would fain know whether the potency of [rich] men do not this, and so keep them under the greatest tyranny that was [ever] thought of in the world. And therefore I think that to that it is fully answered: God hath set down that thing as to propriety with this law of his, *Thou shalt not steal*. And for my part I am against any such thought, and, as for yourselves, I wish you would not make the world believe that we are for anarchy.

Cromwell: I know nothing but this, that they that are the most yielding have the greatest wisdom; but really, sir, this is not right as it should be. No man says that you have a mind to anarchy, but [that] the consequence of this rule tends to anarchy, must end in anarchy; for where is there any bound or limit set if you take away this [limit], that men that have no interest but the interest of breathing [shall have no voice in elections]? Therefore I am confident on 't, we should not be so hot one with another.

Rainborough: I know that some particular men we debate with [believe we] are for anarchy.

Ireton: I profess I must clear myself as to that point. I would not desire, I cannot allow myself, to lay the least scandal upon anybody. And truly, for that gentleman that did take so much offence, I do not know why he should take it so. We speak to the paper—not to persons —and to the matter of the paper. And I hope that no man is so much engaged to the matter of the paper—I hope [that] our persons, and our hearts and judgments, are not [so] pinned to papers but that we are ready to hear what good or ill consequence will flow from it.

I have, with as much plainness and clearness of reason as I could, showed you how I did conceive the doing of this [that the paper advocates] takes away that which is the most original, the most fundamental civil constitution of this kingdom, and which is, above all, that constitution by which I have any property. If you will take away that and set up, as a thing paramount, whatever a man may claim by the Law of Nature, though it be not a thing of necessity to him for the sustenance of nature; if you do make this your rule, I desire clearly to understand where then remains property.

Now then—I would misrepresent nothing—the answer which had

anything of matter in it, the great and main answer upon which that which hath been said against this [objection] rests, seemed to be that it will not make a breach of property, [for this reason]: that there is a law, *Thou shalt not steal.* [But] the same law says, *Honour thy father and* [thy] *mother,* and that law doth likewise hold out that it doth extend to all that (in that place where we are in) are our governors; so that by that there is a forbidding of breaking a civil law when we may live quietly under it, and [that by] a divine law. Again it is said—indeed [was said] before—that there is no law, no divine law, that tells us that such a corporation must have the election of burgesses, such a shire [of knights], or the like. Divine law extends not to particular things. And so, on the other side, if a man were to demonstrate his [right to] property by divine law, it would be very remote. Our [right to] property descends from other things, as well as our right of sending burgesses. That divine law doth not determine particulars but generals in relation to man and man, and to property, and all things else: and we should be as far to seek if we should go to prove a property in [a thing by] divine law, as to prove that I have an interest in choosing burgesses of the Parliament by divine law. And truly, under favour, I refer it to all, whether there be anything of solution to that objection that I made, if it be understood—I submit it to any man's judgment.

Rainborough: To the thing itself—property [in the franchise]. I would fain know how it comes to be the property [of some men, and not of others]. As for estates and those kind of things, and other things that belong to men, it will be granted that they are property; but I deny that that is a property, to a lord, to a gentleman, to any man more than another in the kingdom of England. If it be a property, it is a property by a law—neither do I think that there is very little property in this thing by the law of the land, because I think that the law of the land in that thing is the most tyrannical law under heaven. And I would fain know what we have fought for. [For our laws and liberties?] And this is the old law of England—and that which enslaves the people of England—that they should be bound by laws in which they have no voice at all! . . .

Petty: I desire to add one word concerning the word *property.* It is for something that anarchy is so much talked of. For my own part I cannot believe in the least that it can be clearly derived from that paper. 'Tis true, that somewhat may be derived in the paper against the King, the power of the King, and somewhat against the power of the Lords; and the truth is when I shall see God going about to throw down King and Lords and property, then I shall be contented. But I hope that they may live to see the power of the King and the Lords thrown down, that yet may live to see property preserved. And for this of changing the Representative of the nation, of changing those that choose the Representative, making of them more full, taking more into the number than formerly, I had verily thought we had all agreed in it that more should have chosen—all that had desired a more equal representation than we now have. For now those only choose who have forty shillings freehold. A man may have a lease for one hundred pounds a year, a man may have a lease for three lives, [but he has no voice]. But [as] for this [argument], that it destroys all right [to property] that every Englishman that is an inhabitant of England should choose and have a voice in the representatives, I suppose it is, [on the contrary], the only means to preserve all property. For I judge every man is naturally free; and I judge the reason why men [chose representatives] when they were in so great numbers that every man could not give his voice [directly], was that they who were chosen might preserve property [for all]; and therefore men agreed to come into some form of government that they might preserve property, and I would fain know, if we were to begin a government, [whether you would say], 'You have not forty shillings a year, therefore you shall not have a voice.' Whereas before there was a government every man had such a voice, and afterwards, and for this very cause, they did choose representatives, and put themselves into forms of government that they may preserve property, and therefore it is not to destroy it, [to give every man a voice].

Ireton: I think we shall not be so apt to come to a right understanding in this business, if one man, and another man, and another man do speak their several thoughts and conceptions to the same purpose, as if we do consider where the objection lies, and what the answer is which is made to it; and therefore I desire we may do so. To that which this gentleman spake last. The main thing that he seemed to answer was this: that he would make it appear that the going about to establish this government, [or] such a government, is not a destruction of property, nor does not tend to the destruction of property, because the people's falling into a government is for the preservation of property. What weight there [is in it] lies in this: since there is a falling into a government, and government is to preserve property, therefore this cannot be against property. The objection does not lie in that, the making of the representation more equal, but [in] the introducing of men into an equality of interest in this government, who have no property in this kingdom, or who have no local permanent interest in it.

For if I had said that I would not wish at all that we should have any enlargement of the bounds of those that are to be the electors, then you might have excepted against it. But [what I said was] that I would not go to enlarge it beyond all bounds, so that upon the same ground you may admit of so many men from foreign states as would outvote you. The objection lies still in this. I do not mean that I would have it restrained to that proportion [that now obtains], but to restrain it still to men who have a local, a permanent interest in the kingdom, who have such an interest that they may live upon it as freemen, and who have such an interest as is fixed upon a place, and is not the same equally everywhere. If a man be an inhabitant upon a rack rent for a year, for two years, or twenty years, you cannot think that man hath any fixed or permanent interest. That man, if he pay the rent that his land is worth, and hath no advantage but what he hath by his land, is as good a man, may have as much interest, in another kingdom as here. I do not speak of not enlarging this [representation] at all, but of keeping this to the most fundamental constitution in this kingdom, that is, that no person that hath not a local and permanent interest in the kingdom should have an equal dependence in election [with those that have]. But if you go beyond this law, if you admit any man that hath a breath and being, I did show you how this will destroy property. It may come to destroy property thus. You may have such men chosen, or at least the major part of them, [as have no local and permanent interest]. Why may not those men vote against all property? [Again] you may admit strangers by this rule, if you admit them once to inhabit, and those that have interest in the land may be voted out of their land. It may destroy property that way. . . .

Rainborough: I desire to know how this comes to be a property in some men, and not in others.

Colonel [Nathaniel] Rich: I confess [there is weight in] that objection that the Commissary-General last insisted upon; for you have five to one in this kingdom that have no permanent interest. Some men [have] ten, some twenty servants, some more, some less. If the master and servant shall be equal electors, then clearly those that have no interest in the kingdom will make it their interest to choose those that have no interest. It may happen, that the majority may by law, not in a confusion, destroy property; there may be a law enacted, that there shall be an equality of goods and estate. I think that either of the extremes may be urged to inconveniency; that is, [that] men that have no interest as to estate should have no interest as to election [and that they should have an equal interest]. But there may be a more equitable division and distribution than that he that hath nothing should have an equal voice; and certainly there may be some other way thought of, that there may be a representative of the poor as well as the rich, and not to exclude all. . . .

Wildman: Unless I be very much mistaken we are very much deviated from the first question. Instead of following the first proposition to inquire what is just, I conceive we look to prophecies, and look to what may be the event, and judge of the justness of a thing by the consequence. I desire we may recall [ourselves to the question] whether it be right or no. I conceive all that hath been said against it will be reduced to this [question of consequences], and [to] another reason—that it is against a fundamental law, that every person [choosing] ought to have a permanent interest, because it is not fit that those should choose Parliaments that have no lands to be disposed of by Parliament.

Ireton: If you will take it by the way, it is not fit that the representees should choose [as] the representers, or the persons who shall make the law in the kingdom, [those] who have not a permanent fixed interest in the kingdom. [The reason is the same in the two cases.]

Wildman: Sir, I do so take it; and I conceive that that is brought in for the same reason: that foreigners might [otherwise not only] come to have a voice in our elections as well as the native inhabitants, [but to be elected].

Ireton: That is upon supposition that these [foreigners] should be all inhabitants.

Wildman: I shall begin with the last first. The case is different with the native inhabitant and [the] foreigner. If a foreigner shall be admitted to be an inhabitant in the nation, so he will submit to that form of government as the natives do, he hath the same right as the natives but in this particular. Our case is to be considered thus, that we have been under slavery. That's acknowledged by all. Our very laws were made by our conquerors; and whereas it's spoken much of chronicles, I conceive there is no credit to be given to any of them; and the reason is because those that were our lords, and made us their vassals, would suffer nothing else to be chronicled. We are now engaged for our freedom. That's the end of Parliaments: not to constitute what is already [established, but to act] according to the just rules of government. Every person in England hath as clear a right to elect his representative as the greatest person in England. I conceive that's the undeniable maxim of government: that all government is in the free consent of the people. If [so], then upon that account there is no person that is under a just government, or hath justly his own, unless he by his own free consent be put under that government. This he cannot be unless he be consenting to it, and therefore, according to this maxim, there is never a person in England [but ought to have a voice in elections]. If [this], as that gentleman says, be true, there are no laws that in this strictness and rigour of justice [any man is bound to], that are not made by those who[m] he doth consent to. And therefore I should humbly move, that if the question be stated—which would soonest bring things to an issue—it might rather be thus: Whether any person can justly be bound by law, who doth not give his consent that such persons shall make laws for him?

Ireton: Let the question be so: Whether a man can be bound to any law that he doth not consent to? And I shall tell you, that he may and ought to be [bound to a law] that he doth not give a consent to, nor doth not choose any [to consent to]; and I will make it clear. If a foreigner come within this kingdom, if that stranger will have liberty [to dwell here] who hath no local interest here, he, as a man, it's true, hath air, [the passage of highways, the protection of laws, and all] that by nature; we must not expel [him] our coasts, give him no being amongst us, nor kill him because he comes upon our land, comes up our stream, arrives at our shore. It is a piece of hospitality, of humanity, to receive that man amongst us. But if that man be received to a being amongst us, I think that man may very well be content to submit himself to the law of the land; that is, the law that is made by those people that have a property, a fixed property, in the land. I think, if any man will receive protection from this people though [neither] he nor his ancestors, not any betwixt him and Adam, did ever give concurrence to this constitution, I think this man ought to be subject to those laws, and to be bound by those laws, so long as he continues amongst them. That is my opinion. A man ought to be subject to a law, that did not give his consent, but with this reservation, that if this man do think himself unsatisfied to be subject to this law he may go into another kingdom. And so the same reason doth extend, in my understanding, [to] that man that hath no permanent interest in the kingdom. If he hath money, his money is as good in another place as here; he hath nothing that doth locally fix him to this kingdom. If that man will live in this kingdom, or trade amongst us, that man ought to subject himself to the law made by the people who have the interest of this kingdom in them. And yet I do acknowledge that which you take to be so general a maxim, that in every kingdom, within every land, the original of power of making laws, of determining what shall be law in the land, does lie in the people—[but by the people is meant those] that are possessed of the permanent interest in the land. . . .

Major [William] Rainborough: I think if it can be made to appear that it is a just and reasonable thing, and that it is for the preservation of all the [native] freeborn men, [that they should have an equal voice in election]—I think it ought to be made good unto them. And the reason is: that the chief end of this government is to preserve persons as well as estates, and if any law shall take hold of my person it is more dear than my estate.

Colonel Rainborough: I do very well remember that the gentleman in the window [said] that, if it were so, there were no propriety to be had, because five parts of [the nation], the poor people, are now excluded and would then come in. So one on the other side said [that], if [it were] otherwise, then rich men [only] shall be chosen. Then, I say, the one part shall make hewers of wood and drawers of water of the other five, and so the greatest part of the nation be enslaved. Truly I think we are still where we were; and I do not hear any argument given but only that it is the present law of the kingdom. I say still, what shall become of those many [men] that have laid out themselves for the Parliament of England in this present war, that have ruined themselves by fighting, by hazarding all they had? They are Englishmen. They have now nothing to say for themselves.

Rich: I should be very sorry to speak anything here that should give offence, or that may occasion personal reflection[s] that we spoke against just now. I did not urge anything so far as was represented, and I did not at all urge that there should be a consideration [had of rich men], and that [a] man that is [poor] shall be without consideration, [or that] he deserves to be made poore[r] and not to live [in independence] at all. But all that I urged was this: that I think it worthy consideration, whether they should have an equality in their interest. However, I think we have been a great while upon this point, and if we be as long upon all the rest, it were well if there were no greater difference than this.

Mr. [Hugh] Peter: I think that this [matter of the franchise] may be easily agreed on—that is, there may be a way thought of. I think you would do well to set up all night [if thereby you could effect it], but I think that three or four might be thought of in this company [to form a committee]. You will be forced [only] to put characters upon electors or elected; therefore I do suppose that if there be any here that can make up a Representative to your mind, the thing is gained. But I would fain know whether that will answer the work of your meeting. The question is, whether you can state any one question for [removing] the present danger of the kingdom, whether any one question or no will dispatch the work.

Sir, I desire, [if it be possible], that some question may be stated to finish the present work, to cement us [in the points] wherein lies the distance; and if the thoughts [be] of the commonwealth [and] the people's freedom, I think that's soon cured. I desire that all manner of plainness may be used, that we may not go on with the lapwing and carry one another off the nest. There is something else that must cement us where the awkwardness of our spirits lies.

Rainborough: For my part, I think we cannot engage one way or other in the Army if we do not think of the people's liberties. If we can agree where the liberty and freedom of the people lies, that will do all.

Ireton: I cannot consent so far. As I said before: when I see the hand of God destroying King, and Lords, and Commons too, [or] any foundation of human constitution, when I see God hath done it, I shall, I hope, comfortably acquiesce in it. But first, I cannot give my consent to it, because it is not good. And secondly, as I desire that this Army should have regard to engagements wherever they are lawful, so I would have them have regard to this [as well]: that they should not bring that scandal upon the name of God [and the Saints], that those that call themselves by that name, those whom God hath owned and appeared with—that we should represent ourselves to the world as men so far from being of that peaceable spirit which is suitable to the Gospel, as we should have bought peace of the world upon such terms—[as] we would not have peace in the world but upon such terms—as should destroy all property. If the principle upon which you move this alteration, or the ground upon which you press that we should make this alteration, do destroy all kind of property or whatsoever a man hath by human constitution, [I cannot consent to it]. The Law of God doth not give me property, nor the Law of Nature, but property is of human constitution. I have a property and this I shall enjoy. Constitution founds property. If either the thing itself that you press or the consequence [of] that you press [do destroy property], though I shall acquiesce in having no property, yet I cannot give my heart or hand to it; because it is a thing evil in itself and scandalous to the world, and I desire this Army may be free from both.

Sexby: I see that though liberty were our end, there is a degeneration from it. We have engaged in this kingdom and ventured our lives, and it was all for this: to recover our birthrights and privileges as Englishmen; and by the arguments urged there is none. There are many thousands of us soldiers that have ventured our lives; we have had little propriety in the kingdom as to our estates, yet we have had a birthright. But it seems now, except a man hath a fixed estate in this kingdom, he hath no right in this kingdom. I wonder we were so much deceived. If we had not a right to the kingdom, we were mere mercenary soldiers. There are many in my condition, that have as good a condition [as I have]; it may be little estate they have at present, and yet they have as much a [birth]right as those two who are their lawgivers, as any in this place. I shall tell you in a word my resolution. I am resolved to give my birthright to none. Whatsoever may come in the way, and [whatsoever may] be thought, I will give it to none. If this thing [be denied the poor], that with so much pressing after [they have sought, it will be the greatest scandal]. There was one thing spoken to this effect: that if the poor and those in low condition [were given their birthright it would be the destruction of this kingdom]. I think this was but a distrust of Providence. I do think the poor and meaner of this kingdom—I speak as in relation [to the condition of soldiers], in which we are—have been the means of the preservation of this kingdom. I say, in their stations, and really I think to their utmost possibility; and their lives have not been [held] dear for purchasing the good of the kingdom. [And now they demand the birthright for which they fought.] Those that act to this end are as free from anarchy or confusion as those that oppose it, and they have the Law of God and the law of their conscience [with them]. But truly I shall only sum up [in] this. I desire that we may not spend so much time upon these things. We must be plain. When men come to understand these things, they will not lose that which they have contended for. That which I shall beseech you is to come to a determination of this question.

Ireton: I am very sorry we are come to this point, that from reasoning one to another we should come to express our resolutions. I profess for my part, what I see is good for the kingdom, and becoming a Christian to contend for, I hope through God I shall have strength and resolution to do my part towards it. And yet I will profess direct contrary in some kind to what that gentleman said. For my part, rather than I will make a disturbance to a good constitution of a kingdom wherein I may live in godliness and honesty, and peace and quietness, I will part with a great deal of my birthright. I will part with my own property rather than I will be the man that shall make a disturbance in the kingdom for my property; and therefore if all the people in this kingdom, or [the] representative[s] of them all together, should meet and should give away my property I would submit to it, I would give it away. But that gentleman, and I think every Christian, ought to bear that spirit, to carry that in him, that he will not make a public disturbance upon a private prejudice.

Now let us consider where our difference lies. We all agree that you should have a Representative to govern, and this Representative to be as equal as you can [make it]. But the question is, whether this distribution can be made to all persons equally, or whether [only] amongst those equals that have the interest of England in them. That which I have declared [is] my opinion [still]. I think we ought to keep to that [constitution which we have now], both because it is a civil constitution —it is the most fundamental constitution that we have—and [because] there is so much justice and reason and prudence [in it]—as I dare confidently undertake to demonstrate—that there are many more evils that will follow in case you do alter [it] than there can [be] in the standing of it. . . .

Rainborough: Sir, I see that it is impossible to have liberty but all property must be taken away. If it be laid down for a rule, and if you will say it, it must be so. But I would fain know what the soldier hath fought for all this while? He hath fought to enslave himself, to give power to men of riches, men of estates, to make him a perpetual slave. . . .

Ireton: . . . Give me leave [to say] but this one word. I [will] tell you what the soldier of the kingdom hath fought for. First, the danger that we stood in was that one man's will must be a law. The people of the kingdom must have this right at least, that they should not be concluded [but] by the Representative of those that had the interest of the kingdom. So[m]e men fought in this, because they were immediately concerned and engaged in it. Other men who had no other interest in the kingdom but this, that they should have the benefit of those laws made by the Representative, yet [fought] that they should have the benefit of this Representative. They thought it was better to be concluded by the common consent of those that were fixed men, and settled men, that had the interest of this kingdom [in them]. 'And from that way,' [said they], 'I shall know a law and have a certainty.' Every man that was born [in the country, that] is a denizen in it, that hath a freedom, he was capable of trading to get money, to get estates by; and therefore this man, I think, had a great deal of reason to build up such a foundation of interest to himself: that is, that the will of one man should not be a law, but that the law of this kingdom should be by a choice of persons to represent, and that choice to be made by, the generality of the kingdom. Here was a right that induced men to fight, and those men that had this interest, though this be not the utmost interest that other men have, yet they had *some* interest.

(1647)

The Humble Petition of Divers Well-Affected Women

28.

(May 5, 1649)

This is a Leveller document. Although there is some doubt that it was actually written by women, it presents an interesting viewpoint.

---

from The Humble Petition . . .

TO THE SUPREME AUTHORITY OF ENGLAND THE COMMONS ASSEMBLED IN PARLIAMENT. THE HUMBLE PETITION OF DIVERS WELL-AFFECTED WOMEN OF THE CITIES OF LONDON AND WESTMINSTER, THE BOROUGH OF SOUTHWARK, HAMBLETS AND PARTS ADJACENT. AFFECTERS AND APPROVERS OF THE PETITION OF SEPT. 11. 1648 [May 5, 1649]

Sheweth, that since we are assured of our creation in the image of God, and of an interest in Christ equal unto men, as also of a proportionable share in the freedoms of this commonwealth, we cannot but wonder and grieve that we should appear so despicable in your eyes as to be thought unworthy to petition or represent our grievances to this honourable House. Have we not an equal interest with the men of this nation in those liberties and securities contained in the *Petition of Right,* and other the good laws of the land? Are any of our lives, limbs, liberties, or goods to be taken from us more than from men, but by due process of law and conviction of twelve sworn men of the neighbourhood? And can you imagine us to be so sottish or stupid as not to perceive, or not to be sensible when daily those strong defences of our peace and welfare are broken down and trod underfoot by force and arbitrary power?

Would you have us keep at home in our houses, when men of such faithfulness and integrity as the four prisoners, our friends, in the Tower, are fetched out of their beds and forced from their houses by soldiers, to the affrighting and undoing of themselves, their wives, children, and families? Are not our husbands, ourselves, our children and families, by the same rule as liable to the like unjust cruelties as they?

Shall such men as Capt. Bray be made close prisoners, and such as

Mr. Sawyer snatched up and carried away, beaten and buffeted at the pleasure of some officers of the Army; and such as Mr. Blank kept close prisoner, and after most barbarous usage be forced to run the gauntlet, and be most slave-like and cruelly whipped? And must we keep at home in our houses, as if our lives and liberties and all were not concerned?

Nay, shall such valiant, religious men as Mr. Robert Lockyer be liable to law martial, and to be judged by his adversaries, and most inhumanly shot to death? Shall the blood of war be shed in time of peace? Doth not the word of God expressly condemn it? Doth not the *Petition of Right* declare that no person ought to be judged by law martial (except in time of war) and that all commissions given to execute martial law in time of peace are contrary to the laws and statutes of the land? Doth not Sir Ed. Coke, in his chapter of murder in the third part of his *Institutes,* hold it for good law (and since owned and published by this Parliament) that for a general or other officers of an army in time of peace to put any man (although a soldier) to death by colour of martial law, it is absolute murder in that general? And hath it not by this House in the case of the late Earl of Strafford been adjudged high treason? And are we Christians, and shall we sit still and keep at home, while such men as have borne continual testimony against the injustice of all times and unrighteousness of men, be picked out and be delivered up to the slaughter? And yet must we show no sense of their sufferings, no tenderness of affections, no bowels of compassion, nor bear any testimony against so abominable cruelty and injustice?

Have such men as these continually hazarded their lives, spent their estates and time, lost their liberties, and thought nothing too precious for defence of us, our lives and liberties, been as a guard by day and as a watch by night; and when for this they are in trouble and greatest danger, persecuted and hated even to the death, should we be so basely ungrateful as to neglect them in the day of their affliction? No, far be it from us. Let it be accounted folly, presumption, madness, or whatsoever in us, whilst we have life and breath we will never leave them nor forsake them, nor ever cease to importune you, having yet so much hopes of you as of the unjust judge (mentioned, Luke 18), to obtain justice, if not for justice' sake, yet for importunity, or to use any other means for the enlargement and reparation of those of them that live, and for justice against such as have been the cause of Mr. Lockyer's death.***

And therefore again we entreat you to review our last petition in behalf of our friends above mentioned, and not to slight the things

therein contained because they are presented unto you by the weak
hand of women, it being a usual thing with God, by weak means to
work mighty effects. For we are no whit satisfied with the answer you
gave unto our husbands and friends, but do equally with them remain
liable to those snares laid in your Declaration, which maketh the abet-
ters of the book laid to our friends' charge, no less than traitors, when
hardly any discourse can be touching the affairs of the present times
but falls within the compass of that book; so that all liberty of discourse is thereby utterly taken away, than which there can be no
greater slavery.***

(1649)

Anonymous

More Light Shining in Buckingham-shire (1649)

29.

Although some scholars have attributed this pamphlet to Gerrard Winstanley, it is not likely that he was the author. The pamphlet states the Leveller position that the "kingly power" was contrary to Scripture and, in England, a result of the Norman Conquest.

---

from More Light Shining in Buckingham-shire

The Apostle saith, *Whatsoever things were written, were for our learning.*

It is recorded in Scripture, that man being created male and female after Gods own Image or likeness, *viz.* his Son Jesus, who is said to be the Image of the invisible God, and the first born of every Creature, and by whom all things were made, and to whom all things were to subject, for he being Lord over all the inferior Creatures; God endowed with that excellent Rule of right Reason, which is the pure influence of the Almighty, whereby he should walk in subjection to his Creator and Father, and in Equity towards his own kind, *viz.* to do to another, as the other should do to him, and none to lord or force any arbitrary power one over another, or to assume any priviledge above his brethren; for all men by Gods donation are all alike free by birth, and to have alike priviledg by vertue of his grant: *Gen.* 1. 26. to the end, and *Gen.* 9. 1. to 18. So that as all inferior creatures are given unto man, *viz.* mankind, and that for all necessaries as he should need: So it is as plain, that every man hath a right and propriety in the creatures, one as well as the other; so that for any to inclose them wholly from his kind, to his own use, to the impoverishment of his fellow creatures, whereby they are made his slaves, is altogether unlawful, and it is the cause of all oppressions, whereby many thousands are deprived of their rights which God hath invested withal, wherby they are forced to beg or starve for want; for all grounds being inclosed, and all other things monopolized into a few Mercinarys hands, whereby thousands that would, and desire to live in a lawful Calling lawfully, are of all people most oppressed, because not suffered to keep any thing about them, because of the incroachers before named, who will either hunt it or pownd it, &c. neither can they enjoy the benefit of their own labor, although God commands they should, because of those forenamed oppressors, who have not only inclosed, monopolized, incroached, inhanced all the creatures into their hands, but do likewise extort

119

away the labours of their poor brethren, and take out the bread out of
their mouths, and from their poor wives and children, by their unreasonable, unlawful, unjust and wicked Rates, Taxes, Powls, Towls,
Customs, so that the flower of those industrious mens labors are
boulted out from them, and only the Bran left them to feed on; and if
any seem for all this to maintain his family through his extream industry, then the other Cormorants force offices on him, &c. thereby to more
inslave him and that with most wretched oaths, &c. Oh it would be too
tedious to relate all the slavery they are put to, and sworn [to] perform, as that at their Court-leets, there to appear to do homage, and
acknowledg themselves slave to their Tyrants, called Lords of Mannors; and if they hold any Lands, what extream Rents are they forced
to pay for it, to their extorting Landlords? besides above the 3ᵈ part
of their labor taken from them by the impropriators, besides paying
quitrents, as it is called, whereby in some, as the Lords of the Mannors,
are petty Tyrants and Kings; so they hold all from a supream Lord,
who was none of Gods setting up, *viz.* a King, whom they upholding as
the only dread Soveraign Lord, and allowing him a great and intolerable Revenue, as Lands, Customs, Poles, Toles, Tithes of all sorts,
and quitrents, &c. with Fines, Harriets, and Charters, Patents, Monopolies, &c. by which means they can be Farmers under him, and petty
tyrants over the people: and to secure themselves from being made deliver up their usurped powers and interest; they have their Commissions, Grants, Pattents holding in his name, and they protecting him
from being questioned and his power thrown down; he doth defend,
uphold, maintain and allow them to rend, tear, devour, rob, spoyl,
extort and tyrannize over the poor people, &c. . . .

From whence we observe, That all those oppressors before named
do live altogether out of Gods way, and in Rebellion to his Laws: first,
because they live without a Calling, and so are idle, being Vagabonds,
and wasters of the creatures, by drunkenness, pride, gluttony, and so
but Vermin in a Common-wealth, and by their own Law ought to be
put into a house of Correction, and to be made work. . . .

1. Now for one man to be Lord or King over another, and force
on his Commands of his own authority, he takes on him the place of
Jesus, and so is a Rebel and Traytor to the Crown and Dignity of
Christ.

2. For man to reject the Laws of God, which binds him, *to do to
another as another should do to him,* and force on his own Arbitrary
Laws, such a one is a Rebell in the highest degree, and his power is of
the Beast, and so of the Devil, and he and his followers are said to go
into perdition, and shall be tormented for ever and ever.

3. For a man to inclose all Lands and Creatures from his kind, is utterly unnatural, wicked, and treacherous; for if man shall eat bread by his sweat, then he must needs have ground to sow corn; therefore to inclose all grounds from him, is to starve him, for if no corn, no bread, and if no ground, no corn; then this is theft in the highest degree. Mark this you great Cormudgings, you hang a man for stealing for his wants, when you your selves have stole from your fellow brethren all Lands, Creatures, &c. Now mark what saith the Scripture, *Pull out the beam out of thine own eye, then shalt thou see to pull out the mote out of thy brothers eye:* So first go hang your selves for your great thefts of incloseness and oppressness, and then afterwards that you can go hang your poor brethren for petty thefts, as for a sheep, corn, &c.

So that from those grounds we conclude, first, What God entitleth man with, that is to say, with alike priviledges.

2. All men are to enjoy alike Freedoms, and none more then the other, so that they are equal, and none have to do to command another, no more then another him, but in a Joynt union and agreement: that any be set up, it is but a trusted humane power, and they but servants to the whole, and may be removed at pleasure.

3. Man is to subject himself to one Soveraign Lord Jesus, and is to go by the Rule of Equity, and no otherwise.

4. From all which grounds all men have right to the Creatures, &c. one as well as the other. . . .

Lastly, How it may be removed, is, to give all liberty for godly men to declare against it. 1. Therefore take away all binding Laws, penalties, &c. that men may freely preach against it, even in all publike meetings, that so the Priests may no more delude the people. 2. Utterly abolish these wicked Laws, Terms, &c. with all Patents, Corporations, Grants, Monopolies, &c. For why may not all Controversies be ended by Arbitration of our own Neighbourhood, by the rule of Equity at home, then to be thus abused by the Lawyers? And why may not every man as freely speak, preach that God hath made out to him, as the Priests? And if the Priests will not be quiet, but still stir up strife, let them be set aside, as needless and unprofitable, who keep the people in blindness, as they have done, in preferring a wicked man in the place of a God, as they did *Charls Stuart.*

Lastly, Above all, look to the poor; let not all the Bishops Lands, Crown Lands be swallowed up, nor Commons, Parks, Woods, Forrests, &c. for your great ones gape for to inclose them: but let all be for the poor, until more comes: and all, whosoever, that have oppressed the poor, let them make restitution fourfold. And think on prisoners that perish in prison by merciless Creditors & Jaylors, that they may not be mewd up, and starved, until they are poysoned there. And likewise a way to prevent cozening and cheating one another; and that all Tryals be in every Hundred by twelve men of the same neighbor-hood, and all buying and selling Law put down, as aforesaid: And let a free Trade be in the Nation; All Monopolies, Patents, &c. utterly taken away. And for the rule to go by that which is declared the Rule of Equity, *to do to all men as they should do to others, &c.* and all other false tyrannical rules taken away, and all Laws to be out of the Scriptures, seeing there is but one Law-giver, who is able both to save and destroy. And for Law Executioners, to be only such, who are right godly, honest, wise, moderate, judicious, reasonable, and faithful men, and those chosen by free Election of the People; and so all that bulk of Officers that are by Pattents, as all Judges, Iustices, Sheriffs, Bailies, Mayors, &c. and all other Offices that are not elected by the people, but were forced on us with out our Election, and against our consents, by a Patent: And for-asmuch as the throwing down the Kingly power, all those fell with it; and we looked never to have them more revived, seeing that all power is arbitrary that is not out of the peoples voluntary Election, the people being declared the supream Authority under God; and whom they chuse, to be the lawful Magistrate: yet nevertheless, as if the Parliament intended still to keep the old arbitrary and tyrannical *Norman Laws, Terms* and *Courts,* still to enslave us; and *Lawyers, Patentee Officers* to torment, have made an Act that all *Patents, Grants, Courts, &c.* shall continue as they formerly did, only Writs in the *Judges* and *Keepers names,* although in our Petitions we utterly denied the same: and they have appointed *Commissioners* to be *Justices* without *any election from us.* Likewise the *Grandees in the Army* have preferred a thing called *An Agreement of the People,* which is too low and too shallow to free us at all: for it doth not throw down all those *Arbitrary Courts, Powers and Patents,* as aforesaid: And what stock or way is provided for the *poor, fatherless, widows, and impoverished people?* And what advancement of encouragement for the *laboring and industrious,* as to take off burthens, is there? By all which, and by *Arbitrary Powers* erected anew, we see, that they minde their own *interest, gain, and rotten honor* more then our *absolute Freedom:* This being so, we are enforced to appeal to all our *dear brethren* in *England,* and *Souldiers in the Army,* to stand every one in his place, to oppose *all Tyranny* whatsoever, and by whomsoever, intended against us. . . .

                                                                    (1649)

Thomas Hobbes

30.

(1588-1679)

Hobbes, English philosopher, whose *Leviathan* made him the
first of the great English political theorists, is represented here
by only a brief comment on equality.

from Leviathan

Nature hath made men so equall, in the faculties of body, and
mind; as that though there bee found one man sometimes manifestly
stronger in body, or of quicker mind than another; yet when all is
reckoned together, the difference between man, and man, is not so considerable, as that one man can thereupon claim to himselfe any benefit, to which another may not pretend, as well as he. For as to the
strength of body, the weakest has strength enough to kill the strongest,
either by secret machination, or by confederacy with others, that are in
the same danger with himselfe.

And as to the faculties of the mind, (setting aside the arts grounded
upon words, and especially that skill of proceeding upon generall, and
infallible rules, called Science; which very few have, and but in few
things; as being not a native faculty, born with us; nor attained, (as
Prudence,) while we look after somewhat els,) I find yet a greater equality amongst men, than that of strength. For Prudence is but Experience; which equall time, equally bestowes on all men, in those things
they equally apply themselves unto. That which may perhaps make
such equality incredible, is but a vain conceipt of one's owne wisdome,
which almost all men think they have in a greater degree, than the
Vulgar; that is, than all men but themselves, and a few others, whom
by Fame, or for concurring with themselves, they approve. For such
is the nature of men, that howsoever they may acknowledge many
others to be more witty, or more eloquent, or more learned; Yet they
will hardly believe there be many so wise as themselves: For they see
their own wit at hand, and other men's at a distance. But this proveth
rather that men are in that point equall, than unequall. For there is
not ordinarily a greater signe of the equall distribution of any thing,
than that every man is contented with his share.

(1651)

Gerrard Winstanley
(1609?-?)

31. Winstanley, vigorous pamphleteer and leader of a small English religio-economic movement known as the "Diggers," expressed the view that the root of tyranny is economic and that the "common land" should be given to the poor to cultivate.

from The Law of Freedom in a Platform

Now saith the people, By what Power do these maintain their Title over us? Formerly they held Title from the King, as he was the Conquerors Successor: But have not the Commoners cast out the King, and broke the band of that Conquest? Therefore in equity they are free from the slavery of that Lordly Power.

Secondly, In Parishes where Commons lie, the rich *Norman* Freeholders, or the new (more covetous) Gentry, over-stock the Commons with Sheep and Cattle; so that inferior Tenants and poor Laborers can hardly keep a Cow, but half starve her; so that the poor are kept poor still, and the Common Freedom of the Earth is kept from them, and the poor have no more relief then they had when the King (or Conqueror) was in power.

Thirdly, In many Parishes two or three of the great ones bears all the sway, in making Assessments, over-awing Constables and other Officers; and when time was to quarter Souldiers, they would have a hand in that, to ease themselves, and over-burden the weaker sort; and many times make large sums of money over and above the Justices Warrant in Assessments, and would give no accompt why, neither durst the inferior people demand an accompt, for he that spake should be sure to be crushed the next opportunity; and if any have complained to Committees or Justices, they have been either wearied out by delays and waiting, or else the offence hath been by them smothered up; so that we see one great man favored another, and the poor oppressed have no relief.

Fourthly, There is another grievance which the people are much troubled at, and that is this; Country people cannot sell any Corn or other fruits of the Earth in a Market Town, but they must either pay Toll, or be turned out of Town: Now say they, This is a most shameful thing, that we must part with our estates in Taxes and Free-quarter to purchase the Freedom of the Land, and the Freedom of the Towns, and yet this Freedom must be still given from us, into the hands of a covetous *Norman* Toll-Taker, according to the Kings old burdensom Laws, and contrary to the Liberty of a free Commonwealth.

Now saith the whisperings of the people, The inferior Tenants and Laborers bears all the burdens, in laboring the Earth, in paying Taxes and Free-quarter beyond their strength, and in furnishing the Armies with Souldiers, who bear the greatest burden of the War; and yet the Gentry, who oppress them, and that live idle upon their labours, carry away all the comfortable livelyhood of the Earth.

For is not this a common speech among the people, We have parted with our Estates, we have lost our Friends in the Wars, which we willingly gave up, because Freedom was promised us; and now in the end we have new Task-masters, and our old burdens increased: and though all sorts of people have taken an Engagement to cast out Kingly Power, yet Kingly Power remains in power still in the hands of those who have no more right to the Earth then our selves.

For say the people, If the Lords of Manors and our Task-masters hold Title to the Earth over us from the old Kingly power, behold that power is beaten and cast out.

And two Acts of Parliament are made. The one to cast out Kingly power, back'd by the Engagement against King and House of Lords. The other to make *England* a free Commonwealth.

And if Lords of Mannors lay claim to the earth over us, from the Armies Victories over the King; then we have as much right to the Land as they, because our labours, and blood, and death of friends, were the purchasers of the Earths freedome as well as theirs.

And is not this a slavery, say the People, That though there be Land enough in *England,* to maintain ten times as many people as are in it, yet some must beg of their brethren, or work in hard drudgery for day wages for them, or starve, or steal, and so be hanged out of the way, as men not fit to live in the earth, before they must be suffered to plant the waste land for their livelihood, unlesse they will pay Rent to their brethren for it? wel, this is a burthen the Creation groans under; and the subjects (so called) have not their Birth-right Freedomes granted them from their brethren, who hold it from them by club law, but not by righteousness.

And who now must we be subject to, seeing the Conqueror is gone?

I Answer, we must either be subject to a Law, or to mens wils. If to a Law, then all men in *England* are subjects, or ought to be, thereunto: but what Law that is to which every one ought to be subject is not yet established in execution. If any say the old Kings Laws are the

Rule, then it may be Answered, That those Laws are so full of confusion, that few knows when they obey and when not, because they were the Laws of a Conqueror to hold the people in subjection to the will of the Conqueror; therefore that cannot be the rule for every one: besides, we dayly see many actions done by State Officers, which they have no Law to justifie them in, but their Prerogative will.

And again if we must be subject to men, then what men must we be subject to, seeing one man hath as much right to the earth as another, for no man now stands as a Conqueror over his Brethren by the Law of righteousness?

You will say, We must be subject to the Ruler; it is true, but not to suffer the Rulers to call the Earth theirs and not ours, for by so doing they betray their trust, and run into the line of Tyranny, and we lose our freedome, and from thence Enmity and Wars arise.

A Ruler is worthy double honour when he rules well, that is, when he himself is subject to the Law, and requires all others to be subject thereunto and makes it his work to see the Laws obeyed, and not his own will, and such Rulers are faithfull, and they are to be subjected unto us therein, for all Commonwealth Rulers are servants to, not Lords and Kings over the people. But you will say, Is not the Land your brothers? and you cannot take away another mans Right by claiming a share therein with him.

I Answer, It is his either by creation right, or by right of Conquest: If by Creation right he call the earth his and not mine; then it is mine as well as his, for the Spirit of the whole Creation, who made us both, is no respecter of persons.

And if by Conquest he call the earth his and not mine, it must be either by the Conquest of the Kings over the Commoners, or by the Conquest of the Commoners over the Kings.

If he claim the earth to be his from the Kings Conquest, The Kings are beaten and cast out and that title is undone.

If he claim Title to the earth to be his from the Conquest of the Commoners over the Kings, then I have right to the Land as well as my brother, for my brother without me, nor I without my brother, did not cast out the Kings, but both together assisting with person and purse, we prevailed, so that I have by this Victory as equall a share in the earth which is now redeemed as my brother, by the Law of righteousnesse.

If my brother still say he will be Landlord (through his covetous ambition) and I must pay him Rent, or else I shall not live in the Land, then does he take my right from me, which I have purchased by my money in Taxes, free quarter and blood. And O thou Spirit of the whole Creation, who hath this Title to be called *King of Righteousness, and Prince of Peace;* judge thou between my brother and me, Whether this be righteous, &c.

And now, say the people, is not this a grievous thing that our brethren that will be Landlords right or wrong, will make Laws, and call for a Law to be made to imprison, crush, nay put to death, any that denies God, Christ, and Scripture; and yet they will not practise that golden Rule, *Do to another as thou wouldst have another do to thee,* which God, Christ, and Scriptures, hath Enacted for a Law? are not these men guilty of death by their own Law, which is the words of their own mouth? is it not a flat denyall of God and Scripture?

O the confusion and thick darkness that hath over-spread our Brethren is very great, I have no power to remove it, but lament it in the secrets of my heart; when I see Prayers, Sermons, Fasts, Thanksgiving, directed to this God in words and shews, and when I come to look for actions of obedience to the Righteous Law, suitable to such a profession, I finde them men of another Nation, saying, and not doing; like an old Courtier saying *Your Servant,* when he was an Enemy. I wil say no more, but groan and waite for a restoration.

Thus Sir, I have reckoned up some of those burdens which the people groan under.

And I being sensible hereof was moved in my self, to present this Platform of Commonwealths Government unto you, wherein I have declared a full Commonwealths Freedome, according to the Rule of Righteousness, which is Gods Word. It was intended for your view above two years ago, but the disorder of the Times caused me to lay it aside, with a thought never to bring it to light . . .

I laid aside this in silence, and said, I would not make it publick; but this word was like fire in my bones ever and anon, *Thou shalt not bury thy talent in the earth,* therefore I was stirred up to give it a resurrection, and to pick together as many of my scattered papers as I could finde, and to compile them into this method, which I do here present to you, and do quiet my own spirit.

And now I have set the candle at your door, for you have power in your hand, in this other added opportunity, to Act for Common Freedome if you will; I have no power. . . .

It may be you will say, If Tythes be taken from the Priests and Impropriators, and Copy-hold Services from Lords of Mannors, how shal they be provided for again; for is it not unrighteous to take their estates from them?

I Answer, when Tythes were first enacted, and Lordly power drawn over the backs of the oppressed, the Kings and Conquerors made no scruple of Conscience to take it, though the people lived in sore bondage of poverty for want of it; and can there be scruple of conscience to make restitution of this which hath been so long stoln goods? It is no scruple arising from the Righteous Law, but from covetousness, who goes away sorrowfull to heare he must part with all to follow Righteousness and Peace.

But though you do take away Tythes, and the Power of Lords of Mannors, yet there will be no want to them, for they have the freedome of the Common stock, they may send to the Storehouses for what they want, and live more free then now they do, for now they are in care and vexation by servants, by casualties, by being cheated in buying and selling, and many other incumbrances, but then they will be free from all, for the common Storehouses is every mans riches, not any ones.

Is not buying and selling a righteous Law? No, It is the Law of the Conqueror, but not the righteous Law of Creation: how can that be righteous which is a cheat? for is not this a common practise, when he hath a bad Horse or Cow, or any bad commodity, he will send it to the Market, to cheat some simple plain-hearted man or other, and when he comes home, will laugh at his neighbours hurt, and much more &c.

When Mankinde began to buy and sell, then did he fall from his Innocency; for then they began to oppress and cozen one another of their Creation Birth-right: As for example; if the Land belong to three persons, and two of them buy and sell the Earth, and the third give no consent, his Right is taken from him, and his posterity is engaged in a War.

When the Earth was first bought and sold, many gave no consent: As when our Crown Lands, and Bishops Lands were sold, some foolish Soldiers yeelded, and covetous Officers were active in it, to advance themselves above their Brethren: but many, who payd Taxes and Free-quarter for the purchase of it, gave no consent, but declared against it, as an unrighteous thing, depriving posterity of their Birth-rights and Freedoms.

Therefore this buying and selling did bring in, and still doth bring in, discontents and wars, which have plagued Mankinde sufficiently for so doing. And the Nations of the world will never learn to beat their swords into plowshares, and their spears into pruning hooks, and leave of warring, until this cheating device of buying and selling be cast out among the rubbish of Kingly power.

But shall not one man be richer then another?

There is no need of that; for Riches make men vain-glorious, proud, and to oppress their Brethren; and are the occasion of wars.

No man can be rich, but he must be rich, either by his own labors, or by the labors of other men helping him: If a man have no help from his neighbor, he shall never gather an Estate of hundreds and thousands a year: If other men help him to work, then are those Riches his Neighbors, as well as his; for they be the fruit of other mens labors as well as his own.

But all rich men live at ease, feeding and clothing themselves by the labors of other men, not by their own; which is their shame, and not their Nobility; for it is a more blessed thing to give then to receive: But rich men receive all they have from the laborers hand, and what they give, they give away other mens labors, not their own; Therefore they are not righteous Actors in the Earth.

But shall not one man have more Titles of Honor then another?

Yes: As a man goes through Offices, he rises to Titles of Honor, till he comes to the highest Nobility, to be a faithful Commonwealths man in a Parliament House. Likewise he who findes out any secret in *Nature,* shall have a Title of Honor given him, though he be a young man. But no man shall have any Title of Honor till he win it by industry, or come to it by age, or Office-bearing. Every man that is above sixty years of age shall have respect as a man of Honor by all others that are younger, as is shewed hereafter.

Shall every man count his Neighbors house as his own, and live together as one Family?

No: Though the Earth and Storehouses be common to every Family, yet every Family shall live apart as they do; and every mans house, wife, children, and furniture for ornament of his house, or any thing which he hath fetched in from the Storehouses, or provided for the necessary use of his Family, is all a propriety to that Family, for the peace thereof. And if any man offer to take away a mans wife, children, or furniture of his house, without his consent, or disturb the peace of his dwelling, he shall suffer punishment as an Enemy to the *Commonwealths* Government; as is mentioned in the *Platform* following.

(1652)

32

George Fox

George Fox, the English founder of the Society of Friends, stressed direct personal relation to God through "inner light."

from To The Protector and Parliament of England

And of laying great taxes upon people, take heed lest ye oppresse the just, and lay heavier burthens upon them then they can bear, by which the just comes to groan under, but minde equality, measurable-nesse, true weights, true ballances, and equality in all things, man with man, that whereby you may govern in righteousnesse and in justice. For oppression, and heavy burthens, and heavy taxes from some, give to some the great wages, whereby others are oppressed; therefore wages being lesse, the taxes come lesse, then you all come to the feeling principle of God in you, by which you all feel and consider, that which is exalted with fulnesse, and ease the oppressed, and not feed that which is full and exalted; and the one with his fulnesse is exalted above his measure, and the other with his heavy tax is oppressed through the care. Therefore now you have ease, take heed all you that be in offices, and having fulnesse, *of growing fat and forgetting God,* through places and abundance of riches and great wages; therefore, your wages lesse, your taxes lesse, you keep chaste and low in the fear of God, and then there will be lesse danger. For such as are exalted by high places, or great gifts, the Lord God brings one plague or judgement or other upon them, or upon the Nation where they dwell; therefore keep down in the feare of God, that you may be ordered with wisdome, and come to order in the creation with it, to the glory of the Creator; Here you all feele the blessings of the Lord God of life amongst you, and with you, and both the exactor and the exacted, the one his jawes will be broken, the other will be relieved, and helped, and that which helps is blessed, and the will of men must be crossed in the earthly, and that mountain broken down, as the stone riseth that is cut out of the mountain without hands; for the abundance of judgements must come from the Lord God, and plagues and misery before men be seasoned, and be in the favoury of life, for that which did ever oppresse first, went from that of God in them; for the first Murtherer, he went out of the truth, and destroyer. Therefore Esaus birth, Esaus flock, that looks for the fat of the earth, and beares the sword against Jacob, must be as the stubble, and a wildernesse, and a place for Dragons: Therefore Isaac knew the second birth, which is the seeds called; and Jacob knew that riseth and reignes over the high places of the Earth, that the elder you may come to witnesse to serve the younger; here is the election known.

(1658)

John Locke

(1632-1704)

33.

John Locke, English philosopher and founder of British Empiricism, was the author of *Two Treatises on Government* in which he justified constitutional monarchy and enunciated ideas which ultimately bore fruit in the U. S. Constitution.

from The Second Treatise on Civil Government

4. To understand political power aright, and derive it from its original, we must consider what state all men are naturally in, and that is a state of perfect freedom to order their actions and dispose of their possessions and persons as they think fit, within the bounds of the law of nature, without asking leave, or depending upon the will of any other man.

A state also of equality, wherein all the power and jurisdiction is reciprocal, no one having more than another; there being nothing more evident than that creatures of the same species and rank, promiscuously born to all the same advantages of nature, and the use of the same faculties, should also be equal one amongst another without subordination or subjection, unless the Lord and Master of them all should by any manifest declaration of his will set one above another, and confer on him by an evident and clear appointment an undoubted right to dominion and sovereignty.

5. This equality of men by nature the judicious Hooker looks upon as so evident in itself and beyond all question, that he makes it the foundation of that obligation to mutual love amongst men on which he builds the duties they owe one another, and from whence he derives the great maxims of justice and charity. His words are:

> "The like natural inducement hath brought men to know that it is no less their duty to love others than themselves; for seeing those things which are equal must needs all have one measure, if I cannot but wish to receive good, even as much at every man's hands as any man can wish unto his own soul, how should I look to have any part of my desire herein satisfied, unless myself be careful to satisfy the like desire, which is undoubtedly in other men weak, being of one and the same nature? To have anything offered them repugnant to this desire, must needs

in all respects grieve them as much as me, so that, if I do harm, I must look to suffer, there being no reason that others should show greater measures of love to me than they have by me showed unto them. My desire, therefore, to be loved of my equals in nature as much as possible may be, imposeth upon me a natural duty of bearing to themward fully the like affection; from which relation of equality between ourselves and them that are as ourselves, what several rules and canons natural reason hath drawn for direction of life no man is ignorant." (Ecclesiastical Polity, lib. i.)

6. But though this be a state of liberty, yet it is not a state of licence; though man in that state have an uncontrollable liberty to dispose of his person or possessions, yet he has not liberty to destroy himself, or so much as any creature in his possession, but where some nobler use than its bare preservation calls for it. The state of nature has a law of nature to govern it, which obliges every one; and reason, which is that law, teaches all mankind who will but consult it, that, being all equal and independent, no one ought to harm another in his life, health, liberty, or possessions. For men being all the workmanship of one omnipotent and infinitely wise Maker—all the servants of one sovereign Master, sent into the world by his order, and about his business—they are his property, whose workmanship they are, made to last during his, not one another's pleasure; and being furnished with like faculties, sharing all in one community of nature, there cannot be supposed any such subordination among us, that may authorise us to destroy one another, as if we were made for one another's uses, as the inferior ranks of creatures are for ours. Every one, as he is bound to preserve himself, and not to quit his station wilfully, so, by the like reason, when his own preservation comes not in competition, ought he, as much as he can, to preserve the rest of mankind, and not, unless it be to do justice on an offender, take away or impair the life, or what tends to the preservation of the life, the liberty, health, limb, or goods of another.

7. And that all men may be restrained from invading others' rights, and from doing hurt to one another, and the law of nature be observed, which willeth the peace and preservation of all mankind, the execution of the law of nature is in that state put into every man's hand, whereby every one has a right to punish the transgressors of that law to such a degree as may hinder its violation. For the law of nature would, as all other laws that concern men in this world, be in vain if

there were nobody that, in the state of nature, had a power to execute that law, and thereby preserve the innocent and restrain offenders. And if any one in the state of nature may punish another for any evil he has done, every one may do so. For in that state of perfect equality, where naturally there is no superiority or jurisdiction of one over another, what any may do in prosecution of that law, every one must needs have a right to do.

8. And thus in the state of nature one man comes by a power over another; but yet no absolute or arbitrary power, to use a criminal, when he has got him in his hands, according to the passionate heats or boundless extravagance of his own will; but only to retribute to him so far as calm reason and conscience dictate what is proportionate to his transgression, which is so much as may serve for reparation and restraint. For these two are the only reasons why one man may lawfully do harm to another, which is that we call punishment. In transgressing the law of nature, the offender declares himself to live by another rule than that of common reason and equity, which is that measure God has set to the actions of men, for their mutual security; and so he becomes dangerous to mankind, the tie which is to secure them from injury and violence being slighted and broken by him. Which, being a trespass against the whole species, and the peace and safety of it, provided for by the law of nature, every man upon this score, by the right he hath to preserve mankind in general, may restrain, or, where it is necessary, destroy things noxious to them, and so may bring such evil on any one who hath transgressed that law, as may make him repent the doing of it, and thereby deter him, and by his example others, from doing the like mischief. And in this case, and upon this ground, every man hath a right to punish the offender, and be executioner of the law of nature.

·   ·   ·   ·   ·   ·   ·

54. Though I have said above (Chapter 2) that all men by nature are equal, I cannot be supposed to understand all sorts of equality. Age or virtue may give men a just precedency. Excellency of parts and merit may place others above the common level. Birth may subject some, and alliance or benefits others, to pay an observance to those to whom nature, gratitude, or other respects may have made it due. And yet all this consists with the equality which all men are in, in respect of jurisdiction or dominion, one over another; which was the equality I there spoke of as proper to the business in hand, being that equal right that every man hath to his natural freedom, without being subjected to the will or authority of any other man.

55. Children, I confess, are not born in this full state of equality, though they are born to it. Their parents have a sort of rule and jurisdiction over them when they come into the world, and for some time after, but 'tis but a temporary one. The bonds of this subjection are like the swaddling clothes they are wrapped up in and supported by in the weakness of their infancy. Age and reason, as they grow up loosen them, till at length they drop quite off, and leave a man at his own free disposal.

.   .   .   .

87. Man being born, as has been proved, with a title to perfect freedom, and an uncontrolled enjoyment of all the rights and privileges of the law of nature equally with any other man or number of men in the world, hath by nature a power not only to preserve his property— that is, his life, liberty, and estate—against the injuries and attempts of other men, but to judge of and punish the breaches of that law in others as he is persuaded the offence deserves, even with death itself, in crimes where the heinousness of the fact in his opinion requires it. But because no political society can be nor subsist without having in itself the power to preserve the property, and, in order thereunto, punish the offences of all those of that society, there, and there only, is political society, where every one of the members hath quitted this natural power, resigned it up into the hands of the community in all cases that exclude him not from appealing for protection to the law established by it; and thus all private judgment of every particular member being excluded, the community comes to be umpire; and by understanding indifferent rules and men authorised by the community for their execution, decides all the differences that may happen between any members of that society concerning any matter of right, and punishes those offences which any member hath committed against the society with such penalties as the law has established; whereby it is easy to discern who are and who are not in political society together. Those who are united into one body, and have a common established law and judicature to appeal to, with authority to decide controversies between them and punish offenders, are in civil society one with another; but those who have no such common appeal—I mean on earth— are still in the state of nature, each being, where there is no other, judge for himself and executioner, which is, as I have before shown it, the perfect state of nature.

88. And thus the commonwealth comes by a power to set down what punishment shall belong to the several transgressions which they

think worthy of it committed amongst the members of that society, which is the power of making laws, as well as it has the power to punish any injury done unto any of its members by any one that is not of it, which is the power of war and peace; and all this for the preservation of the property of all the members of that society as far as is possible. But though every man who has entered into civil society, and has become a member of any commonwealth, has thereby quitted his power to punish offences against the law of nature in prosecution of his own private judgment, yet with the judgment of offences, which he has given up to the legislative in all cases where he can appeal to the magistrate, he has given a right to the commonwealth to employ his force for the execution of the judgments of the commonwealth whenever he shall be called to it; which, indeed, are his own judgments, they being made by himself or his representative. And herein we have the original of the legislative and executive power of civil society, which is to judge by standing laws how far offences are to be punished when committed within the commonwealth, and also to determine by occasional judgments founded on the present circumstances of the fact, how far injuries from without are to be vindicated; and in both these to employ all the force of all the members when there shall be need.

89. Wherever, therefore, any number of men so unite into one society, as to quit every one his executive power of the law of nature, and to resign it to the public, there, and there only, is a political, or civil society. And this is done wherever any number of men, in the state of nature, enter into society to make one people, one body politic, under one supreme government, or else when any one joins himself to, and incorporates with, any government already made. For hereby he authorises the society, or, which is all one, the legislative thereof, to make laws for him, as the public good of the society shall require, to the execution whereof his own assistance (as to his own decrees) is due. And this puts men out of a state of nature into that of a commonwealth, by setting up a judge on earth with authority to determine all the controversies and redress the injuries that may happen to any member of the commonwealth; which judge is the legislative, or magistrates appointed by it. And wherever there are any number of men, however associated, that have no such decisive power to appeal to, there they are still in the state of nature.

· · · · · · ·

95. Men being, as has been said, by nature all free, equal, and independent, no one can be put out of this estate, and subjected to the

political power of another, without his own consent, which is done by agreeing with other men to join and unite into a community for their comfortable, safe, and peaceable living one amongst another, in a secure enjoyment of their properties, and a greater security against any that are not of it. This any number of men may do, because it injures not the freedom of the rest; they arc lcft as thcy were in the liberty of the state of nature. When any number of men have so consented to make one community or government, they are thereby presently incorporated, and make one body politic, wherein the majority have a right to act and conclude the rest.

96. For when any number of men have, by the consent of every individual, made a community, they have thereby made that community one body, with a power to act as one body, which is only by the will and determination of the majority. For that which acts any community being only thc consent of the individuals of it, and it being one body must move one way, it is necessary the body should move that way whither the greater force carries it, which is the consent of the majority; or else it is impossible it should act or continue one body, one community, which the consent of every individual that united into it agreed that it should; and so every one is bound by that consent to be concluded by the majority. And therefore we see that in assemblies empowered to act by positive laws, where no number is set by that positive law which empowers them, the act of the majority passes for the act of thc wholc, and of course determines, as having by the law of nature and reason the power of the whole.

97. And thus every man, by consenting with others to make one body politic under one government, puts himself under an obligation to every one of that society, to submit to the determination of the majority, and to be concluded by it; or else this original compact, whereby he with others incorporates into one society, would signify nothing, and be no compact, if he be left free and under no other ties than he was in before in the state of nature. For what appearance would there be of any compact? What new engagement if he were no farther tied by any decrees of the society, than he himself thought fit, and did actually consent to? This would be still as great a liberty as he himself had before his compact, or any one else in the state of nature hath, who may submit himself and consent to any acts of it if he thinks fit.

. . . .

123. If man in the state of nature be so free, as has been said, if he be absolute lord of his own person and possessions, equal to the great-

est, and subject to nobody, why will he part with his freedom, this empire, and subject himself to the dominion and control of any other power? To which it is obvious to answer, that though in the state of nature he hath such a right, yet the enjoyment of it is very uncertain, and constantly exposed to the invasions of others. For all being kings as much as he, every man his equal, and the greater part no strict observers of equity and justice, the enjoyment of the property he has in this state is very unsafe, very unsecure. This makes him willing to quit this condition, which, however free, is full of fears and continual dangers; and it is not without reason that he seeks out and is willing to join in society with others, who are already united, or have a mind to unite, for the mutual preservation of their lives, liberties, and estates, which I call by the general name, property.

(1690)

John Wise

(1652-1725)

34.

An American Congregationalist clergyman, sometimes called "the first great American democrat," opposed the plan of Increase and Cotton Mather to put individual churches under the jurisdiction of an association of ministers. He derived his ideas on church government from a general theory concerning the natural rights of man, the justification of authority, and the different forms of civil polity.

from A Vindication of the Government of New England Churches

I shall disclose several principles of natural knowledge, plainly discovering the law of nature, or the true sentiments of natural reason, with respect to man's being and government. And in this essay I shall peculiarly confine the discourse to two heads: viz.

I. Of the natural (in distinction to the civil), and then,

II. Of the civil being of man. And I shall principally take Baron Puffendorff for my chief guide and spokesman.

I. I shall consider man in a state of natural being, as a free-born subject under the crown of Heaven, and owing homage to none but God himself. It is certain civil government in general is a very admirable result of Providence, and an incomparable benefit to mankind, yet must needs be acknowledged to be the effect of human free-compacts and not of divine institution; it is the produce of man's reason, of human and rational combinations, and not from any direct orders of infinite wisdom, in any positive law wherein is drawn up this or that scheme of civil government. Government (says the Lord Warrington) is necessary—in that no society of men can subsist without it; and that particular form of government is necessary which best suits the temper and inclination of a people. Nothing can be God's ordinance but what he has particularly declared to be such; there is no particular form of civil government described in God's Word, neither does nature prompt it. The government of the Jews was changed five times. Government is not formed by nature, as other births or productions; if it were, it would be the same in all countries, because nature keeps the same method, in the same thing, in all climates. If a commonwealth be changed into a monarchy, is it nature that forms and brings forth the monarch? Or if a royal family be wholly extinct (as in Noah's case, being not heir apparent from descent from Adam) is it nature that must go to work (with the king bees, who themselves alone preserve the royal race in that empire) to breed a monarch before the people can have a king or a government set over them? And thus we must leave kings to resolve which is their best title to their crowns, whether natural right, or the constitution of government settled by human compacts, under the direction and conduct of reason. But to proceed under the head of a state of natural being, I shall more distinctly explain the state of human nature in its original capacity, as man is placed on earth by his Maker, and clothed with many investitures and immunities which properly belong to man separately considered. As:

1. The prime immunity in man's state is that he is most properly the subject of the law of nature. He is the favorite animal on earth, in that this part of God's image: viz., Reason, is congenate with his nature, wherein by a law immutable, enstamped upon his frame, God has provided a rule for men in all their actions, obliging each one to the performance of that which is right, not only as to justice, but likewise as to all other moral virtues, the which is nothing but the dictate of right reason founded in the soul of man. . . . That which is to be drawn from man's reason, flowing from the true current of that faculty, when unperverted, may be said to be the law of nature, on which account the Holy Scriptures declare it written on men's hearts. For being endowed with a soul, you may know from yourself how and what you ought to act (Rom. ii. 14): *These having not a law are a law to themselves.* So that the meaning is, when we acknowledge the law of nature to be the dictate of right reason, we must mean that the understanding of man is endowed with such a power as to be able from the contemplation of human condition to discover a necessity of living agreeably with this law. . . . If a man anyways doubts whether what he is going to do to another man to be agreeable to the law of nature, then let him suppose himself to be in that other man's room, and by this rule effectually executed. A man must be a very dull scholar to nature not to make proficiency in the knowledge of her laws. But more particularly in pursuing our condition for the discovery of the law of nature, this is very obvious to view: viz.,

1. A principle of self-love and self-preservation is very predominant in every man's being.

2. A sociable disposition.

3. An affection or love to mankind in general. And to give such sentiments the force of a law, we must suppose a God who takes care of

all mankind and has thus obliged each one as a subject of higher principles of being than mere instincts. For that all law, properly considered, supposes a capable subject and a superior power; and the law of
God, which is binding, is published by the dictates of right reason as
other ways: therefore, says Plutarch, *To follow God and obey reason is
the same thing*. But moreover that God has established the law of
nature as the general rule of government is further illustrated from
the many sanctions in Providence, and from the peace and guilt of
conscience in them that either obey, or violate the law of nature. But,
moreover, the foundation of the law of nature with relation to government may be thus discovered: *scil.,* Man is a creature extremely de-
sirous of his own preservation; of himself he is plainly exposed to many
wants, unable to secure his own safety and maintenance without the
assistance of his fellows; and he is also able of returning kindness by
the furtherance of mutual good; but yet man is often found to be
malicious, insolent, and easily provoked, and as powerful in effecting
mischief as he is ready in designing it. Now, that such a creature may
be preserved, it is necessary that he be sociable; that is, that he be
capable and disposed to unite himself to those of his own species, and
to regulate himself towards them, that they may have no fair reason to
do him harm, but rather incline to promote his interests, and secure
his rights and concerns. This, then, is a fundamental law of nature,
that every man as far as in him lies, do maintain a sociableness with
others, agreeable with the main end and disposition of human nature
in general. For this is very apparent, that reason and society render
man the most potent of all creatures. And finally, from the principles
of sociableness, it follows as a fundamental law of nature that man is
not so wedded to his own interest, but that he can make the common
good the mark of his aim; and hence he becomes capacitated to enter
into a civil state by the law of nature; for without his property in nature: viz., sociableness, which is for cementing of parts, every government would soon molder and dissolve.

2. The second great immunity of man is an original liberty enstamped upon his rational nature. He that intrudes upon this liberty
violates the law of nature. In this discourse I shall waive the consideration of man's moral turpitude, but shall view him physically as a
creature which God has made and furnished essentially with many
ennobling immunities, which render him the most august animal in
the world, and still, whatever has happened since his creation, he remains at the upper end of nature, and as such is a creature of a very
noble character. For as to his dominion, the whole frame of the lower

part of the universe is devoted to his use and at his command; and his liberty under the conduct of right reason is equal with his trust. Which liberty may be briefly considered, internally as to his mind, and externally as to his person.

1. The internal native liberty of man's nature in general implies a faculty of doing or omitting things according to the direction of his judgment. But in a more special meaning, this liberty does not consist in a loose and ungovernable freedom, or in an unbounded license of acting. Such license is disagreeing with the condition and dignity of man and would make man of a lower and meaner constitution than brute creatures, who in all their liberties are kept under a better and more rational government by their instincts. Therefore, as Plutarch says, *Those persons only who live in obedience to reason are worthy to be accounted free; they alone live as they will,* who have learned what they ought to will. So that the true natural liberty of man, such as really and truly agrees to him, must be understood as he is guided and restrained by the ties of reason and laws of nature; all the rest is brutal, if not worse.

2. Man's external personal, natural liberty, antecedent to all human parts or alliances, must also be considered. And so every man must be conceived to be perfectly in his own power and disposal, and not to be controlled by the authority of any other. And thus every man must be acknowledged equal to every man, since all subjection and all command are equally banished on both sides; and considering all men thus at liberty, every man has a prerogative to judge for himself: viz., what shall be most for his behoof, happiness, and well-being.

3. The third capital immunity belonging to man's nature is an equality amongst men, which is not to be denied by the law of nature till man has resigned himself with all his rights for the sake of a civil state, and then his personal liberty and equality is to be cherished and preserved to the highest degree as will consist with all just distinctions amongst men of honor and shall be agreeable with the public good. For man has a high valuation of himself, and the passion seems to lay its first foundation, not in pride, but really in the high and admirable frame and constitution of human nature. The word *man,* says my author, is thought to carry somewhat of dignity in its sound; and we commonly make use of this as the most proper and prevailing argument against a rude insulter: viz., *I am not a beast or a dog, but am a man as well as yourself.* Since then human nature agrees equally with all persons; and since no one can live a sociable life with another that does not own or respect him as a man, it follows as a command of the

law of nature that every man esteem and treat another as one who is naturally his equal, or who is a man as well as he. There be many popular or plausible reasons that greatly illustrate this equality: viz., that we all derive our being from one stock, the same common father of human race. On this consideration Boethius checks the pride of the insulting nobility.

Quid genus et proavos strepitis?
Si primordia vestra,
Auteremque Deum spectas,
Nullus degener extat
Nisi vitiis pejora fovens,
Proprium deserat ortum.

Fondly our first descent we boast;
   If whence at first our breath we drew,
   The common springs of life we view,
The airy notion soon is lost.

The Almighty made us equal all;
   But he that slavishly complies
   To do the drudgery of vice,
Denies his high original.

And also that our bodies are composed of matter, frail, brittle, and liable to be destroyed by thousand accidents; we all owe our existence to the same method of propagation. The noblest mortal in his entrance on to the stage of life is not distinguished by any pomp or of passage from the lowest of mankind; and our life hastens to the same general mark: death observes no ceremony, but knocks as loud at the barriers of the court as at the door of the cottage. This equality being admitted bears a great force in maintaining peace and friendship amongst men. For that he who would use the assistance of others in promoting his own advantage ought as freely to be at their service when they want his help on the like occasions. *One good turn requires another* is the common proverb, for otherwise he must need esteem others unequal to himself who constantly demands their aid and as constantly denies his own. And whoever is of this insolent temper cannot but highly displease those about him and soon give occasion of the breach of the common peace. It was a manly reproof which Caractacus gave the Romans: *Num si vos omnibus,* etc. What! because you desire to be masters of all men, does it follow therefore that all men should desire to be your slaves, for that it is a command of nature's law that no man that has not obtained a particular and special right shall arrogate to himself a larger share than his fellows, but shall admit others to equal privileges with himself. So that the principle of equality in a natural state is peculiarly transgressed by pride, which is when a man without sufficient reason prefers himself to others. And though as Hensius paraphrases upon Aristotle's *Politics* to this purpose: viz., *Nothing is more suitable to nature than that those who excel in understanding and prudence should rule and control those who are less happy in those advantages,* etc., yet we must note that there is room for an answer: *scil.,* that it would be the greatest absurdity to believe that nature actually invests the wise with a sovereignty over the weak; or with a right of forcing them against their wills; for that no sovereignty can be established unless some human deed or covenant precede; nor does natural fitness for government make a man presently governor over another; for that, as Ulpian says, *by a natural right all men are born free;* and nature having set all men upon a level and made them equals, no servitude or subjection can be conceived without inequality; and this cannot be made without usurpation or force in others, or voluntary compliance in those who resign their freedom and give away their degree of natural being. . . .

(1717)

John Woolman

35.

(1720-1772)

The American Quaker leader traveled through the colonies preaching against slavery, war, poverty, and greed. This selection is from his classic *Journal*.

from The Journal of John Woolman

Ninth of fifth month [*1757*].—A Friend at whose house we breakfasted setting us a little on our way, I had conversation with him, in the fear of the Lord, concerning his slaves, in which my heart was tender; I used much plainness of speech with him, and he appeared to take it kindly. We pursued our journey without appointing meetings, being pressed in my mind to be at the Yearly Meeting in Virginia. In my traveling on the road I often felt a cry rise from the center of my mind, thus: "O Lord, I am a stranger on the earth, hide not Thy face from me." On the 11th we crossed the rivers Patowmack and Rapahannock and lodged at Port Royal. On the way we had the company of a colonel of the militia, who appeared to be a thoughtful man. I took occasion to remark on the difference in general betwixt a people used to labor moderately for their living, training up their children in frugality and business, and those who live on the labor of slaves—the former, in my view, being the most happy life. He concurred in the remark, and mentioned the trouble arising from the untoward, slothful disposition of the Negroes, adding that one of our laborers would do as much in a day as two of their slaves. I replied that free men, whose minds were properly on their business, found a satisfaction in improving, cultivating, and providing for their families; but Negroes, laboring to support others who claim them as their property, and expecting nothing but slavery during life, had not the like inducement to be industrious.

After some further conversation I said that men having power too often misapplied it; that though we made slaves of the Negroes, and the Turks made slaves of the Christians, I believed that liberty was the natural right of all men equally. This he did not deny, but said the lives of the Negroes were so wretched in their own country that many of them lived better here than there. I replied, "There is great odds in regard to us on what principle we act"; and so the conversation on that subject ended. I may here add that another person, some time after-

145

wards, mentioned the wretchedness of the Negroes, occasioned by their intestine wars, as an argument in favor of our fetching them away for slaves. To which I replied: if compassion for the Africans, on account of their domestic troubles, was the real motive of our purchasing them, that spirit of tenderness being attended to would incite us to use them kindly, that, as strangers brought out of affliction, their lives might be happy among us. And as they are human creatures, whose souls are as precious as ours and who may receive the same help and comfort from the Holy Scriptures as we do, we could not omit suitable endeavors to instruct them therein; but that while we manifest by our conduct that our views in purchasing them are to advance ourselves, and while our buying captives taken in war animates those parties to push on the war and increase desolation amongst them, to say they live unhappily in Africa is far from being an argument in our favor. I further said, the present circumstances of these provinces to me appear difficult; the slaves look like a burdensome stone to such as burden themselves with them; and that if the white people retain a resolution to prefer their outward prospects of gain to all other considerations, and do not act conscientiously towards them as fellow creatures, I believe that burden will grow heavier and heavier, until times change in a way disagreeable to us. The person appeared very serious, and owned that in considering their condition and the manner of their treatment in these provinces he had sometimes thought it might be just in the Almighty so to order it.

(1757)

Declaration of Independence

36.
(1776)

The Declaration of Independence was adopted July 4, 1776, by delegates of the Thirteen Colonies. It was written almost entirely by Thomas Jefferson.

THE UNANIMOUS DECLARATION OF THE THIRTEEN UNITED STATES OF AMERICA

When in the Course of human events, it becomes necessary for one people to dissolve the political bands which have connected them with another, and to assume among the powers of the earth, the separate and equal station to which the Laws of Nature and of Nature's God entitle them, a decent respect to the opinions of mankind requires that they should declare the causes which impel them to the separation. We hold these truths to be self-evident, that all men are created equal, that they are endowed by their Creator with certain unalienable Rights, that among these are Life, Liberty and the pursuit of Happiness. That to secure these rights, Governments are instituted among Men, deriving their just powers from the consent of the governed, That whenever any Form of Government becomes destructive of these ends, it is the Right of the People to alter or to abolish it, and to institute new Government, laying its foundation on such principles and organizing its powers in such form, as to them shall seem most likely to effect their Safety and Happiness. Prudence, indeed, will dictate that Governments long established should not be changed for light and transient causes; and accordingly all experience hath shewn, that mankind are more disposed to suffer, while evils are sufferable, than to right themselves by abolishing the forms to which they are accustomed. But when a long train of abuses and usurpations, pursuing invariably the same Object, evinces a design to reduce them under absolute Despotism, it is their right, it is their duty, to throw off such Government, and to provide new Guards for their future security. Such has been the patient sufferance of these Colonies; and such is now the necessity which constrains them to alter their former Systems of Government. The history of the present King of Great Britain is a history of repeated injuries and usurpations, all having in direct object the establishment of an absolute Tyranny over these States. To prove this, let Facts be submitted to a candid world.

He has refused his Assent to Laws, the most wholesome and necessary for the public good.

He has forbidden his Governors to pass Laws of immediate and pressing importance, unless suspended in their operation till his Assent should be obtained; and when so suspended, he has utterly neglected to attend to them.

He has refused to pass other Laws for the accommodation of large districts of people, unless those people would relinquish the right of Representation in the Legislature, a right inestimable to them and formidable to tyrants only.

He has called together legislative bodies at places unusual, uncomfortable, and distant from the depository of their public Records, for the sole purpose of fatiguing them into compliance with his measures.

He has dissolved Representative Houses repeatedly, for opposing with manly firmness his invasions on the rights of the people.

He has refused for a long time, after such dissolutions, to cause others to be elected; whereby the Legislative powers, incapable of Annihilation, have returned to the People at large for their exercise; the State remaining in the mean time exposed to all the dangers of invasion from without, and convulsions within.

He has endeavoured to prevent the population of these States; for that purpose obstructing the Laws of Naturalization of Foreigners; refusing to pass others to encourage their migrations hither, and raising the conditions of new Appropriations of Lands.

He has obstructed the Administration of Justice, by refusing his Assent to Laws for establishing Judiciary powers.

He has made Judges dependent on his Will alone, for the tenure of their offices, and the amount and payment of their salaries.

He has erected a multitude of New Offices, and sent hither swarms of Officers to harrass our people, and eat out their substance.

He has kept among us, in times of peace, standing Armies without the Consent of our legislatures.

He has affected to render the Military independent of and superior to the Civil power.

He has combined with others to subject us to a jurisdiction foreign to our constitution, and unacknowledged by our laws; giving his Assent to their Acts of pretended Legislation:

For Quartering large bodies of armed troops among us:

For protecting them, by a mock Trial, from punishment for any Murders which they should commit on the Inhabitants of these States:

For cutting off our Trade with all parts of the world:

For imposing Taxes on us without our Consent:

For depriving us in many cases of the benefits of Trial by Jury:

For transporting us beyond Seas to be tried for pretended offences:

For abolishing the free System of English Laws in a neighbouring Province, establishing therein an Arbitrary government, and enlarging its Boundaries so as to render it at once an example and fit instrument for introducing the same absolute rule into these Colonies:

For taking away our Charters, abolishing our most valuable Laws, and altering fundamentally the Forms of our Governments:

For suspending our own Legislatures, and declaring themselves invested with power to legislate for us in all cases whatsoever.

He has abdicated Government here, by declaring us out of his Protection and waging War against us.

He has plundered our seas, ravaged our Coasts, burnt our towns, and destroyed the Lives of our people.

He is at this time transporting large Armies of foreign Mercenaries to compleat the works of death, desolation and tyranny, already begun with circumstances of Cruelty & perfidy scarcely paralleled in the most barbarous ages, and totally unworthy the Head of a civilized nation.

He has constrained our fellow Citizens taken Captive on the high Seas to bear Arms against their Country, to become the executioners of their friends and Brethren, or to fall themselves by their Hands.

He has excited domestic insurrections amongst us, and has endeavoured to bring on the inhabitants of our frontiers, the merciless Indian Savages, whose known rule of warfare, is an undistinguished destruction of all ages, sexes and conditions.

In every stage of these Oppressions We have Petitioned for Redress in the most humble terms: Our repeated Petitions have been answered only by repeated injury. A Prince, whose character is thus marked by every act which may define a Tyrant, is unfit to be the ruler of a free people.

Nor have We been wanting in attentions to our Brittish brethren. We have warned them from time to time of attempts by their legislature to extend an unwarrantable jurisdiction over us. We have reminded them of the circumstances of our emigration and settlement here. We have appealed to their native justice and magnanimity, and we have conjured them by the ties of our common kindred to disavow these usurpations, which, would inevitably interrupt our connections and correspondence. They too have been deaf to the voice of justice and of consanguinity. We must, therefore, acquiesce in the necessity, which denounces our Separation, and hold them, as we hold the rest of mankind, Enemies in War, in Peace Friends.

We, therefore, the Representatives of the united States of America, in General Congress, Assembled, appealing to the Supreme Judge of the world for the rectitude of our intentions, do, in the Name, and by Authority of the good People of these Colonies, solemnly publish and declare, That these United Colonies are, and of Right ought to be Free and Independent States; that they are Absolved from all Allegiance to the British Crown, and that all political connection between them and the State of Great Britain, is and ought to be totally dissolved; and that as Free and Independent States, they have full Power to levy War, conclude Peace, contract Alliances, establish Commerce, and to do all other Acts and Things which Independent States may of right do. And for the support of this Declaration, with a firm reliance on the protection of divine Providence, we mutually pledge to each other our Lives, our Fortunes and our sacred Honor.

(1776)

Thomas Jefferson
(1743-1826)

37.

Thomas Jefferson, third President of the United States, philosopher-statesman, architect and scientist, was the author of the Declaration of Independence and the Virginia Statute for Religious Freedom.

from A Letter to Rev. James Madison (October 28, 1785)*

Fontainebleau Oct. 28, 1795

Dear Sir,—Seven o'clock, and retired to my fireside, I have determined to enter into conversation with you; this is a village of about 5,000 inhabitants . . . This being the first trip, I set out yesterday morning to take a view of the place. . . . As soon as I had got clear of the town I fell in with a poor woman walking at the same rate with myself & going the same course. . . . She told me she was a day labourer, at 8. sous or 4ᵈ sterling the day; that she had two children to maintain, & to pay a rent of 30 livres for her house (which would consume the hire of 75 days), that often she could get no emploiment, and of course was without bread. As we had walked together near a mile & she had so far served me as a guide, I gave her, on parting 24 sous. She burst into tears of a gratitude which I could perceive was unfeigned, because she was unable to utter a word. . . . This little attendrissement, with the solitude of my walk led me into a train of reflections on that unequal division of property which occasions the numberless instances of wretchedness which I had observed in this country & is to be observed all over Europe. The property of this country is absolutely concentrated in a very few hands, having revenues of from half a million of guineas a year downwards. These employ the flower of the country as servants, some of them having as many as 200 domestics, not labouring. They employ also a great number of manufacturers, & tradesmen, & lastly the class of labouring husbandmen. But after all these comes the most numerous of all the classes, that is, the poor who cannot find work. I asked myself what could be the reason that so many should be permitted to beg who are willing to work, in a country where there is a very considerable proportion of uncultivated lands? These lands are

---

* Jefferson dated this letter 1795 but the contents of the letter make it clear that he wrote it in 1785.

kept idle mostly for the sake of game. It should seem then that it must be because of the enormous wealth of the proprietors which places them above attention to the increase of their revenues by permitting these lands to be laboured. I am conscious that an equal division of property is impracticable. But the consequences of this enormous inequality producing so much misery to the bulk of mankind, legislators cannot invent too many devices for subdividing property, only taking care to let their subdivisions go hand in hand with the natural affections of the human mind. The descent of property of every kind therefore to all the children, or to all the brothers & sisters, or other relations in equal degree is a politic measure, and a practicable one. Another means of silently lessening the inequality of property is to exempt all from taxation below a certain point, & to tax the higher portions of property in geometrical progression as they rise. Whenever there is in any country, uncultivated lands and unemployed poor, it is clear that the laws of property have been so far extended as to violate natural right. The earth is given as a common stock for man to labour & live on. If, for the encouragement of industry we allow it to be appropriated, we must take care that other employment be provided to those excluded from the appropriation. If we do not the fundamental right to labour the earth returns to the unemployed. It is too soon yet in our country to say that every man who cannot find employment but who can find uncultivated land, shall be at liberty to cultivate it, paying a moderate rent. But it is not too soon to provide by every possible means that as few as possible shall be without a little portion of land. The small landholders are the most precious part of a state. . . .

(1785)

38

Immanuel Kant

(1724-1804)

Immanuel Kant, the great German philosopher, developed in his
ethical theory the position that in all actions men are to be
treated as ends in themselves rather than as merely means.

---

from The Fundamental Principles of the Metaphysics of Morals

... The question then is this: Is it a necessary law *for all rational
beings* that they should always judge of their actions by maxims of
which they can themselves will that they should serve as universal
laws? If it is so, then it must be connected (altogether *a priori*) with the
very conception of the will of a rational being generally. But in order
to discover this connection we must, however reluctantly, take a step
into metaphysic, although into a domain of it which is distinct from
speculative philosophy, namely, the metaphysic of morals. In a practical philosophy, where it is not the reasons of what *happens* that we
have to ascertain, but the laws of what *ought to happen,* even although
it never does, i.e. objective practical laws, there it is not necessary to
inquire into the reasons why anything pleases or displeases, how the
pleasure of mere sensation differs from taste, and whether the latter is
distinct from a general satisfaction of reason; on what the feeling of
pleasure or pain rests, and how from it desires and inclinations arise,
and from these again maxims by the co-operation of reason: for all this
belongs to an empirical psychology, which would constitute the second
part of physics, if we regard physics as the *philosophy of nature,* so far
as it is based on *empirical laws.* But here we are concerned with objective practical laws, and consequently with the relation of the will to
itself so far as it is determined by reason alone, in which case whatever
has reference to anything empirical is necessarily excluded; since if
reason of itself alone determines the conduct (and it is the possibility
of this that we are now investigating), it must necessarily do so *a priori.*

The will is conceived as a faculty of determining oneself to action
in accordance with the conception of certain laws. And such a faculty
can be found only in rational beings. Now that which serves the will
as the objective ground of its self-determination is the *end,* and if this
is assigned by reason alone, it must hold for all rational beings. On the

other hand, that which merely contains the ground of possibility of the action of which the effect is the end, this is called the *means*. The subjective ground of the desire is the *spring*, the objective ground of the volition is the motive; hence the distinction between subjective ends which rest on springs, and objective ends which depend on motives valid for every rational being. Practical principles are *formal* when they abstract from all subjective ends, they are *material* when they assume these, and therefore particular springs of action. The ends which a rational being proposes to himself at pleasure as *effects* of his actions (material ends) are all only relative, for it is only their relation to the particular desires of the subject that gives them their worth, which therefore cannot furnish principles universal and necessary for all rational beings and for every volition, that is to say practical laws. Hence all these relative ends can give rise only to hypothetical imperatives.

Supposing, however, that there were something *whose existence* has *in itself* an absolute worth, something which, being *an end in itself,* could be a source of definite laws, then in this and this alone would lie the source of a possible categorical imperative, i.e. a practical law.

Now I say: man and generally any rational being *exists* as an end in himself, *not merely as a means* to be arbitrarily used by this or that will, but in all his actions, whether they concern himself or other rational beings, must be always regarded at the same time as an end. All objects of the inclinations have only a conditional worth, for if the inclinations and the wants founded on them did not exist, then their object would be without value. But the inclinations themselves being sources of want, are so far from having an absolute worth for which they should be desired, that on the contrary it must be the universal wish of every rational being to be wholly free from them. Thus the worth of any object which is *to be acquired* by our action is always conditional. Beings whose existence depends not on our will but on Nature's, have nevertheless, if they are irrational beings, only a relative value as means, and are therefore called *things;* rational beings, on the contrary, are called *persons,* because their very nature points them out as ends in themselves, that is as something which must not be used merely as means, and so far therefore restricts freedom of action (and is an object of respect). These, therefore, are not merely subjective ends whose existence has a worth *for us* as an effect of our action, but *objective ends,* that is, things whose existence is an end in itself: an end moreover for which no other can be substituted, which they should subserve *merely* as means, for otherwise nothing whatever would possess *absolute worth;* but if all worth were conditioned and therefore contingent, then there would be no supreme practical principle of reason whatever.

If then there is a supreme practical principle or, in respect of the human will, a categorical imperative, it must be one which, being drawn from the conception of that which is necessarily an end for every one because it is *an end in itself,* constitutes an *objective* principle of will, and can therefore serve as a universal practical law. The foundation of this principle is: *rational nature exists as an end in itself.* Man necessarily conceives his own existence as being so: so far then this is a *subjective* principle of human actions. But every other rational being regards its existence similarly, just on the same rational principle that holds for me: so that it is at the same time an objective principle, from which as a supreme practical law all laws of the will must be capable of being deduced. Accordingly the practical imperative will be as follows: *So act as to treat humanity, whether in thine own person or in that of any other, in every case as an end withal, never as means only.* We will now inquire whether this can be practically carried out. . . .

(1785)

Declaration of the Rights of Man and of the Citizen

39.

(1789)

This historic French document was drafted by Sieyès and embodied as a preamble of the French Constitution of 1791. It was based on Rousseau's theories and on the American Declaration of Independence.

DECLARATION OF THE RIGHTS OF MAN AND OF THE CITIZEN

The representatives of the people of France, formed into a National Assembly, considering that ignorance, neglect, or contempt of human rights, are the sole causes of public misfortunes and corruptions of government, have resolved to set forth in a solemn declaration these natural, imprescriptible, and inalienable rights, that this declaration being constantly present to the minds of the members of the body social, they may be ever kept attentive to their rights and their duties; that the acts of the legislative and executive powers of government, being capable of being every moment compared with the end of political institutions, may be more respected; and also, that the future claims of the citizens, being directed by simple and incontestable principles, may always tend to the maintenance of the Constitution and the general happiness.

For these reasons the National Assembly doth recognize and declare, in the presence of the Supreme Being, and with the hope of His blessing and favor, the following *sacred* rights of men and of citizens:

I. Men are born, and always continue, free and equal in respect of their rights. Civil distinctions, therefore, can be founded only on public utility.

II. The end of all political associations is the preservation of the natural and imprescriptible rights of man; and these rights are Liberty, Property, Security, and Resistance of Oppression.

III. The nation is essentially the source of all sovereignty; nor can any individual, or any body of men, be entitled to any authority which is not expressly derived from it.

IV. Political Liberty consists in the power of doing whatever does not injure another. The exercise of the natural rights of every man has no other limits than those which are necessary to secure to every *other* man the free exercise of the same rights; and these limits are determinable only by the law.

V. The law ought to prohibit only actions hurtful to society. What is not prohibited by the law should not be hindered; nor should anyone be compelled to that which the law does not require.

VI. The law is an expression of the will of the community. All citizens have a right to concur, either personally or by their representatives, in its formation. It should be the same to all, whether it protects or punishes; and all being equal in its sight, are equally eligible to all honors, places, and employments, according to their different abilities, without any other distinction than that created by their virtues and talents.

VII. No man should be accused, arrested, or held in confinement, except in cases determined by the law, and according to the forms which it has prescribed. All who promote, solicit, execute, or cause to be executed, arbitrary orders, ought to be punished, and every citizen called upon, or apprehended by virtue of the law, ought immediately to obey, and renders himself culpable by resistance.

VIII. The law ought to impose no other penalties but such as are absolutely and evidently necessary; and no one ought to be punished, but in virtue of a law promulgated before the offense, and legally applied.

IX. Every man being presumed innocent till he has been convicted, whenever his detention becomes indispensable, all rigor to him, more than is necessary to secure his person, ought to be provided against by the law.

X. No man ought to be molested on account of his opinions, not even on account of his religious opinions, provided his avowal of them does not disturb the public order established by the law.

XI. The unrestrained communication of thoughts and opinions being one of the most precious rights of man, every citizen may speak, write, and publish freely, provided he is responsible for the abuse of this liberty, in cases determined by the law.

XII. A public force being necessary to give security to the rights of men and of citizens, that force is instituted for the benefit of the community and not for the particular benefit of the persons with whom it is intrusted.

XIII. A common contribution being necessary for the support of the public force, and for defraying the other expenses of government, it ought to be divided equally among the members of the community, according to their abilities.

XIV. Every citizen has a right, either by himself or his representative, to a free voice in determining the necessity of public contributions, the appropriations of them, and their amount, mode of assessment, and duration.

XV. Every community has a right to demand of all its agents an account of their conduct.

XVI. Every community in which a separation of powers and a security of rights is not provided for, wants a constitution.

XVII. The right to property being inviolable and sacred, no one ought to be deprived of it, except in cases of evident public necessity, legally ascertained, and on condition of a previous just indemnity.

(1789)

John Adams

40.

(1735-1826)

John Adams was a signer of the Declaration of Independence
and the second President of the United States.

---

from A Letter to Thomas Brand-Hollis
(June 11, 1790)

New York, 11 June, 1790

. . . The great revolution in France is wonderful, but not supernatural. The hand of Providence is in it, I doubt not, working, however, by natural and ordinary means, such as produced the reformation
in religion in the sixteenth century. That all men have one common
nature, is a principle which will now universally prevail, and equal
rights and equal duties will in a just sense, I hope, be inferred from
it. But equal ranks and equal property never can be inferred from it,
any more than equal understanding, agility, vigor, or beauty. Equal
laws are all that ever can be derived from human equality. . . . The
great and perpetual distinction in civilized societies, has been between
the rich, who are few, and the poor, who are many. When the many are
masters, they are too unruly, and then the few are too tame, and afraid
to speak out the truth. When the few are masters, they are too severe,
and then the many are too servile. This is the strict truth. The few have
had most art and union, and therefore have generally prevailed in the
end. The inference of wisdom from these premises is, that neither the
poor nor the rich should ever be suffered to be masters. They should
have equal power to defend themselves; and that their power may be
always equal, there should be an independent mediator between them,
always ready, always able, and always interested to assist the weakest.
Equal laws can never be made or maintained without this balance. You
see I still hold fast my scales, and weigh everything in them. The
French must finally become my disciples, or rather the disciples of
Zeno, or they will have no equal laws, no personal liberty, no property,
no lives. . . .

. . . In this country the pendulum has vibrated too far to the popular side, driven by men without experience or judgment, and horrid
ravages have been made upon property by arbitrary multitudes or majorities of multitudes. France has severe trials to endure from the same

159

cause. Both have found, or will find, that to place property at the mercy of a majority who have no property, is "committere agnum lupo." My fundamental maxim of government is, never to trust the lamb to the custody of the wolf. If you are not perfectly of my mind at present, I hereby promise and assure you that you will live to see that I am precisely right. Thus arrogantly concludes your assured friend.

(1790)

Thomas Paine

41.

(1737-1809)

Tom Paine, British-born pamphleteer and propagandist for the American Revolution, wrote *The Rights of Man* in defense of the French Revolution.

from The Rights of Man

Every history of the creation, and every traditionary account, whether from the lettered or unlettered world, however they may vary in their opinion or belief of certain particulars, all agree in establishing one point, *the unity of man;* by which I mean that men are all of *one degree,* and consequently that all men are born equal, and with equal natural right, in the same manner as if posterity had been continued by *creation* instead of *generation,* the latter being the only mode by which the former is carried forward; and consequently every child born into the world must be considered as deriving its existence from God. The world is as new to him as it was to the first man that existed, and his natural right in it is of the same kind.

The Mosaic account of the creation, whether taken as divine authority or merely historical, is full to this point, *the unity or equality of man.* The expression admits of no controversy. "And God said, Let us make man in our own image. In the image of God created he him; male and female created he them." The distinction of sexes is pointed out, but no other distinction is even implied. If this be not divine authority, it is at least historical authority, and shews that the equality of man, so far from being a modern doctrine, is the oldest upon record.

It is also to be observed that all the religions known in the world are founded, so far as they relate to man, on the *unity of man,* as being all of one degree. Whether in heaven or in hell, or in whatever state man may be supposed to exist hereafter, the good and the bad are the only distinctions. Nay, even the laws of governments are obliged to slide into this principle, by making degrees to consist in crimes and not in persons.

It is one of the greatest of all truths, and of the highest advantage to cultivate. By considering man in this light, and by instructing him to consider himself in this light, it places him in a close connection with all his duties, whether to his Creator or to the creation, of which he is a part; and it is only when he forgets his origin, or, to use a more fashionable phrase, his *birth and family,* that he becomes dissolute. It is not among the least of the evils of the present existing governments in all parts of Europe that man, considered as man, is thrown back to a vast distance from his Maker, and the artificial chasm filled up with a succession of barriers, or sort of turnpike gates, through which he has to pass. I will quote Mr. Burke's catalogue of barriers that he has set up between man and his Maker. Putting himself in the character of a herald, he says: "We fear God—we look with *awe* to kings—with affection to Parliaments—with duty to magistrates—with reverence to priests, and with respect to nobility." Mr. Burke has forgotten to put in "chivalry." He has also forgotten to put in Peter.

The duty of man is not a wilderness of turnpike gates, through which he is to pass by tickets from one to the other. It is plain and simple, and consists but of two points. His duty to God, which every man must feel; and with respect to his neighbor, to do as he would be done by. If those to whom power is delegated do well, they will be respected: if not, they will be despised; and with regard to those to whom no power is delegated, but who assume it, the rational world can know nothing of them.

Hitherto we have spoken only (and that but in part) of the natural rights of man. We have now to consider the civil rights of man, and to show how the one originates from the other. Man did not enter into society to become *worse* than he was before, nor to have fewer rights than he had before, but to have those rights better secured. His natural rights are the foundation of all his civil rights. But in order to pursue this distinction with more precision, it will be necessary to mark the different qualities of natural and civil rights.

A few words will explain this. Natural rights are those which appertain to man in right of his existence. Of this kind are all the intellectual rights, or rights of the mind, and also all those rights of acting as an individual for his own comfort and happiness, which are not injurious to the natural rights of others. Civil rights are those which appertain to man in right of his being a member of society. Every civil right has for its foundation some natural right pre-existing in the individual, but to the enjoyment of which his individual power is not, in all cases, sufficiently competent. Of this kind are all those which relate to security and protection.

From this short review it will be easy to distinguish between that class of natural rights which man retains after entering into society and those which he throws into the common stock as a member of society.

The natural rights which he retains are all those in which the *power* to execute is as perfect in the individual as the right itself. Among this class, as is before mentioned, are all the intellectual rights, or rights of the mind; consequently religion is one of those rights. The natural rights which are not retained, are all those in which, though the right is perfect in the individual, the power to execute them is defective. They answer not his purpose. A man, by natural right, has a right to judge in his own cause; and so far as the right of the mind is concerned, he never surrenders it. But what availeth it him to judge, if he has not power to redress? He therefore deposits this right in the common stock of society, and takes the arm of society, of which he is a part, in preference and in addition to his own. Society *grants* him nothing. Every man is a proprietor in society, and draws on the capital as a matter of right.

From these premises two or three certain conclusions will follow:

First, That every civil right grows out of a natural right; or, in other words, is a natural right exchanged.

Secondly, That civil power properly considered as such is made up of the aggregate of that class of the natural rights of man, which becomes defective in the individual in point of power, and answers not his purpose, but when collected to a focus becomes competent to the purpose of every one.

Thirdly, That the power produced from the aggregate of natural rights, imperfect in power in the individual, cannot be applied to invade the natural rights which are retained in the individual, and in which the power to execute is as perfect as the right itself.

We have now, in a few words, traced man from a natural individual to a member of society, and shewn, or endeavoured to shew, the quality of the natural rights retained, and of those which are exchanged for civil rights. . . .

(1792)

42. Georg Wilhelm Friedrich Hegel
(1770-1831)

Hegel, German philosopher, formulated an idealistic philosophy against which both Kierkegaard and Marx reacted.

from The Positivity of the Christian Religion

Equality was a principle with the early Christians; the slave was the brother of his owner; humility, the principle of not elevating one's self above anyone else, the sense of one's own unworthiness, was the first law of a Christian; men were to be valued not by honors or dignity, not by talents or other brilliant qualities, but by the strength of their faith. This theory, to be sure, has been retained in all its comprehensiveness, but with the clever addition that it is in the eyes of Heaven that all men are equal in this sense. For this reason, it receives no further notice in this earthly life. A simple-minded man may hear his bishop or superintendent preaching with touching eloquence about these principles of humility, about the abhorrence of all pride and all vanity, and he may see the edified expressions with which the lords and ladies in the congregation listen to this; but if, when the sermon is over, he approaches his prelate and the gentry with the hope of finding them humble brothers and friends, he will soon read in their laughing or contemptuous faces that all this is not to be taken *au pied de la lettre* and that only in Heaven will it find its literal application. And if even today eminent Christian prelates annually wash the feet of a number of the poor, this is little more than a comedy which leaves things as they are and which has also lost much of its meaning, because washing the feet is in our social life no longer what it was with the Jews, namely, a daily action and a courtesy to guests, performed as a rule only by slaves or servants. On the other hand, while the Chinese emperor's annual turn at the plow may equally have sunk to the level of a comedy, it has yet retained a greater and a more direct significance for every onlooker, because plowing must always be one of the chief occupations of his subjects.

(1796)

Jeremy Bentham

43.

(1748-1832)

Jeremy Bentham, the founder of Utilitarianism, was an English legal reformer and advocate of political democracy.

from Principles of the Civil Code

To judge of the effect of a portion of wealth upon happiness, it is necessary to consider it in three different states:—

1st. When it has always been in the hands of the holder.

2nd. When it is leaving his hands.

3rd. When it is coming into them.

It is to be observed in general, that in speaking of the effect of a portion of wealth upon happiness, abstraction is always to be made of the particular sensibility of individuals, and of the exterior circumstances in which they may be placed. Differences of character are inscrutable; and such is the diversity of circumstances, that they are never the same for two individuals. Unless we begin by dropping these two considerations, it will be impossible to announce any general proposition. But though each of these propositions may prove false or inexact in a given individual case, that will furnish no argument against their speculative truth and practical utility. It is enough for the justification of these propositions—1st, If they approach nearer the truth than any others which can be substituted for them; 2nd, If with less inconvenience than any others they can be made the basis of legislation.

I. Let us pass to the first case. The object being to examine the effect of a portion of wealth, when it has always been in the hands of the holder, we may lay down the following propositions:—

1st. *Each portion of wealth has a corresponding portion of happiness.*

2nd. *Of two individuals with unequal fortunes, he who has the most wealth has the most happiness.*

3rd. *The excess in happiness of the richer will not be so great as the excess of his wealth.*

4th. *For the same reasons, the greater the disproportion is between the two masses of wealth, the less is it probable that there exists a disproportion equally great between the corresponding masses of happiness.*

5th. *The nearer the actual proportion approaches to equality, the greater will be the total mass of happiness.*

It is not necessary to limit what is here said of wealth to the condition of those who are called wealthy. This word has a more extensive signification. It embraces everything which serves either for subsistence or abundance. It is for the sake of brevity that the phrase *portion of wealth* is used instead of *portion of the matter of wealth.*

I have said that for *each portion of wealth there is a corresponding portion of happiness.* To speak more exactly, it ought rather to be said, *a certain chance of happiness.* For the efficacy of a cause of happiness is always precarious; or, in other words, a cause of happiness has not its ordinary effect, nor the same effect, upon all persons. Here is the place for making an application of what has been said concerning the sensibility and the character of individuals, and the variety of circumstances in which they are found.

The second proposition is a direct consequence of the first. *Of two individuals, he who is the richer is the happier or has the greater chance of being so.* This is a fact proved by the experience of all the world. The first who doubts it shall be the very witness I will call to prove it. Let him give all his superfluous wealth to the first comer who asks him for it; for this superfluity, according to his system, is but dust in his hands; it is a burden and nothing more. The manna of the desert putrefied, if any one collected a greater quantity than he could eat. If wealth resembled that manna, and after passing a certain point was no longer productive in happiness, no one would wish for it; and the desire of accumulation would be a thing unknown.

The third proposition is less likely to be disputed. Put on one side a thousand farmers, having enough to live upon, and a little more. Put on the other side a king, or, not to be encumbered with the cares of government, a prince, well portioned, himself as rich as all the farmers taken together. It is probable, I say, that his happiness is greater than the average happiness of the thousand farmers; but it is by no means probable that it is equal to the sum total of their happiness, or, what amounts to the same thing, a thousand times greater than the average happiness of one of them. It would be remarkable if his happiness were ten times, or even five times greater. The man who is born in the bosom of opulence, is not so sensible of its pleasures as he who is the artisan of his own fortune. It is the pleasure of acquisition, not the satisfaction of possessing, which gives the greatest delights. The one is a lively sentiment, pricked on by the desires, and by anterior privations, which rushes toward an unknown good; the other is a feeble sentiment, weakened by use, which is not animated by contrasts, and which borrows nothing from the imagination.

II. Passing to the second case, let us examine the effect of a portion of wealth, when it enters for the first time into the hands of a new possessor. It is to be observed that we must lay expectation out of view. It is necessary to suppose that this augmentation of fortune comes unexpectedly, as a gift of chance.

1st. *A portion of wealth may be so far divided as to produce no happiness at all for any of the participants.* This is what would happen, rigorously speaking, if the portion of each was less in value than the smallest known coin. But it is not necessary to carry the thing to that extreme, in order to make the proposition true.

2nd. *Among participants of equal fortunes, the more perfectly equality is preserved in the distribution of a new portion of wealth, the greater will be the total mass of happiness.*

3rd. *Among participants of unequal fortunes, the more the distribution of new wealth tends to do away that inequality, the greater will be the total mass of happiness.*

III. The third case requires us to examine the effect produced by a portion of wealth which is leaving the hands of its former possessor. Here, too, we must lay expectation out of view, and suppose the loss to be unforeseen;—and a loss almost always is so, because every man naturally expects to keep what he has. This expectation is founded upon the ordinary course of things. For in a general view of human affairs, wealth already acquired is not only preserved, but increased. This is proved by the extreme difference between the primitive poverty of every community and its actual wealth.

1st. *The loss of a portion of wealth will produce, in the total happiness of the loser, a defalcation greater or less, according to the proportion of the part lost to the part which remains.*

Take away from a man the fourth part of his fortune, and you take away the fourth part of his happiness, and so on.

But there are cases in which the proportion would not be the same. If, in taking away from me three-fourths of my fortune, you take away what is necessary for my physical support, and if, in taking away half of it, you would have left that necessary portion untouched, the defalcation of happiness, instead of being twice as great in the first case as in the second, will be four times, ten times, indefinitely greater.

2nd. *This granted, fortunes being equal, the greater the number of persons among whom a loss is shared, the less considerable will be the defalcation from the sum total of happiness.*

3rd. *After passing a certain point, division renders the several quotas impalpable, and the defalcation in the sum total of happiness amounts to nothing.*

4th. *Fortunes being unequal, the loss of happiness produced by a given loss of wealth will become less in proportion as the distribution of the loss shall tend towards the production of an exact equality.* But in this case we must lay out of view the inconveniences attendant on the violation of security.

Governments, profiting by the progress of knowledge, have favoured, in many respects, the principle of equality in the distribution of losses. It is thus that they have taken under the protection of the laws *policies of insurance,* those useful contracts by which individuals assess themselves beforehand to provide against possible losses. The principle of insurance, founded upon a calculation of probabilities, is but the art of distributing losses among so great a number of associates as to make them very light, and almost nothing.

The same spirit has influenced sovereigns when they have indemnified, at the expense of the state, those of their subjects who have suffered either by public calamities or by the devastations of war. We have seen nothing of this kind wiser or better managed than the administration of the great Frederic. It is one of the finest points of view under which the social art can be considered.

Some attempts have been made to indemnify individuals for losses caused by the offences of malefactors. But examples of this kind are yet very rare. It is an object which merits the attention of legislators; for it is the means of reducing almost to nothing the evil of offences which attack property. To prevent it from becoming injurious, such a system must be arranged with care. It will not do to encourage indolence and imprudence in the neglect of precautions against offences, by making them sure of an indemnification; and it is necessary to guard even more cautiously against fraud and secret connivances which might counterfeit offences, and even produce them, for the sake of the indemnity. The utility of this remedial process would depend entirely on the way in which it was administered; yet the rejection of a means so salutary can only originate in a culpable indifference, anxious to save itself the trouble of discovering expedients.

The principles we have laid down may equally serve to regulate the distribution of a loss among many persons charged with a common responsibility. If their respective contributions correspond to the respective quantity of their fortunes, their relative state will be the same as before; but if it is desired to improve this occasion for the purposes of an approach towards equality, it is necessary to adopt a different proportion. To levy an equal impost, without regard to differences of fortune, would be a third plan, which would be agreeable neither to equality nor security.

To place this subject in a clearer light, I shall present a mixed case, in which it is necessary to decide between two individuals, of whom one demands a profit at the expense of the other. The question is to determine the effect of a portion of wealth which, passing into the hands of one individual under the form of gain, must come out of the hands of another in the form of loss.

1st. *Among competitors of equal fortunes, when that which is gained by one must be lost by another, the arrangement productive of the greatest sum of good will be that which favours the old possessor to the exclusion of the new demandant.*

For, in the first place, the sum to be lost, bearing a greater proportion to the reduced fortune than the same sum to the augmented fortune, the diminution of happiness for the one will be greater than the augmentation of happiness for the other; in one word, equality will be violated by the contrary arrangement.

In the second place, the loser will experience a pain of disappointment; the other merely does not gain. Now the negative evil of not acquiring is not equal to the positive evil of losing. If it were, as every man would experience this evil for all that he does not acquire, the causes of suffering would be infinite, and men would be infinitely miserable.

In the third place, men in general appear to be more sensitive to pain than to pleasure, even when the cause is equal. To such a degree, indeed, does this extend, that a loss which diminishes a man's fortune by one-fourth, will take away more happiness than he could gain by doubling his property.

2nd. *Fortunes being unequal, if the loser is the poorer, the evil of the loss will be aggravated by that inequality.*

3rd. *If the loser is the richer, the evil done by an attack upon security will be compensated in part by a good which will be great in proportion to the progress towards equality.*

By the aid of these maxims, which, to a certain point, have the character and the certainty of mathematical propositions, there might be at last produced a regular and constant art of indemnities and satisfactions. Legislators have frequently shown a disposition to promote equality under the name of *equity,* a word to which a greater latitude has been given than to *justice.* But this idea of equity, vague and half developed, has rather appeared an affair of instinct than of calculation. It was only by much patience and method that it was found possible to reduce to rigorous propositions an incoherent multitude of confused sentiments.

(1802)

Thomas Skidmore

(?-c. 1832)

44.

Thomas Skidmore, self-educated mechanic, was the leader of the wage earners' faction in the new Workingman's Party in New York in 1829. His book reveals his indebtedness for basic conceptions to Thomas Paine and Robert Owen.

from The Rights of Man to Property

If a man were to ask me, to what I would compare the unequal distribution of property which prevails in the world, and has ever prevailed, I would say, that it reminds me of a large party of gentlemen, who should have a common right to dine at one and the same public table; a part of whom should arrive first, sit down and eat what they chose; and then, because the remaining part came later to dinner, should undertake to monopolize the whole; and deprive them of the opportunity of satisfying their hunger, but upon terms such as those who had feasted, should be pleased to prescribe.

Such, now, is the actual condition of the whole human race. Those who have gone before us, have been the first to sit down to the table, and to enjoy themselves, without interruption, from those who came afterwards; and not content with this enjoyment, they have disposed of the whole dinner, in such a manner, that nine-tenths of the beings that now people this globe, have not wherewith to dine, but upon terms such as these first monopolisers, or those to whom they pretend they have conferred their own power as successors, shall choose to dictate. It is, as if, after dining till they were satisfied, a general scramble ensued, for what remained on the table; and those who succeeded in filling their pockets and other receptacles, with provisions, should have something to give to their children; but those who should have the misfortune to get none, or having got it, should lose it again, through fraud, calamity, or force, should have none for theirs, to the latest generation.

Such is the exact resemblance of the present order of things. Ye proud and rich possessors of the earth, look at this, and see if it be not so; and being so, and seeing that it is in your power to consent to a more *honorable* method of obtaining title to possession; say, if ye will not do so? I do not ask you, because it is in your power to confer any favor by giving such consent; for, this community, and every other, whenever they shall understand their rights, will have power enough in their own hands to do what they shall think fit, without seeking for any acquisition from you; but because it will be more agreeable to your own true happiness, to give such consent freely; than, with the ill, but unavailing grace of reluctance. Three hundred thousand freemen, in this State, hold votes in their hands, which no power that you can command can take out; and of these freemen, more than two hundred and fifty thousand are men whom a preceding generation, together with yourselves and their own ignorance of their rights have conspired to place in situations such that they have no property in the State of which they are citizens; although their title to such property is as good as that of any man that breathes. . . .

Let the poor and middling classes understand that their oppressions come from the overgrown wealth that exists among them, on the one hand, and from entire destitution on the other; and that as this overgrown wealth is continually augmenting its possessions, in a rapid ratio, the public sufferings are continually augmenting also; and must continue to augment, until the equal and unalienable rights of the people shall order otherwise. Let the parent reflect, if he be now a man of toil, that his children must be, ninety-nine cases in a hundred, slaves, *and worse,* to some rich proprietor; and that there is no alternative, but the change proposed. Let him not cheat himself with empty pretensions; for, *he who commands the property of a State, or even an inordinate portion of it,* HAS THE LIBERTY AND THE HAPPINESS OF ITS CITIZENS IN HIS OWN KEEPING. And if there be some dozen, or fifty, or five hundred of these large proprietors, they are neither more nor less than so many additional keepers. He who can feed me, or starve me; give me employment, or bid me wander about in idleness; is my master; and it is the utmost folly for me to boast of being any thing but a slave.

In fine, let the people awake to their rights; let them understand in what they consist; let them see the course they must pursue to obtain them; let them follow up that course, by informing each as many as he can, his fellow citizens, of the truth which this Work contains; let all co-operate in the early and effectual accomplishment of the objects it recommends, and these objects will easily and speedily be achieved, and none will have labored in vain.

At the moment of taking leave of the reader, it occurs to me, that it would be well to add a single remark. If ever the principles of this Work are to prevail; if ever they are to find their way among men, and to restore to them their rights, it is only to be done, by each doing all

he can, single and separately, to open the eyes of his fellows, to the perception of the evil that oppresses him, its origin and cure. While this
is doing, and doing too in many parts of the State, of the Union, and
the World, at one and the same time; for such is the co-extensive and
contemporary energy; with which the productions of the press operate; the rich, now and then, will cast their eyes on this Work; and they,
too, will see that the system which it proposes, must, sooner, or later,
take place. Ultimately, the whole of them will come to the same conclusion. So many of them as shall dread its approach, and shall not
have the moral honesty to surrender up to the disposition of their
fellow citizens, all that they have, will, of course, conceal as much as
they can. And that which is the most desirable to conceal, and the
easiest concealed, is money. Now, whenever it shall appear, correctly
or otherwise, it is no matter, to the rich generally, that the great mass
of the people have very nearly awakened to the determination to re-
sume their rights, and pursuant thereto, to order a General Division of
property; these concealments will take place very suddenly; and, perhaps, to such an extent as to withdraw the precious metals entirely
from circulation, out of the banks, as well as elsewhere. In such an
event, the banks would be broken; and as there would be no circulating
medium, all business would be instantly suspended. Those who now
carry on extensive business, would have nothing with which to pay off
their hands; and if they had, *they* might be as willing as others, to bury
it in the earth, for the purpose of defrauding the community out of it.

(1829)

William Ellery Channing

45.

(1780-1842)

Channing, Unitarian minister in Boston, wrote extensively and lucidly on education, labor problems, slavery, and religious tolerance.

from Honor Due to All Men

Among the many and inestimable blessings of Christianity, I regard as not the least the new sentiment with which it teaches man to look upon his fellow-beings; the new interest which it awakens in us towards everything human; the new importance which it gives to the soul; the new relation which it establishes between man and man. In this respect it began a mighty revolution, which has been silently spreading itself through society, and which, I believe, is not to stop until new ties shall have taken the place of those which have hitherto, in the main, connected the human race. Christianity has as yet but begun its work of reformation. Under its influences a new order of society is advancing, surely though slowly; and this beneficent change it is to accomplish in no small measure by revealing to men their own nature, and teaching them to "honor all" who partake it.

As yet Christianity has done little, compared with what it is to do, in establishing the true bond of union between man and man. The old bonds of society still continue in a great degree. They are instinct, interest, force. The true tie, which is mutual respect, calling forth mutual, growing, never-failing acts of love, is as yet little known. A new revelation, if I may so speak, remains to be made; or rather, the truths of the old revelation in regard to the greatness of human nature are to be brought out from obscurity and neglect. The soul is to be regarded with a religious reverence hitherto unfelt; and the solemn claims of every being to whom this divine principle is imparted are to be established on the ruins of those pernicious principles, both in church and state, which have so long divided mankind into the classes of the abject many and the self-exalting few. . . .

It may be said that Christianity has done much to awaken benevolence, and that it has taught men to call one another brethren. Yes, to *call* one another so; but has it as yet given the true feeling of brotherhood? We undoubtedly feel ourselves to be all of one race, and this is well. We trace ourselves up to one pair, and feel the same blood flowing in our veins. But do we understand our spiritual brotherhood? Do we feel ourselves to be derived from one Heavenly Parent, in whose image we are all made, and whose perfection we may constantly approach? Do we feel that there is one divine life in our own and in all souls? This seems to me the only true bond of man to man. Here is a tie more sacred, more enduring, than all the ties of this earth. Is it felt, and do we in consequence truly honor one another?

Sometimes, indeed, we see men giving sincere, profound, and almost unmeasured respect to their fellow-creatures; but to whom? To great men; to men distinguished by a broad line from the multitude; to men pre-eminent by genius, force of character, daring effort, high station, brilliant success. To such honor is given; but this is not to "honor all men"; and the homage paid to such is generally unfriendly to that Christian estimate of human beings for which I am now pleading. The great are honored at the expense of their race. They absorb and concentrate the world's admiration, and their less gifted fellow-beings are thrown by their brightness into a deeper shade, and passed over with a colder contempt. Now I have no desire to derogate from the honor paid to great men, but I say, Let them not rise by the depression of the multitude. I say that great men, justly regarded, exalt our estimate of the human race, and bind us to the multitude of men more closely; and when they are not so regarded, when they are converted into idols, when they serve to wean our interest from ordinary men, they corrupt us, they sever the sacred bond of humanity which should attach us to all, and our characters become vitiated by our very admiration of greatness. The true view of great men is that they are only examples and manifestations of our common nature, showing what belongs to all souls, though unfolded as yet only in a few. The light which shines from them is, after all, but a faint revelation of the power which is treasured up in every human being. They are not prodigies, not miracles, but natural developments of the human soul. They are indeed as men among children, but the children have a principle of growth which leads to manhood.

That great men and the multitude of minds are of one family is apparent, I think, in the admiration which the great inspire into the multitude. A sincere, enlightened admiration always springs from something congenial in him who feels it with him who inspires it. He that can understand and delight in greatness was created to partake of it; the germ is in him; and sometimes this admiration, in what we deem inferior minds, discovers a nobler spirit than belongs to the great man who awakens it; for sometimes the great man is so absorbed in his own greatness as to admire no other; and I should not hesitate to say that a common mind, which is yet capable of a generous admiration, is destined to rise higher than the man of eminent capacities, who can enjoy no power or excellence but his own. When I hear of great men, I wish not to separate them from their race, but to blend them with it. I esteem it no small benefit of the philosophy of mind that it teaches us that the elements of the greatest thoughts of the man of genius exist in his humbler brethren, and that the faculties which the scientific exert in the profoundest discoveries are precisely the same with those which common men employ in the daily labors of life.

To show the grounds on which the obligation to honor all men rests, I might take a minute survey of that human nature which is common to all, and set forth its claims to reverence. But, leaving this wide range, I observe that there is one principle of the soul which makes all men essentially equal, which places all on a level as to means of happiness, which may place in the first rank of human beings those who are the most depressed in worldly condition, and which therefore gives the most depressed a title to interest and respect. I refer to the sense of duty, to the power of discerning and doing right, to the moral and religious principle, to the inward monitor which speaks in the name of God, to the capacity of virtue or excellence. This is the great gift of God. We can conceive no greater. In seraph and archangel we can conceive no higher energy than the power of virtue, or the power of forming themselves after the will and moral perfections of God. This power breaks down all barriers between the seraph and the lowest human being; it makes them brethren. Whoever has derived from God this perception and capacity of rectitude has a bond of union with the spiritual world stronger than all the ties of nature. He possesses a principle which, if he is faithful to it, must carry him forward forever, and insures to him the improvement and happiness of the highest order of beings.

It is this moral power which makes all men essentially equal, which annihilates all the distinctions of this world. Through this, the ignorant and the poor may become the greatest of the race; for the greatest is he who is most true to the principle of duty. It is not improbable that the noblest human beings are to be found in the least favored conditions of society, among those whose names are never uttered beyond the narrow circle in which they toil and suffer, who have but "two mites" to give away, who have perhaps not even that, but who "desire to be fed with the crumbs which fall from the rich man's table"; for in this class may be found those who have withstood the severest temptation, who have practised the most arduous duties, who have confided in God under the heaviest trials, who have been most wronged and have forgiven most; and these are the great, the exalted. It matters nothing what the particular duties are to which the individual is called,—how minute or obscure in their outward form. Greatness in God's sight lies, not in the extent of the sphere which is filled, or of the effect which is produced, but altogether in the power of virtue in the soul, in the energy with which God's will is chosen, with which trial is borne, and goodness loved and pursued. . . .

(1832)

Alexis de Tocqueville

46.

(1805-1859)

Alexis de Tocqueville was a French liberal politician and writer whose observations on American life have become classic.

from Democracy in America

It is possible to imagine an extreme point at which freedom and equality would meet and blend. Let us suppose that all the people take a part in the government, and that each one of them has an equal right to take a part in it. As no one is different from his fellows, none can exercise a tyrannical power; men will be perfectly free because they will all be entirely equal; and they will all be perfectly equal because they are entirely free. To this ideal state democratic nations tend. This is the only complete form that equality can assume upon earth; but there are a thousand others which, without being equally perfect, are not less cherished by those nations.

The principle of equality may be established in civil society without prevailing in the political world. There may be equal rights of indulging in the same pleasures, of entering the same professions, of frequenting the same places; in a word, of living in the same manner and seeking wealth by the same means, although all men do not take an equal share in the government. A kind of equality may even be established in the political world though there should be no political freedom there. A man may be the equal of all his countrymen save one, who is the master of all without distinction and who selects equally from among them all the agents of his power. Several other combinations might be easily imagined by which very great equality would be united to institutions more or less free or even to institutions wholly without freedom.

Although men cannot become absolutely equal unless they are entirely free, and consequently equality, pushed to its furthest extent, may be confounded with freedom, yet there is good reason for distinguishing the one from the other. The taste which men have for liberty and that which they feel for equality are, in fact, two different things; and I am not afraid to add that among democratic nations they are two unequal things.

Upon close inspection it will be seen that there is in every age some peculiar and preponderant fact with which all others are connected; this fact almost always gives birth to some pregnant idea or some ruling passion, which attracts to itself and bears away in its course all the feelings and opinions of the time; it is like a great stream towards which each of the neighboring rivulets seems to flow.

Freedom has appeared in the world at different times and under various forms; it has not been exclusively bound to any social condition, and it is not confined to democracies. Freedom cannot, therefore, form the distinguishing characteristic of democratic ages. The peculiar and preponderant fact that marks those ages as its own is the equality of conditions; the ruling passion of men in those periods is the love of this equality. Do not ask what singular charm the men of democratic ages find in being equal, or what special reasons they may have for clinging so tenaciously to equality rather than to the other advantages that society holds out to them: equality is the distinguishing characteristic of the age they live in; that of itself is enough to explain that they prefer it to all the rest.

But independently of this reason there are several others which will at all times habitually lead men to prefer equality to freedom.

If a people could ever succeed in destroying, or even in diminishing, the equality that prevails in its own body, they could do so only by long and laborious efforts. Their social condition must be modified, their laws abolished, their opinions superseded, their habits changed, their manners corrupted. But political liberty is more easily lost; to neglect to hold it fast is to allow it to escape. Therefore not only do men cling to equality because it is dear to them; they also adhere to it because they think it will last forever.

That political freedom in its excesses may compromise the tranquillity, the property, the lives of individuals is obvious even to narrow and unthinking minds. On the contrary, none but attentive and clearsighted men perceive the perils with which equality threatens us, and they commonly avoid pointing them out. They know that the calamities they apprehend are remote and flatter themselves that they will only fall upon future generations, for which the present generation takes but little thought. The evils that freedom sometimes brings with it are immediate; they are apparent to all, and all are more or less affected by them. The evils that extreme equality may produce are slowly disclosed; they creep gradually into the social frame; they are seen only at intervals; and at the moment at which they become most violent, habit already causes them to be no longer felt.

The advantages that freedom brings are shown only by the lapse of time, and it is always easy to mistake the cause in which they originate. The advantages of equality are immediate, and they may always be traced from their source.

Political liberty bestows exalted pleasures from time to time upon a certain number of citizens. Equality every day confers a number of small enjoyments on every man. The charms of equality are every instant felt and are within the reach of all; the noblest hearts are not insensible to them, and the most vulgar souls exult in them. The passion that equality creates must therefore be at once strong and general. Men cannot enjoy political liberty unpurchased by some sacrifices, and they never obtain it without great exertions. But the pleasures of equality are self-proffered; each of the petty incidents of life seems to occasion them, and in order to taste them nothing is required but to live.

Democratic nations are at all times fond of equality, but there are certain epochs at which the passion they entertain for it swells to the height of fury. This occurs at the moment when the old social system, long menaced, is overthrown after a severe internal struggle, and the barriers of rank are at length thrown down. At such times men pounce upon equality as their booty, and they cling to it as to some precious treasure which they fear to lose. The passion for equality penetrates on every side into men's hearts, expands there, and fills them entirely. Tell them not that by this blind surrender of themselves to an exclusive passion they risk their dearest interests; they are deaf. Show them not freedom escaping from their grasp while they are looking another way; they are blind, or rather they can discern but one object to be desired in the universe. . . .

I think that democratic communities have a natural taste for freedom; left to themselves, they will seek it, cherish it, and view any privation of it with regret. But for equality their passion is ardent, insatiable, incessant, invincible; they call for equality in freedom; and if they cannot obtain that, they still call for equality in slavery. They will endure poverty, servitude, barbarism, but they will not endure aristocracy.

This is true at all times, and especially in our own day. All men and all powers seeking to cope with this irresistible passion will be overthrown and destroyed by it. In our age freedom cannot be established without it, and despotism itself cannot reign without its support. . . .

It is possible to conceive of men arrived at a degree of freedom that should completely content them; they would then enjoy their independence without anxiety and without impatience. But men will never establish any equality with which they can be contented. Whatever efforts a people may make, they will never succeed in reducing all the conditions of society to a perfect level; and even if they unhappily attained that absolute and complete equality of position, the inequality of minds would still remain, which, coming directly from the hand of God, will forever escape the laws of man. However democratic, then, the social state and the political constitution of a people may be, it is certain that every member of the community will always find out several points about him which overlook his own position; and we may foresee that his looks will be doggedly fixed in that direction. When inequality of conditions is the common law of society, the most marked inequalities do not strike the eye; when everything is nearly on the same level, the slightest are marked enough to hurt it. Hence the desire of equality always becomes more insatiable in proportion as equality is more complete.

Among democratic nations, men easily attain a certain equality of condition, but they can never attain as much as they desire. It perpetually retires from before them, yet without hiding itself from their sight, and in retiring draws them on. At every moment they think they are about to grasp it; it escapes at every moment from their hold. They are near enough to see its charms, but too far off to enjoy them; and before they have fully tasted its delights, they die.

To these causes must be attributed that strange melancholy which often haunts the inhabitants of democratic countries in the midst of their abundance, and that disgust at life which sometimes seizes upon them in the midst of calm and easy circumstances. Complaints are made in France that the number of suicides increases; in America suicide is rare, but insanity is said to be more common there than anywhere else. These are all different symptoms of the same disease. The Americans do not put an end to their lives, however disquieted they may be, because their religion forbids it; and among them materialism may be said hardly to exist, notwithstanding the general passion for physical gratification. The will resists, but reason frequently gives way. . . .

In democracies servants are not only equal among themselves, but it may be said that they are, in some sort, the equals of their masters. This requires explanation in order to be rightly understood. At any moment a servant may become a master, and he aspires to rise to that condition; the servant is therefore not a different man from the master. Why, then, has the former a right to command, and what compels the latter to obey except the free and temporary consent of both their wills? Neither of them is by nature inferior to the other; they only become so for a time, by covenant. Within the terms of this covenant the one is a servant, the other a master; beyond it they are two citizens of the commonwealth, two men.

I beg the reader particularly to observe that this is not only the notion which servants themselves entertain of their own condition; domestic service is looked upon by masters in the same light, and the precise limits of authority and obedience are as clearly settled in the mind of the one as in that of the other.

When the greater part of the community have long attained a condition nearly alike and when equality is an old and acknowledged fact, the public mind, which is never affected by exceptions, assigns certain general limits to the value of man, above or below which no man can long remain placed. It is in vain that wealth and poverty, authority and obedience, accidentally interpose great distances between two men; public opinion, founded upon the usual order of things, draws them to a common level and creates a species of imaginary equality between them, in spite of the real inequality of their conditions. This all-powerful opinion penetrates at length even into the hearts of those whose interest might arm them to resist it; it affects their judgment while it subdues their will.

In their inmost convictions the master and the servant no longer perceive any deep-seated difference between them, and they neither hope nor fear to meet with either at any time. They are therefore subject neither to disdain nor to anger, and they discern in each other neither humility nor pride. The master holds the contract of service to be the only source of his power, and the servant regards it as the only cause of his obedience. They do not quarrel about their reciprocal situations, but each knows his own and keeps it. . . .

(1835)

47.

The Seneca Falls Declaration of Sentiments
(1848)

The platform adopted by the first woman's rights convention in the United States, held in Seneca Falls, New York.

THE SENECA FALLS DECLARATION OF SENTIMENTS

When, in the course of human events, it becomes necessary for one portion of the family of man to assume among the people of the earth a position different from that which they have hitherto occupied, but one to which the laws of nature and of nature's God entitle them, a decent respect to the opinions of mankind requires that they should declare the causes that impel them to such a course.

We hold these truths to be self-evident: that all men and women are created equal; that they are endowed by their Creator with certain inalienable rights; that among these are life, liberty, and the pursuit of happiness; that to secure these rights governments are instituted, deriving their just powers from the consent of the governed. Whenever any form of government becomes destructive of these ends, it is the right of those who suffer from it to refuse allegiance to it, and to insist upon the institution of a new government, laying its foundation on such principles, and organizing its powers in such form, as to them shall seem most likely to effect their safety and happiness. Prudence, indeed, will dictate that governments long established should not be changed for light and transient causes; and accordingly all experience hath shown that mankind are more disposed to suffer while evils are sufferable, than to right themselves by abolishing the forms to which they are accustomed. But when a long train of abuses and usurpations, pursuing invariably the same object, evinces a design to reduce them under absolute despotism, it is their duty to throw off such government, and to provide new guards for their future security. Such has been the patient sufferance of the women under this government, and such is now the necessity which constrains them to demand the equal station to which they are entitled.

The history of mankind is a history of repeated injuries and usurpations on the part of man toward woman, having in direct object the establishment of an absolute tyranny over her. To prove this, let facts be submitted to a candid world.

He has never permitted her to exercise her inalienable right to the elective franchise.

He has compelled her to submit to laws, in the formation of which she had no voice.

He has withheld from her rights which are given to the most ignorant and degraded men—both natives and foreigners.

Having deprived her of this first right of a citizen, the elective franchise, thereby leaving her without representation in the halls of legislation, he has oppressed her on all sides.

He has made her, if married, in the eye of the law, civilly dead.

He has taken from her all right in property, even to the wages she earns.

He has made her, morally, an irresponsible being, as she can commit many crimes with impunity, provided they be done in the presence of her husband. In the covenant of marriage, she is compelled to promise obedience to her husband, he becoming, to all intents and purposes, her master—the law giving him power to deprive her of her liberty, and to administer chastisement.

He has so framed the laws of divorce, as to what shall be the proper causes, and in case of separation, to whom the guardianship of the children shall be given, as to be wholly regardless of the happiness of women—the law, in all cases, going upon a false supposition of the supremacy of man, and giving all power into his hands.

After depriving her of all rights as a married woman, if single, and the owner of property, he has taxed her to support a government which recognizes her only when her property can be made profitable to it.

He has monopolized nearly all the profitable employments, and from those she is permitted to follow, she receives but a scanty remuneration. He closes against her all the avenues to wealth and distinction which he considers most honorable to himself. As a teacher of theology, medicine, or law, she is not known.

He has denied her the facilities for obtaining a thorough education, all colleges being closed against her.

He allows her in Church, as well as State, but a subordinate position, claiming Apostolic authority for her exclusion from the ministry, and, with some exceptions, from any public participation in the affairs of the Church.

He has created a false public sentiment by giving to the world a different code of morals for men and women, by which moral delinquencies which exclude women from society, are not only tolerated, but deemed of little account in man.

He has usurped the prerogative of Jehovah himself, claiming it as his right to assign for her a sphere of action, when that belongs to her conscience and to her God.

He has endeavored, in every way that he could, to destroy her confidence in her own powers, to lessen her self-respect and to make her willing to lead a dependent and abject life.

Now, in view of this entire disfranchisement of one-half the people of this country, their social and religious degradation—in view of the unjust laws above mentioned, and because women do feel themselves aggrieved, oppressed, and fraudulently deprived of their most sacred rights, we insist that they have immediate admission to all the rights and privileges which belong to them as citizens of the United States.

In entering upon the great work before us, we anticipate no small amount of misconception, misrepresentation, and ridicule; but we shall use every instrumentality within our power to effect our object. We shall employ agents, circulate tracts, petition the State and National legislatures, and endeavor to enlist the pulpit and the press in our behalf. We hope this Convention will be followed by a series of Conventions embracing every part of the country.

(1848)

Abraham Lincoln

48.

(1809-1865)

Abraham Lincoln, 16th President of the United States and author of the Emancipation Proclamation, comments on equality in several public addresses which are reprinted here.

from An Address Delivered at Springfield, June 26, 1857

I think the authors of that notable instrument [the Declaration of Independence] intended to include *all* men, but they did not intend to declare all men equal *in all respects.* They did not mean to say all were equal in color, size, intellect, moral developments, or social capacity. They defined with tolerable distinctness in what respects they did consider all men created equal—equal with "certain inalienable rights, among which are life, liberty, and the pursuit of happiness." This they said, and this they meant. They did not mean to assert the obvious untruth that all were then actually enjoying that equality, nor yet that they were about to confer it immediately upon them. In fact, they had no power to confer such a boon. They meant simply to declare the right, so that enforcement of it might follow as fast as circumstances should permit.

They meant to set up a standard maxim for free society, which should be familiar to all, and revered by all; constantly looked to, constantly labored for, and even though never perfectly attained, constantly approximated, and thereby constantly spreading and deepening its influence and augmenting the happiness and value of life to all people of all colors everywhere. The assertion that "all men are created equal" was of no practical use in effecting our separation from Great Britain; and it was placed in the Declaration not for that, but for future use. Its authors meant it to be—as, thank God, it is now proving itself—a stumbling-block to all those who in after times might seek to turn a free people back into the hateful paths of despotism. They knew the proneness of prosperity to breed tyrants, and they meant when such should reappear in this fair land and commence their vocation, they should find left for them at least one hard nut to crack.

(1857)

185

from Lincoln's Reply in the First Joint Debate with Douglas, in 1858

. . . I have no purpose to introduce political and social equality between the white and the black races. There is a physical difference between the two, which, in my judgment, will probably forever forbid their living together upon the footing of perfect equality; and inasmuch as it becomes a necessity that there must be a difference, I, as well as Judge Douglas, am in favor of the race to which I belong having the superior position. I have never said anything to the contrary, but I hold that, notwithstanding all this, there is no reason in the world why the Negro is not entitled to all the natural rights enumerated in the Declaration of Independence—the right to life, liberty, and the pursuit of happiness. . . . I agree with Judge Douglas he is not my equal in many respects—certainly not in color, perhaps not in moral or intellectual endowment. But in the right to eat the bread, without the leave of anybody else, which his own hand earns, he is my equal and the equal of Judge Douglas, and the equal of every living man.

(1858)

from An Address Delivered at New Haven, March 6, 1860

What is the true condition of the laborer? I take it that it is best for all to leave each man free to acquire property as fast as he can. Some will get wealthy. I don't believe in a law to prevent a man from getting rich; it would do more harm than good. So while we do not propose any war upon capital, we do wish to allow the humblest man an equal chance to get rich with everybody else. When one starts poor, as most do in the race of life, free society is such that he knows he can better his condition; he knows that there is no fixed condition of labor for his whole life. . . . I want every man to have a chance—and I believe a black man is entitled to it—in which he can better his condition—when he may look forward and hope to be a hired laborer this year and the next, work for himself afterward, and finally to hire men to work for him. That is the true system.

(1860)

Henry J. S. Maine

49.

(1822-1888)

Henry J. S. Maine was an English jurist and historian who traced the history of laws as the history of civilization.

from Ancient Law

There is a single example which very strikingly illustrates the effects of the theory of natural law on modern society, and indicates how very far are those effects from being exhausted. There cannot, I conceive, be any question that to the assumption of the Law Natural we owe the doctrine of the fundamental equality of human beings. That "all men are equal" is one of a large number of legal provisions which, in progress of time, have become political. The Roman jurisconsults of the Antonine era lay down that "omnes homines naturâ aequales sunt," but in their eyes this is a strictly juridical axiom. They intend to affirm that under the hypothetical Law of Nature, and in so far as positive law approximates to it, the arbitrary distinctions which the Roman Civil Law maintained between classes of persons cease to have a legal existence. The rule was one of considerable importance to the Roman practitioner, who required to be reminded that, wherever Roman jurisprudence was assumed to conform itself exactly to the code of Nature, there was no difference in the contemplation of the Roman tribunals between citizen and foreigner, between freeman and slave, Agnate and Cognate. The jurisconsults who thus expressed themselves most certainly never intended to censure the social arrangements under which civil law fell somewhat short of its speculative type; nor did they apparently believe that the world would ever see human society completely assimilated to the economy of nature. But when the doctrine of human equality makes its appearance in a modern dress it has evidently clothed itself with a new shade of meaning. Where the Roman jurisconsult had written "aequales sunt," meaning exactly what he said, the modern civilian wrote "all men are equal" in the sense of "all men ought to be equal." The peculiar Roman idea that natural law coexisted with civil law and gradually absorbed it, had evidently been lost sight of, or had become unintelligible, and the words which had at most conveyed a theory concerning the origin, composition and development of human institutions, were beginning to express the sense of a great standing wrong suffered by mankind. As early as the beginning of the fourteenth century, the current language concerning the birth-state of men, though visibly intended to be identical with that of Ulpian and his contemporaries has assumed an altogether different form and meaning. The preamble to the celebrated ordinance of King Louis Hutin, enfranchising the serfs of the royal domains, would have sounded strangely to Roman ears. "Whereas, according to natural law, everybody ought to be born free; and by some usages and customs which, from long antiquity, have been introduced and kept until now in our realm, and peradventure by reason of the misdeeds of their predecessors, many persons of our common people have fallen into servitude, therefore, We," etc. This is the enunciation not of a legal rule but of a political dogma; and from this time the equality of men is spoken of by the French lawyers just as if it were a political truth which happened to have been preserved among the archives of their science. Like all other deductions from the hypothesis of a Law Natural, and like the belief itself in a Law of Nature, it was languidly assented to and suffered to have little influence on opinion and practice until it passed out of the possession of the lawyers into that of the literary men of the eighteenth century and of the public which sat at their feet. With them it became the most distinct tenet of their creed, and was even regarded as a summary of all the others. It is probable, however, that the power which it ultimately acquired over the events of 1789 was not entirely owing to its popularity in France, for in the middle of the century it passed over to America. The American lawyers of the time, and particularly those of Virginia, appear to have possessed a stock of knowledge which differed chiefly from that of their English contemporaries in including much which could only have been derived from the legal literature of continental Europe. A very few glances at the writings of Jefferson will show how strongly his mind was affected by the semi-juridical, semi-popular opinions which were fashionable in France, and we cannot doubt that it was sympathy with the peculiar ideas of the French jurists which led him and the other colonial lawyers who guided the course of events in America to join the specially French assumption that "all men are born equal" with the assumption, more familiar to Englishmen, that all men are born free, in the very first lines of their Declaration of Independence. The passage was one of great importance to the history of the doctrine before us. The American lawyers, in thus prominently and emphatically affirming the fundamental equality of human beings, gave an impulse to political movements in their own country, and in a less degree in Great Britain, which is far from having yet spent itself; but beside this they returned the dogma they had adopted to its home in France, endowed with vastly greater energy and enjoying much greater claims on general reception and respect. Even the more cautious politicians of the first Constituent Assembly repeated Ulpian's proposition as if it at once commended itself to the instincts and intuitions of mankind; and of all the "principles of 1789" it is the one which has been least strenuously assailed, which has most thoroughly leavened modern opinion, and which promises to modify most deeply the constitution of societies and the politics of states.

(1861)

John Stuart Mill

50.
(1806-1873)

J. S. Mill, an employee of the East India Company, member of Parliament, and liberal philosopher, wrote books which were influential in philosophy, economics, and political theory.

from Utilitarianism

Nearly allied to the idea of impartiality is that of *equality;* which often enters as a component part both into the conception of justice and into the practice of it, and, in the eyes of many persons, constitutes its essence. But in this, still more than in any other case, the notion of justice varies in different persons, and always conforms in its variations to their notion of utility. Each person maintains that equality is the dictate of justice, except where he thinks that expediency requires inequality. The justice of giving equal protection to the rights of all, is maintained by those who support the most outrageous inequality in the rights themselves. Even in slave countries it is theoretically admitted that the rights of the slave, such as they are, ought to be as sacred as those of the master; and that a tribunal which fails to enforce them with equal strictness is wanting in justice; while, at the same time, institutions which leave to the slave scarcely any rights to enforce, are not deemed unjust, because they are not deemed inexpedient. Those who think that utility requires distinctions of rank, do not consider it unjust that riches and social privileges should be unequally dispensed; but those who think this inequality inexpedient, think it unjust also. Whoever thinks that government is necessary, sees no injustice in as much inequality as is constituted by giving to the magistrate powers not granted to other people. Even among those who hold leveling doctrines, there are as many questions of justice as there are differences of opinion about expediency. Some communists consider it unjust that the produce of the labor of the community should be shared on any other principle than that of exact equality; others think it just that those should receive most whose wants are greatest; while others hold that those who work harder, or who produce more, or whose services are more valuable to the community, may justly claim a larger quota in the division of the produce. And the sense of natural justice may be plausibly appealed to in behalf of every one of these opinions

.   .   .   .

That first of judicial virtues, impartiality, is an obligation of justice, partly for the reason last mentioned, as being a necessary condition of the fulfilment of the other obligations of justice. But this is not the only source of the exalted rank, among human obligations, of those maxims of equality and impartiality which, both in popular estimation and in that of the most enlightened, are included among the precepts of justice. In one point of view, they may be considered as corollaries from the principles already laid down. If it is a duty to do to each according to his deserts, returning good for good as well as repressing evil by evil, it necessarily follows that we should treat all equally well (when no higher duty forbids) who have deserved equally well of *us,* and that society should treat all equally well who have deserved equally well of *it,* that is, who have deserved equally well absolutely. This is the highest abstract standard of social and distributive justice; towards which all institutions, and the efforts of all virtuous citizens, should be made in the utmost possible degree to converge. But this great moral duty rests upon a still deeper foundation, being a direct emanation from the first principle of morals, and not a mere logical corollary from secondary or derivative doctrines. It is involved in the very meaning of utility, or the greatest happiness principle. That principle is a mere form of words without rational signification, unless one person's happiness, supposed equal in degree (with the proper allowance made for kind), is counted for exactly as much as another's. Those conditions being supplied, Bentham's dictum, "everybody to count for one, nobody for more than one," might be written under the principle of utility as an explanatory commentary. The equal claim of everybody to happiness in the estimation of the moralist and of the legislator, involves an equal claim to all the means of happiness, except in so far as the inevitable conditions of human life, and the general interest, in which that of every individual is included, set limits to the maxim; and those limits ought to be strictly construed. As every other maxim of justice, so this is by no means applied or held applicable universally; on the contrary, as I have already remarked, it bends to every person's ideas of social expediency. But in whatever case it is deemed applicable at all, it is held to be the dictate of justice. All persons are deemed to have a *right* to equality of treatment, except when some recognized social expediency requires the reverse. And hence all social inequalities which have ceased to be considered expedient, assume the character not of simple inexpediency, but of injustice, and appear so tyrannical, that people are apt to wonder how they ever could have been tolerated;

forgetful that they themselves perhaps tolerate other inequalities under an equally mistaken notion of expediency, the correction of which would make that which they approve seem quite as monstrous as what they have at last learnt to condemn. The entire history of social improvement has been a series of transitions, by which one custom or institution after another, from being a supposed primary necessity of social existence, has passed into the rank of a universally stigmatized injustice and tyranny. So it has been with the distinctions of slaves and freemen, nobles and serfs, patricians and plebeians; and so it will be, and in part already is, with the aristocracies of color, race, and sex.

(1863)

Karl Marx
(1818-1883)

51.

Marx was a German social philosopher and the chief theoretician of modern socialism. The best introduction to his views on the State and Socialist policy is in his *Criticism of the Gotha Program,* written as an attack on the policy of his German followers in connection with the fusion of the Marxian and Lassallean Socialist Parties in Germany.

from The Criticism of the Gotha Program

What is "equitable distribution"?

Does not the bourgeoisie maintain that the distribution now prevailing is "equitable"? And is it not, in fact, the only "equitable" distribution on the basis of the present mode of production? Are economic relations regulated by juridical conceptions or on the contrary do not the juridical relations arise out of the economic relations? Do not the sectarian socialists also entertain the most variegated notions of what constitutes "equitable" distribution?

In order to know what to understand in this instance by the phrase "equitable distribution," we must connect the first sentence with it. The phrase assumes a society in which the means of labor are common property and the total social labor is regulated coöperatively, whereas we learn from the first sentence that the "proceeds of labor belong to all the members of society, uncurtailed and with equal right."

"To all the members of society"? Even to those who do not work? Then what becomes of the "uncurtailed proceeds of labor"? Only to the working members of society? Then what becomes of the "equal right" of all the members of society?

Obviously, "all the members of society" and the "equal right" are only methods of expression. The essence of the matter consists in this, that in this Communistic society every worker must receive the "uncurtailed" Lassallean "proceeds of labor." . . .

What we are dealing with here is a Communist society, not as it has *developed* upon its own foundation, but on the contrary, just as it is *emerging* out of capitalist society; consequently, a society which still bears, in every respect, economic, moral and intellectual, the birthmarks of the old society from whose womb it is issuing. Accordingly, the individual producer gets back—once the deductions are made—exactly as much as he has given it. What he has given is his individual amount of labor. For example, the social working day consists of the sum of the individual working hours; the individual working time of each producer is the portion of the social working day supplied by him, his share of it. He receives from society a check signifying that he has supplied so much labor (after deduction of his work done for the common fund), and with this check he draws from the social stores as much of the means of consumption as costs an equal amount of labor. The same quantity of labor which he has given society in one form, he receives back in another.

Evidently the same principle prevails here that today regulates the exchange of commodities in so far as it is an exchange of equal values. Substance and form are changed because under the changed conditions no one can give anything except his labor and because, on the other hand, nothing can become the property of the individual except the individual means of consumption. But so far as the distribution of the latter among the individual producers is concerned, the same principle prevails as in the exchange of equivalent commodities: an equal quantity of labor in one form is exchanged for an equal quantity of labor in another form.

Equal right, therefore, is here still according to the principle of *bourgeois right,* although principle and practice are no longer at odds, whereas today the exchange of equivalents in the exchange of commodities exists only for the average and not for individual cases.

Notwithstanding this progress, the *equal right* is still encumbered with bourgeois limitations. The right of the producers is *proportional* to the labor they supply; the equality consists in measuring this right by an *equal standard:* labor.

But one individual is physically or mentally superior to another and consequently supplies more labor in the same time or can work for a longer time; and in order to serve as a measure, labor must be determined according to its duration or its intensity, otherwise it would cease to be a standard. This *equal* right is an unequal right for unequal labor. It recognizes no class distinctions because everyone is only a worker like everybody else; but it tacitly recognizes the inequality of individual endowment and therefore productive capacity, as natural privileges. *It is therefore a right of inequality, in its substance, as is all right.* By its very nature, right can only consist in the application of an equal standard; but the unequal individuals (and they would not be different individuals if they were not unequal) can be measured by an equal standard only in so far as they are considered from the same point of view, or are regarded from a *definite* aspect, for example, in the given instance, if they are regarded *only as workers,* no more than that and regardless of anything else. Furthermore: one worker is married, the other is not; one has more children than the other, etc., etc. Hence, with an equal contribution of labor and consequently an equal share of the social consumption fund, one actually gets more than the other, one is richer than the other, etc. In order to avoid all these shortcomings, right would have to be unequal, and not equal.

But these shortcomings are unavoidable in the first phase of Communist society, as it issues forth from capitalist society after a long and painful travail. Right can never be on a higher level than the economic state of society and the stage of social civilization conditioned by it.

In a higher phase of Communist society, after the enslaving subordination of the individual to the division of labor shall have disappeared, and with it the antagonism between intellectual and manual labor, after labor has become not only a means of life but also the primary necessity of life; when, with the development of the individual in every sense, the productive forces also increase and all the springs of collective wealth flow with abundance—only then can the limited horizon of bourgeois right be left behind entirely and society inscribe upon its banner: "From each according to his abilities, to each according to his needs!"

(1875)

Friedrich Engels
(1820-1895)

52.

Engels, German socialist, collaborated with Marx on the *Communist Manifesto* and edited the 2nd and 3rd volumes of *Das Kapital*. His *Anti-Dühring* illustrates the Marxian emphasis on the need for economic equality as a basis for social and political freedom.

---

from Anti-Dühring

. . . The idea that all men, as men, have something in common, and that they are therefore equal so far as these common characteristics go, is of course primeval. But the modern demand for equality is something entirely different from that; this consists rather in deducing from those common characteristics of humanity, from that equality of men as men, a claim to equal political or social status for all human beings, or at least for all citizens of a state or all members of a society. Before the original conception of relative quality could lead to the conclusion that men should have equal rights in the state and in society, before this conclusion could appear to be something even natural and self-evident, however, thousands of years had to pass and did pass. In the oldest natural communities equality of rights existed at most for members of the community; women, slaves and strangers were excluded from this equality as a matter of course. Among the Greeks and Romans the inequalities of men were of greater importance than any form of equality. It would necessarily have seemed idiotic to the ancients that Greeks and barbarians, freemen and slaves, citizens and dependents, Roman citizens and Roman subjects (to use a comprehensive term) should have a claim to equal political status. Under the Roman Empire all these distinctions gradually disappeared, except the distinction between freemen and slaves, and there arose, for the freemen at least, that equality as between private individuals on the basis of which Roman law developed—the completest elaboration of law based on private property which we know. But so long as the distinction between freemen and slaves existed, there could be no talk of drawing legal conclusions from the fact of general equality *as men;* and we saw this again quite recently, in the slave-owning states of the North American Union.

Christianity knew only *one* point in which all men were equal: that all were equally born in original sin—which corresponded perfectly with its character as the religion of the slaves and the oppressed. Apart from this it recognised, at most, the equality of the elect, which however was only stressed at the very beginning. The traces of common ownership which are also found in the early stages of the new religion can be ascribed to the solidarity of a proscribed sect rather than to real equalitarian ideas. Within a very short time the establishment of the distinction between priests and laymen put an end even to this tendency to Christian equality.—The overruning of Western Europe by the Germans abolished for centuries all ideas of equality, through the gradual building up of such a complicated social and political hierarchy as had never before existed. But at the same time the invasion drew Western and Central Europe into the course of historical development, created for the first time a compact cultural area, and within this area also for the first time a system of predominantly national states exerting mutual influence on each other and mutually holding each other in check. Thereby it prepared the ground on which alone the question of the equal status of men, of the rights of man, could at a later period be raised.

The feudal middle ages also developed in its womb the class which was destined in the future course of its evolution to be the standard-bearer of the modern demand for equality: the bourgeoisie. Itself in its origin one of the "estates" of the feudal order, the bourgeoisie developed the predominantly handicraft industry and the exchange of products within feudal society to a relatively high level, when at the end of the fifteenth century the great maritime discoveries opened to it a new and more far-reaching career. Trade beyond the confines of Europe, which had previously been carried on only between Italy and the Levant, was now extended to America and India, and soon surpassed in importance both the mutual exchange between the various European countries and the internal trade within each separate country. American gold and silver flooded Europe and forced its way like a disintegrating element into every fissure, hole and pore of feudal society. Handicraft industry could no longer satisfy the rising demands; in the leading industries of the most advanced countries it was replaced by manufacture.

But this mighty revolution in the economic conditions of society was not followed by any immediate corresponding change in its political structure. The state order remained feudal, while society became more and more bourgeois. Trade on a large scale, that is to

say, international and, even more, world trade, requires free owners
of commodities who are unrestricted in their movements and have
equal rights as traders to exchange their commodities on the basis
of laws that are equal for them all, at least in each separate place.
The transition from handicraft to manufacture presupposes the existence of a number of free workers—free on the one hand from the
fetters of the guild and on the other from the means whereby they
could themselves utilise their labour power: workers who can contract with their employers for the hire of their labour power, and
as parties to the contract have rights equal with his. And finally the
equality and equal status of all human labour, because and in so far
as it is *human* labour, found its unconscious but clearest expression
in the law of value of modern bourgeois economy, according to which
the value of a commodity is measured by the socially necessary labour
embodied in it. But where economic relations required freedom and
equality of rights, the political system opposed them at every step
with guild restrictions and special privileges. Local privileges, differential duties, exceptional laws of all kinds in trade affected not only
foreigners or people living in the colonies, but often enough also
whole categories of the nationals of each country; the privileges of
the guilds everywhere and ever anew formed barriers to the path
of development of manufacture. Nowhere was the path open and
the chances equal for all the bourgeois competitors—and yet this was
the first and ever more pressing need.

The demand for liberation from feudal fetters and the establishment of equality of rights by the abolition of feudal inequalities was
bound soon to assume wider dimensions from the moment when the
economic advance of society first placed it on the order of the day.
If it was raised in the interests of industry and trade, it was also
necessary to demand the same equality of rights for the great mass
of the peasantry who, in every degree of bondage from total serfdom
upwards, were compelled to give the greater part of their labour time
to their feudal lord without payment and in addition to pay innu-
merable other dues to him and to the state. On the other hand, it
was impossible to avoid the demand for the abolition also of feudal
privileges, the freedom from taxation of the nobility, the political
privileges of the various feudal estates. And as people were no longer
living in a world empire such as the Roman Empire had been, but
in a system of independent states dealing with each other on an equal
footing and at approximately the same stage of bourgeois development, it was a matter of course that the demand for equality should

assume a general character reaching out beyond the individual state, that freedom and equality should be proclaimed as *human rights*. And it is significant of the specifically bourgeois character of these human rights that the American Constitution, the first to recognise the rights of man, in the same breath confirmed the slavery of the coloured races then existing in America: class privileges were prescribed, race privileges sanctioned.

As is well known, however, from the moment when, like a butterfly from the chrysalis, the bourgeoisie arose out of the burghers of the feudal period, when this "estate" of the Middle Ages developed into a class of modern society, it was always and inevitably accompanied by its shadow, the proletariat. And in the same way the bourgeois demand for equality was accompanied by the proletarian demand for equality. From the moment when the bourgeois demand for the abolition of class privileges was put forward, alongside of it appeared the proletarian demand for the abolition of the *classes themselves*—at first in religious form, basing itself on primitive Christianity, and later drawing support from the bourgeois equalitarian theories themselves. The proletarians took the bourgeoisie at their word: equality must not be merely apparent, must not apply merely to the sphere of the state, but must also be real, must be extended to the social and economic sphere. And especially since the French bourgeoisie, from the great revolution on, brought bourgeois equality to the forefront, the French proletariat answered blow for blow with the demand for social and economic equality, and equality became the battle-cry particularly of the French proletariat.

The demand for equality in the mouth of the proletariat has therefore a double meaning. It is either—as was the case at the very start, for example in the peasants' war—the spontaneous reaction against the crying social inequalities, against the contrast of rich and poor, the feudal lords and their serfs, surfeit and starvation; as such it is the simple expression of the revolutionary instinct, and finds its justification in that, and indeed only in that. Or, on the other hand, the proletarian demand for equality has arisen as the reaction against the bourgeois demand for equality, drawing more or less correct and more far-reaching demands from this bourgeois demand, and serving as an agitational means in order to rouse the workers against the capitalists on the basis of the capitalists' own assertions; and in this case it stands and falls with bourgeois equality itself. In both cases the real content of the proletarian demand for equality is the demand for the *abolition of classes*. Any demand for equality which goes beyond that, of necessity passes into absurdity. . . .

The idea of equality, therefore, both in its bourgeois and in its proletarian form, is itself a historical product, the creation of which required definite historical conditions which in turn themselves presuppose a long previous historical development. It is therefore anything but an eternal truth. And if to-day it is taken for granted by the general public—in one sense or another—if, as Marx says, it "already possesses the fixity of a popular prejudice," this is not the consequence of its axiomatic truth, but the result of the general diffusion and the continued appropriateness of the ideas of the eighteenth century. . . .

(1877)

Henry George

53.

(1839-1897)

Henry George, American economist and reformer, founded the single-tax movement in the belief that a single tax on land would meet all costs of government and even leave a surplus.

from Progress and Poverty

What has destroyed every previous civilization has been the tendency to the unequal distribution of wealth and power. This same tendency, operating with increasing force, is observable in our civilization to-day, showing itself in every progressive community, and with greater intensity the more progressive the community. Wages and interest tend constantly to fall, rent to rise, the rich to become very much richer, the poor to become more helpless and hopeless, and the middle class to be swept away.

I have traced this tendency to its cause. I have shown by what simple means this cause may be removed. I now wish to point out *how*, if this is not done, progress must turn to decadence, and modern civilization decline to barbarism, as have all previous civilizations. It is worth while to point out *how* this may occur, as many people, being unable to see how progress may pass into retrogression, conceive such a thing impossible. Gibbon, for instance, thought that modern civilization could never be destroyed because there remained no barbarians to overrun it, and it is a common idea that the invention of printing by so multiplying books has prevented the possibility of knowledge ever again being lost.

The conditions of social progress, as we have traced the law, are association and equality. The general tendency of modern development, since the time when we can first discern the gleams of civilization in the darkness which followed the fall of the Western Empire, has been towards political and legal equality—to the abolition of slavery; to the abrogation of status; to the sweeping away of hereditary privileges; to the substitution of parliamentary for arbitrary government; to the right of private judgment in matters of religion; to the more equal security in person and property of high and low, weak and strong; to the greater freedom of movement and occupation, of speech and of the press. The history of modern civilization is the history of advances in this direction—of the struggles and triumphs of personal, political, and religious freedom. And the general law is shown by the fact that just as this tendency has asserted itself civilization has advanced, while just as it has been repressed or forced back civilization has been checked.

This tendency has reached its full expression in the American Republic, where political and legal rights are absolutely equal, and, owing to the system of rotation in office, even the growth of a bureaucracy is prevented; where every religious belief or non-belief stands on the same footing; where every boy may hope to be President, every man has an equal voice in public affairs, and every official is mediately or immediately dependent for the short lease of his place upon a popular vote. This tendency has yet some triumphs to win in England, in extending the suffrage, and sweeping away the vestiges of monarchy, aristocracy, and prelacy; while in such countries as Germany and Russia, where divine right is yet a good deal more than a legal fiction, it has a considerable distance to go. But it is the prevailing tendency, and how soon Europe will be completely republican is only a matter of time, or rather of accident. The United States are therefore, in this respect, the most advanced of all the great nations, in a direction in which all are advancing, and in the United States we see just how much this tendency to personal and political freedom can of itself accomplish.

Now, the first effect of the tendency to political equality was to the more equal distribution of wealth and power; for, while population is comparatively sparse, inequality in the distribution of wealth is principally due to the inequality of personal rights, and it is only as material progress goes on that the tendency to inequality involved in the reduction of land to private ownership strongly appears. But it is now manifest that absolute political equality does not in itself prevent the tendency to inequality involved in the private ownership of land, and it is further evident that political equality, co-existing with an increasing tendency to the unequal distribution of wealth, must ultimately beget either the despotism of organized tyranny or the worse despotism of anarchy.

To turn a republican government into a despotism the basest and most brutal, it is not necessary to formally change its constitution or abandon popular elections. It was centuries after Caesar before the absolute master of the Roman world pretended to rule other than by authority of a Senate that trembled before him.

But forms are nothing when substance has gone, and the forms of popular government are those from which the substance of freedom may most easily go. Extremes meet, and a government of universal suffrage and theoretical equality, may, under conditions which impel the change, most readily become a despotism. For there, despotism advances in the name and with the might of the people. The single source of power once secured, everything is secured. There is no unfranchised class to whom appeal may be made, no privileged orders who in defending their own rights may defend those of all. No bulwark remains to stay the flood, no eminence to rise above it. They were belted barons led by a mitered archbishop who curbed the Plantagenet with Magna Charta; it was the middle classes who broke the pride of the Stuarts; but a mere aristocracy of wealth will never struggle while it can hope to bribe a tyrant.

And when the disparity of condition increases, so does universal suffrage make it easy to seize the source of power, for the greater is the proportion of power in the hands of those who feel no direct interest in the conduct of government; who, tortured by want and embruted by poverty, are ready to sell their votes to the highest bidder or follow the lead of the most blatant demagogue; or who, made bitter by hardships, may even look upon profligate and tyrannous government with the satisfaction we may imagine the proletarians and slaves of Rome to have felt, as they saw a Caligula or Nero raging among the rich patricians. Given a community with republican institutions, in which one class is too rich to be shorn of their luxuries, no matter how public affairs are administered, and another so poor that a few dollars on election day will seem more than any abstract consideration; in which the few roll in wealth and the many seethe with discontent at a condition of things they know not how to remedy, and power must pass into the hands of jobbers who will buy and sell it as the Praetorians sold the Roman purple, or into the hands of demagogues who will seize and wield it for a time, only to be displaced by worse demagogues.

Where there is anything like an equal distribution of wealth—that is to say, where there is general patriotism, virtue, and intelligence—the more democratic the government the better it will be; but where there is gross inequality in the distribution of wealth, the more democratic the government the worse it will be; for, while rotten democracy may not in itself be worse than rotten autocracy, its effects upon national character will be worse. To give the suffrage to tramps, to paupers, to men to whom the chance to labor is a boon, to men who must beg, or steal, or starve, is to invoke destruction. To put political power in the hands of men embittered and degraded by poverty is to tie firebrands to foxes and turn them loose amid the standing corn; it is to put out the eyes of a Samson and to twine his arms around the pillars of national life. . . .

Now this transformation of popular government into despotism of the vilest and most degrading kind, which must inevitably result from the unequal distribution of wealth, is not a thing of the far future. It has already begun in the United States, and is rapidly going on under our eyes. That our legislative bodies are steadily deteriorating in standard; that men of the highest ability and character are compelled to eschew politics, and the arts of the jobber count for more than the reputation of the statesman; that voting is done more recklessly and the power of money is increasing; that it is harder to arouse the people to the necessity of reforms and more difficult to carry them out; that political differences are ceasing to be differences of principle, and abstract ideas are losing their power; that parties are passing into the control of what in general government would be oligarchies and dictatorships; are all evidences of political decline. . . .

This truth involves both a menace and a promise. It shows that the evils arising from the unjust and unequal distribution of wealth, which are becoming more and more apparent as modern civilization goes on, are not incidents of progress, but tendencies which must bring progress to a halt; that they will not cure themselves, but, on the contrary, must, unless their cause is removed, grow greater and greater, until they sweep us back into barbarism by the road every previous civilization has trod. But it also shows that these evils are not imposed by natural laws; that they spring solely from social maladjustments which ignore natural laws, and that in removing their cause we shall be giving an enormous impetus to progress.

The poverty which in the midst of abundance, pinches and imbrutes men, and all the manifold evils which flow from it, spring from a denial of justice. In permitting the monopolization of the natural opportunities which nature freely offers to all, we have ignored the fundamental law of justice—for so far as we can see, when we view things upon a large scale, justice seems to be the supreme law of the universe. But by sweeping away this injustice and asserting the rights of all men to natural opportunities, we shall conform ourselves to the law—we shall remove the great cause of unnatural inequality in the distribution of wealth and power; we shall abolish poverty; tame the ruthless passions of greed; dry up the springs of vice and misery; light in dark places the lamp of knowledge; give new vigor to invention and a fresh impulse to discovery; substitute political strength for political weakness; and make tyranny and anarchy impossible.

The reform I have proposed accords with all that is politically, socially, or morally desirable. It has the qualities of a true reform, for it will make all other reforms easier. What is it but the carrying out in letter and spirit of the truth enunciated in the Declaration of Independence—the "self-evident" truth that is the heart and soul of the Declaration—*"That all men are created equal; that they are endowed by their Creator with certain inalienable rights; that among them are life, liberty, and the pursuit of happiness"!*

These rights are denied when the equal right to land—on which and by which men alone can live—is denied. Equality of political rights will not compensate for the denial of the equal right to the bounty of nature. Political liberty, when the equal right to land is denied, becomes, as population increases and invention goes on, merely the liberty to compete for employment at starvation wages. This is the truth that we have ignored. And so there come beggars in our streets and tramps on our roads; and poverty enslaves men whom we boast are political sovereigns; and want breeds ignorance that our schools cannot enlighten; and citizens vote as their masters dictate; and the demagogue usurps the part of the statesman; and gold weighs in the scales of justice; and in high places sit those who do not pay to civic virtue even the compliment of hypocrisy; and the pillars of the republic that we thought so strong already bend under an increasing strain.

(1879)

Franz Boas

(1858-1942)

Franz Boas, leading American anthropologist, did rigorous work in linguistics and physical and cultural anthropology which influenced the work of other anthropologists.

from The Mind of Primitive Man

. . . In how far are we justified in considering those anatomical traits in regard to which foreign races differ from the white race as marks of inferiority? . . . We have recognized that achievement alone does not justify us in assuming greater mental ability for the white race than for others, unless we can sustain our claim by other proofs. It follows from this, that differences between the white race and other races must not be interpreted to mean superiority of the former, inferiority of the latter, unless this relation can be proved by anatomical or physiological considerations.

It may not be amiss to illustrate by an example the logical error which is committed with great ease and great frequency. In a painstaking investigation made a few years ago, Mr. R. B. Bean demonstrated certain characteristic differences between the form of the whole and of the parts of the brain of the Baltimore Negro and of the Baltimore white,—differences which consist in the form and relative size of the frontal and occipital lobes and in the size of the *corpus callosum*. The interpretation of the difference is, that the smaller size of the anterior lobes and of the *callosum* indicates a lower mental development, a conclusion which has been refuted by Franklin P. Mall. It may suffice here, where we are interested chiefly in the logical fallacy of such conclusions, to call attention to the fact that a comparison of long-headed and short-headed individuals of the same race—or, let us say, of long-headed North French and of short-headed Central French—would result in similar differences, but that in a case of this kind the inference regarding greater or lesser ability would not be made with the same readiness.

There is, of course, no doubt that great differences exist in the physical characteristics of the races of man. The color of the skin, the form of the hair, and the configuration of lips and nose, distinguish the African clearly from the European. The question to decide is, What relations have these features to the mental aptitude of a race?

Two points of view may be brought forward in relation to this question. First, we may claim that a race in which peculiarities are found that are characteristic of lower stages in the animal series will be in all respects of an inferior type. Secondly, we may direct our attention primarily to the central nervous system, and investigate whether the anatomical structure in one race is superior to that found in another race.

To illustrate the former viewpoint, I will mention a few of the formations in man which have been described as characterizing lower races, because they are found as typical developments in animals. One of these is a variation in the form of the temporal bone, which in man is ordinarily separated from the frontal bone by the sphenoid and parietal bones. It has been found that in some individuals the temporal bone encroaches upon the sphenoid and parietal, and comes into contact with the frontal bone. This formation is the prevalent one among the apes. It has been proved that this variation is found among all races, but with unequal frequency.

The peculiar formation of the tibia known as platycnemism (lateral flatness) has been observed in skeletons of the oldest remains of man in Europe, and also in the skeletons of various races. Other characteristics which remind us of lower forms are peculiarities in the formation of the articular surfaces of tibia and femur, which have been found in a number of human types; the os Incæ, or interparietal bone, which occurs among all races, but most frequently among the Peruvians and the inhabitants of the ancient pueblos; the smallness of the nasal bones and their synostosis with the maxilla; the so-called pre-nasal fossae; and certain variations in the arrangement of arteries and of muscles. All these variable features are found among all races, but the degree of variability is not everywhere the same. Presumably such variations may be considered human characteristics which have not yet had time to become stable, and which in this sense may be considered as still in process of evolution. If this interpretation be correct, it might seem that we can consider those races in which the characteristic human features are more stable as those which are more highly organized.

It is also possible to arrange the races according to various typical features in such a manner that one appears farthest removed from the types of higher animals, others less so. In all these arrangements the gap between man and animal is a wide one, and the variations between the races are slight as compared to it. Thus we find, that, in comparison to the skull, the face of the Negro is larger than that of the American [Indian], whose face is, in turn, larger than that of the white. The lower portion of his face has larger dimensions. The alveolar arch is pushed forward, and thus gains an appearance which reminds us of the higher apes. There is no denying that this feature is a most constant character of the black races, and that it represents a type slightly nearer the animal than the European type. The same may be said of the broadness and flatness of the noses of the Negro and the Mongol.

If we accept the general theories of Klaatsch, Stratz, and Schoeten-sack, who consider the Australian as the oldest and most generalized type of man, we might also call attention to the slenderness of the vertebrae, the undeveloped curvature of the vertebral column, to which Cunningham first called attention, and the traits of the foot, which recall the needs of an animal living in trees, and whose feet had to serve the purpose of climbing from branch to branch.

In relation to the interpretation of all these observations, it must be strongly emphasized that the races which we are accustomed to call "higher races" do not by any means stand in all respects at the end of the series, and are farthest removed from the animal. The European and the Mongol have the largest brains; the European has a small face and a high nose;—all features farther removed from the probable animal ancestor of man than the corresponding features of other races. On the other hand, the European shares lower characteristics with the Australian, both retaining in the strongest degree the hairiness of the animal ancestor, while the specifically human development of the red lip is developed most markedly in the Negro. The proportions of the limbs of the Negro are also more markedly distinct from the corresponding proportions in the higher apes than are those of the European.

When we interpret these data in the light of modern biological concepts, we may say that the specifically human features appear with varying intensity in various races, and that the divergence from the animal ancestor has developed in varying directions.

When all these differences between races are given, the question arises, whether they have significance in regard to mental faculty. I may be permitted to disregard for the moment differences in the size and structural development of the nervous system, and confine myself to the mental significance of other traits. The general analogy of mental development of animals and of man prompts us to associate lower mental traits with theromorphic features. In our naïve, every-day parlance, brutish features and brutality are closely connected. We must distinguish here, however, between the anatomical characteristics of which we have been speaking and the muscular development of the face, trunk, and limbs, due to habitual activity. The hand, which is never employed in activities requiring those refined adjustments which are characteristic of psychologically complex actions, will lack the modelling brought about by the development of each muscle. The face whose muscles have not responded to the innervations accompanying deep thought and refined sentiment will lack in individuality and refinement. The neck that has supported heavy loads, and has not responded to the varied requirements of delicate changes of position of head and body, will appear massive and clumsy. These physiognomic differences must not mislead us in our interpretations. But even without them, we are inclined to draw inferences in regard to mentality from a receding forehead, a heavy jaw, large and heavy teeth, perhaps even from an inordinate length of arms or an unusual development of hairiness.

From a strictly scientific point of view, these inferences seem to be open to the most serious doubt. Only a few investigations have been made in relation to these problems, but their results have been entirely negative. Most important among them is the elaborate attempt made by Karl Pearson to investigate the relationship of intelligence to size and shape of the head. His conclusions are so significant that I will repeat them here: "The onus of proof that other measurements and more subtle psychological observations would lead to more definite results may now, I think, be left to those who *a priori* regard such an association as probable. Personally, the result of the present inquiry has convinced me that there is little relationship between the external physical and the psychical character in man." I think all the investigations that have been made up to the present time compel us to assume that the characteristics of the osseous, muscular, visceral, or circulatory system, have practically no direct relation to the mental ability of man (Manouvrier).

We will now turn to the important subject of the size of the brain, which seems to be the one anatomical feature which bears directly upon the question at issue. It seems plausible that the greater the central nervous system, the higher the faculty of the race, and the greater its aptitude to mental achievements. Let us review the known facts. Two methods are open for ascertaining the size of the central nervous system,—the determination of the weight of the brain and that of the capacity of the cranial cavity. The first of these methods is the one which promises the most accurate results. Naturally, the number of Europeans whose brain-weights have been taken is much larger than that of individuals of other races. There are, however, sufficient data available to establish beyond a doubt the fact that the brain-weight of the whites is larger than that of most other races, particularly larger than that of the Negroes. That of the white male is about 1360 grams. The investigations of cranial capacities are quite in accord with these results. According to Topinard, the capacity of the skull of males of the neolithic period in Europe is about 1560 cc. (44 cases); that of modern Europeans is the same (347 cases); of the Mongoloid race, 1510 cc. (68 cases); of African Negroes, 1405 cc. (83 cases); and of Negroes of the Pacific Ocean, 1460 cc. (46 cases). Here we have, therefore, a decided difference in favor of the white race.

In interpreting these facts, we must ask, Does the increase in the size of the brain prove an increase in faculty? This would seem highly probable, and facts may be adduced which speak in favor of this assumption. First among these is the relatively large size of the brain among the higher animals, and the still larger size in man. Furthermore, Manouvrier has measured the capacity of the skulls of thirty-five eminent men. He found that they averaged 1665 cc. as compared to 1560 cc. general average, which was derived from 110 individuals. On the other hand, he found that the cranial capacity of forty-five murderers was 1580 cc., also superior to the general average. The same result has been obtained through weighings of brains of eminent men. The brains of thirty-four of these showed an average increase of 93 grams over the average brain-weight of 1357 grams. Another fact which may be adduced in favor of the theory that greater brains are accompanied by higher faculty is that the heads of the best English students are larger than those of the average class of students (Galton). The force of the arguments furnished by these observations must, however, not be overestimated.

First of all, the brains of not all eminent men are unusually large. On the contrary, a few unusually small brains have been found in the series. Furthermore, most of the brain-weights constituting the general series are obtained in anatomical institutes; and the individuals who find their way there are poorly developed, on account of malnutrition and of life under unfavorable circumstances, while the eminent men represent a much better nourished class. As poor nourishment reduces the weight and size of the whole body, it will also reduce the size and weight of the brain. It is not certain, therefore, that the observed difference is entirely due to the higher ability of the eminent men. This may also explain the larger size of the brains of the professional classes as compared to those of unskilled laborers (Ferraira). An additional number of restricting facts must be enumerated. The most important among these is the difference in brain-weight between men and women. When men and women of the same stature are compared, it is found that the brain of woman is much lighter than that of man. Nevertheless the faculty of woman while perhaps qualitatively different from that of man, cannot be deemed to be of an inferior character. This is therefore a case in which smaller brain-weight is accompanied throughout by equal faculty. We conclude from this fact that it is not impossible that the smaller brains of males of other races should do the same work as is done by the larger brain of the white race. But this comparison is not quite on equal terms, as we may assume that there is a certain structural difference between male and female, which causes the difference in size between the sexes; so that comparison between male and female is not the same as comparison between male and male.

Notwithstanding these restrictions, the increase of the size of the brain in the higher animals, and the lack of development in microcephalic individuals, are fundamental facts which make it more than probable that increased size of the brain causes increased faculty, although the relation is not quite as immediate as is often assumed.

The reason for a lack of close correlation between brain-weight and mental faculties is not far to seek. The functioning of the brain depends upon the nerve cells and fibres, which do not constitute, by any means, the whole mass of the brain. A brain with many cells and complex connections between the cells may contain less connective tissue than another one of simpler nervous structure. In other words, if there is a close relation between form and ability, it must be looked for rather in the morphological traits of the brain than in its size. A correlation exists between size of brain and number of cells and fibres, but the correlation is weak (Donaldson).

Notwithstanding the numerous attempts that have been made to find structural differences between the brains of different races of man that could be directly interpreted in psychological terms, no conclusive results of any kind have been attained. The status of our present knowledge has been well summed up by Franklin P. Mall, to whose investigation I referred before. He holds, that, on account of the great variability of the individuals constituting each race, racial differences are exceedingly difficult to discover, and that up to the present time none have been found that will endure serious criticism.

.   .   .   .   .   .

When we turn our attention to the Negro problem as it presents itself in the United States, we must remember our previous considerations, in which we found that no proof of an inferiority of the Negro type could be given, except that it seemed possible that perhaps the race would not produce quite so many men of highest genius as other races, while there was nothing at all that could be interpreted as suggesting any material difference in the mental capacity of the bulk of the Negro population as compared to the bulk of the white population.

Much has been said about the shorter period of growth of the Negro child as compared to the white child, but no convincing data have been forthcoming. Considering the great variation in the duration of growth and development in different individuals and in various social classes, according to the more or less favorable nutrition of the child, the information that we possess in regard to the Negro child is practically without value. We have not even evidence that would prove that a shorter period of development must be unfavorable in its results. Neither do we know at what period and in what manner develop the typical Negroid features, which are much less pronounced in the new-born than in adults.

It is surprising, that, notwithstanding their importance, no attempts have been made to gain a better insight into these anatomical and physiological problems, some of which might be solved without much difficulty. As it is, almost all we can say with certainty is, that the differences between the average types of the white and of the Negro, that have a bearing upon vitality and mental ability, are much less than the individual variations in each race.

This result is, however, of great importance, and is quite in accord with the result of ethnological observation. A survey of African tribes exhibits to our view cultural achievements of no mean order. To those unfamiliar with the products of native African art and industry, a walk through one of the large museums of Europe would be a revelation. None of our American museums has made collections that exhibit this subject in any way worthily. The blacksmith, the wood-carver, the weaver, the potter,—these all produce ware original in form, executed with great care, and exhibiting that love of labor, and interest in the results of work, which are apparently so often lacking among the Negroes in our American surroundings. No less instructive are the records of travelers, reporting the thrift of the native villages, of the extended trade of the country, and of its markets. The power of organization as illustrated in the government of native states is of no mean order, and when wielded by men of great personality has led to the foundation of extended empires. All the different kinds of activities that we consider valuable in the citizens of our country may be found in aboriginal Africa. Neither is the wisdom of the philosopher absent. A perusal of any of the collections of African proverbs that have been published will demonstrate the homely practical philosophy of the Negro, which is often proof of sound feeling and judgment.

It would be out of place to enlarge on this subject, because the essential point that anthropology can contribute to the practical discussion of the adaptability of the Negro is a decision of the question how far the undesirable traits that are at present undoubtedly found in our Negro population are due to racial traits, and how far they are due to social surroundings for which we are responsible. To this question anthropology can give the decided answer that the traits of African culture as observed in the aboriginal home of the Negro are those of a healthy primitive people, with a considerable degree of personal initiative, with a talent for organization, and with imaginative power, with technical skill and thrift. Neither is a warlike spirit absent in the race, as is proved by the mighty conquerors who overthrew states and founded new empires, and by the courage of the armies that follow the bidding of their leaders. There is nothing to prove that licentiousness, shiftless laziness, lack of initiative, are fundamental characteristics of the race. Everything points out that these qualities are the result of social conditions rather than of hereditary traits.

It may be well to state here once more with some emphasis that it would be erroneous to assume that there are no differences in the mental make-up of the Negro race and of other races, and that their activities should run in the same lines. On the contrary, if there is any meaning in correlation of anatomical structure and physiological function, we must expect that differences exist. There is, however, no evidence whatever that would stigmatize the Negro as of weaker build, or as subject to inclinations and powers that are opposed to our social organization. An unbiassed estimate of the anthropological evidence so far brought forward does not permit us to countenance the belief in a racial inferiority which would unfit an individual of the Negro race to take his part in modern civilization. We do not know of any demand made on the human body or mind in modern life that anatomical or ethnological evidence would prove to be beyond the powers of the Negro.

The traits of the American Negro are adequately explained on the basis of his history and social status. The tearing-away from the African soil and the consequent complete loss of the old standards of life, which were replaced by the dependency of slavery and by all it entailed, followed by a period of disorganization and by a severe economic struggle against heavy odds, are sufficient to explain the inferiority of the status of the race, without falling back upon the theory of hereditary inferiority.

In short, there is every reason to believe that the Negro, when given facility and opportunity, will be perfectly able to fulfil the duties of citizenship as well as his white neighbor. It may be that he will not produce as many great men as the white race, and that his average achievement will not quite reach the level of the average achievement of the white race; but there will be endless numbers who will be able to outrun their white competitors, and who will do better than the defectives whom we permit to drag down and to retard the healthy children of our public schools.

The anthropological discussion of the Negro problem requires also a word on the "race instinct" of the whites, which plays a most important part in the practical aspect of the problem. Ultimately this phenomenon is a repetition of the old instinct and fear of the connubium of patricians and plebeians, of the European nobility and the common people, or of the castes of India. The emotions and reasonings concerned are the same in every respect. In our case they relate particularly to the necessity of maintaining a distinct social status in order to avoid race-mixture. As in the other cases mentioned, the so-called instinct is not a physiological dislike. This is proved by the existence of our large mulatto population, as well as by the more ready amalgamation of the Latin peoples. It is rather an expression of social conditions that are so deeply ingrained in us that they assume a strong emotional value; and this, I presume, is meant when we call such feelings instinctive. The feeling certainly has nothing to do with the question of the vitality and ability of the mulatto.

Still the questions of race-mixture and of the Negro's adaptability to our environment represent a number of important problems.

I think we have reason to be ashamed to confess that the scientific study of these questions has never received the support either of our government or of any of our great scientific institutions; and it is hard to understand why we are so indifferent toward a question which is of paramount importance to the welfare of our nation. The anatomy of the American Negro is not well known; and, notwithstanding the oft-repeated assertions regarding the hereditary inferiority of the mulatto, we know hardly anything on this subject. If his vitality is lower than that of the full-blooded Negro, this may be as much due to social causes as to hereditary causes. Owing to the very large number of mulattoes in our country, it would not be a difficult matter to investigate the biological aspects of this question thoroughly. The importance of researches on this subject cannot be too strongly urged, since the desirability or undesirability of race-mixture should be known. Looking into a distant future, it seems reasonably certain that with the increasing mobility of the Negro, the number of full-bloods will rapidly decrease; and since there is no introduction of new Negro blood, there cannot be the slightest doubt that the ultimate effect of the contact between the two races must necessarily be a continued increase of the amount of white blood in the Negro community.

This process will go on most rapidly inside of the colored community, owing to intermarriages between mulattoes and full-blooded Negroes. Whether or not the addition of white blood to the colored population is sufficiently large to counterbalance this levelling effect, which will make the mixed bloods with a slight strain of Negro blood darker, is difficult to tell; but it is quite obvious that, although our laws may retard the influx of white blood considerably, they cannot hinder the gradual progress of intermixture. If the powerful caste system of India has not been able to prevent intermixture, our laws, which recognize a greater amount of individual liberty, will certainly not be able to do so; and that there is no racial sexual antipathy is made sufficiently clear by the size of our mulatto population. A candid consideration of the manner in which intermixture takes place shows very clearly that the probability of the infusion of white blood into the colored population is considerable. While the large body of the white population will always, at least for a very long time to come, be entirely remote from any possibility of intermixture with Negroes, I think that we may predict with a fair degree of certainty a condition in which the contrast between colored people and whites will be less marked than it is at the present time. Notwithstanding all the obstacles that may be laid in the way of intermixture, the conditions are such that the persistence of the pure Negro type is practically impossible. Not even an excessively high mortality and lack of fertility among the mixed type, as compared with the pure types, could prevent this result. Since it is impossible to change these conditions, they should be faced squarely, and we ought to demand a careful and critical investigation of the whole problem.

It seems to my mind that the policy of many of our Southern States that try to prevent all racial intermixture is based on an erroneous view of the process involved. The alleged reason for this type of legislation is the necessity of protecting the white race against the infusion of Negro blood. As a matter of fact, this danger does not exist. With very few exceptions, the unions between whites and Negroes are those of white men and Negro women. The increase of races, however, is such that the number of children born does not depend upon the number of men, but upon the number of women. Given, therefore, a certain number of Negro women, the increase of the colored population will depend upon their number; and if a considerable number of their children are those of white fathers, the race as a whole must necessarily lose its pure Negro type. At the same time no such infusion of Negro blood into the white race through the maternal line occurs, so that the process is actually one of lightening the Negro race without corresponding admixture in the white race.

It appears from this consideration that the most important practical questions relating to the Negro problem have reference to the mulattoes and other mixed bloods,—to their physical types, their mental and moral qualities, and their vitality. When the bulky literature of this subject is carefully sifted, little remains that will endure serious criticism; and I do not believe that I claim too much when I say that the whole work on this subject remains to be done. The development of modern methods of research makes it certain that by careful inquiry definite answers to our problems may be found. Is it not, then, our plain duty to inform ourselves, that, so far as that can be done, deliberate consideration of observations may take the place of heated discussion of beliefs in matters that concern not only ourselves, but also the welfare of millions of Negroes?

(1911)

Louis D. Brandeis

(1856-1941)

Louis D. Brandeis, Associate Justice of the U. S. Supreme Court (1916-1939), was known for judicial liberalism. This selection was written at a time when he was known in Boston as "the people's lawyer" by virtue of his championing popular interests against the encroachments of big business.

55.

from "On Industrial Relations"

My observation leads me to believe that while there are many contributing causes to unrest, that there is one cause which is fundamental. That is the necessary conflict—the contrast between our political liberty and our industrial absolutism. We are as free politically, perhaps, as free as it is possible for us to be. Every male has his voice and vote; and the law has endeavored to enable, and has succeeded practically, in enabling him to exercise his political franchise without fear. He therefore has his part; and certainly can secure an adequate part in the government of the country in all of its political relations; that is, in all relations which are determined directly by legislation or governmental administration.

On the other hand, in dealing with industrial problems the position of the ordinary worker is exactly the reverse. The individual employee has no effective voice or vote. And the main objection, as I see it, to the very large corporation is, that it makes possible—and in many cases makes inevitable—the exercise of industrial absolutism. It is not merely the case of the individual worker against the employer which, even if he is a reasonably sized employer, presents a serious situation calling for the interposition of a union to protect the individual. But we have the situation of an employer so potent, so well organized, with such concentrated forces and with such extraordinary powers of reserve and the ability to endure against strikes and other efforts of a union, that the relatively loosely organized masses of even strong unions are unable to cope with the situation. We are dealing here with a question, not of motive, but of condition. Now, the large corporation and the managers of the powerful corporation are probably in large part actuated by motives just the same as an employer of a tenth of their size. Neither of them, as a rule, wishes to have his liberty abridged; but the smaller concern usually comes to the conclusion that it is necessary that it should be, where an important union must be dealt with. But when a great financial power has developed—when there exists these powerful organizations, which can successfully summon forces from all parts of the country, which can afford to use tremendous amounts of money in any conflict to carry out what they deem to be their business principle, and can also afford to suffer large losses—you have necessarily a condition of inequality between the two contending forces. Such contests, though undertaken with the best motives and with strong conviction on the part of the corporate managers that they are seeking what is for the best interests not only of the company but of the community, lead to absolutism. The result, in the cases of these large corporations, may be to develop a benevolent absolutism, but it is an absolutism all the same; and it is that which makes the great corporation so dangerous. There develops within the State a state so powerful that the ordinary social and industrial forces existing are insufficient to cope with it.

. . . Unrest, to my mind, never can be removed—and fortunately never can be removed—by mere improvement of the physical and material condition of the workingman. If it were possible we should run great risk of improving their material condition and reducing their manhood. We must bear in mind all the time, that however much we may desire material improvement and must desire it for the comfort of the individual, that the United States is a democracy, and that we must have, above all things, men. It is the development of manhood to which any industrial and social system should be directed. We Americans are committed not only to social justice in the sense of avoiding things which bring suffering and harm, like unjust distribution of wealth; but we are committed primarily to democracy. The social justice for which we are striving is an incident of our democracy, not the main end. It is rather the result of democracy—perhaps its finest expression—but it rests upon democracy, which implies the rule by the people. And therefore the end for which we must strive is the attainment of rule by the people, and that involves industrial democracy as well as political democracy. That means that the problems of a trade should be no longer the problems of the employer alone. The problems of his business, and it is not the employer's business alone, are the problems of all in it. The union cannot shift upon the employer the responsibility for conditions, nor can the employer insist upon determining, according to his will, the conditions which shall exist. The problems which exist are the problems of the trade; they are the problems of employer and employee. Profit sharing, however liberal, cannot meet the situation. That would mean merely dividing the profits of business. Such a division may do harm or it might do good, dependent on how it is applied.

There must be a division not only of profits, but a division also of responsibilities. The employees must have the opportunity of participating in the decisions as to what shall be their condition and how the business shall be run. They must learn also in sharing that responsibility that they, too, must bear the suffering arising from grave mistakes, just as the employer must. But the right to assist in making the decisions, the right of making their own mistakes, if mistakes there must be, is a privilege which should not be denied to labor. We must insist upon labor sharing the responsibilities for the result of the business.

Now, to a certain extent we are gradually getting it—in smaller businesses. The grave objection to the large business is that, almost inevitably, the form of organization, the absentee stock holdings, and its remote directorship prevent participation, ordinarily, of the employees in such management. The executive officials become stewards in charge of the details of the operation of the business, they alone coming into direct relation with labor. Thus we lose that necessary co-operation which naturally flows from contact between employers and employees—and which the American aspirations for democracy demand. It is in the resultant absolutism that you will find the fundamental cause of prevailing unrest; no matter what is done with the superstructure, no matter how it may be improved in one way or the other, unless we eradicate that fundamental difficulty, unrest will not only continue, but, in my opinion, will grow worse. . . .

It is almost inconceivable to my mind that a corporation with powers so concentrated as the Steel Corporation could get to a point where it would be willing to treat with the employees on equal terms. And unless they treat on equal terms then there is no such thing as democratization. The treatment on equal terms with them involves not merely the making of a contract; it must develop into a continuing relation. The making of a contract with a union is a long step. It is collective bargaining—a great advance. But it is only the first step. In order that collective bargaining should result in industrial democracy it must go further and create practically an industrial government—a relation between employer and employee where the problems as they arise from day to day, or from month to month, or from year to year, may come up for consideration and solution as they come up in our political government. . . .

I think all of our human experience shows that no one with absolute power can be trusted to give it up even in part. That has been the experience with political absolutism; it must prove the same with industrial absolutism. Industrial democracy will not come by gift. It has got to be won by those who desire it. And if the situation is such that a voluntary organization like a labor union is powerless to bring about the democratization of a business, I think we have in this fact some proof that the employing organization is larger than is consistent with the public interest. I mean by larger, is more powerful, has a financial influence too great to be useful to the State; and the State must in some way come to the aid of the workingmen if democratization is to be secured. . . .

(1915)

Harold J. Laski

(1893-1950)

56.

H. J. Laski, English political scientist, one-time Chairman of the British Labor Party, and left-wing intellectual, was a frequent lecturer in the United States. This selection is from one of his early and more systematic works in political theory.

from A Grammar of Politics

... To minds so ardent for liberty as Tocqueville and Lord Acton liberty and equality were antithetic things. It is a drastic conclusion. But it turns, in the case of both men, upon a misunderstanding of what equality implies. Equality does not mean identity of treatment. There can be no ultimate identity of treatment so long as men are different in want and capacity and need. The purpose of society would be frustrated at the outset if the nature of a mathematician met an identical response with that to the nature of a bricklayer. Equality does not even imply identity of reward for effort so long as the difference in reward does not enable me, by its magnitude, to invade the rights of others.

Equality, broadly, is a coherence of ideas each one of which needs special examination. Undoubtedly, it implies fundamentally a certain levelling process. It means that no man shall be so placed in society that he can overreach his neighbour to the extent which constitutes a denial of the latter's citizenship. It means that my realisation of my best self must involve as its logical result the realisation by others of their best selves. It means such an ordering of social forces as will balance a share in the toil of living with a share in its gain also. It means that my share in that gain must be adequate for the purposes of citizenship. It implies that even if my voice be weighed as less weighty than that of another, it must yet receive consideration in the decisions that are made. The meaning, ultimately, of equality surely lies in the fact that the very differences in the nature of men require mechanisms for the expression of their wills that give to each its due hearing. The power, in fact, of the ideal of equality lies in the historical evidence that so far in the record of the State the wills of men have been unequally answered. Their freedom, where it has been gained, has accordingly been built upon the unfreedom of others. Inequality, in a word, means the rule of limited numbers because it secures freedom only to those whose will is secure of respect. They will dominate the State and use its power for their own purposes. They will make the fulfilment of their private desires the criterion of public good.

Equality, therefore, means first of all the absence of special privilege. . . . In the penumbra of equality, it means, in the political sphere, that my will, as a factor in the counting of heads, is equal to the will of any other. It means that I can move forward to any office in the State for which men are prepared to choose me. It means that I am not to find that there are persons in the State whose authority is qualitatively different from my own. Whatever rights inhere in another by virtue of his being a citizen must inhere, and to the same extent, in me also. There is no justification in such a view for the existence of an hereditary second chamber. For, obviously, in the second generation of such an assembly men exercise political authority not in virtue of their own qualities, but by reason of parental accident. So, also, no office that carries with it power can ever be rightly regarded as an incorporeal hereditament, for that is to associate important functions with qualities other than fitness for their performance. The exclusion of any man, or body of men, from access to the avenues of authority is always, that is to say, a denial of their freedom.

Equality means, in the second place, that adequate opportunities are laid open to all. By adequate opportunities we cannot imply equal opportunities in a sense that implies identity of original chance. The native endowments of men are by no means equal. Children who are brought up in an atmosphere where things of the mind are accounted highly are bound to start the race of life with advantages no legislation can secure. Parental character will inevitably affect profoundly the quality of the children whom it touches. So long, therefore, as the family endures—and there seems little reason to anticipate or to desire its disappearance—the varying environments it will create make the notion of equal opportunities a fantastic one.

But that is not to say that the opportunities created may not be adequate. We can at least see first that all men are given such training as seems, in the light of experience, most likely to develop their faculties to the full. We can at least surround those circumstances with the physical media without which the training of the mind can hardly be successful. We can, where we discover talent, at least make it certain that it does not perish for want of encouragement. These conditions do not exist today. Children who come hungry to school cannot, on the average, profit by education in like degree to those who are well fed. The student who is trying to do his work in a room which serves for the various tasks of life cannot find that essential isolation without which the habit of thought can rarely be cultivated. The boy or girl who has to assume that at fourteen they are bound to pass into the industrial world rarely acquires that frame of mind which searches with eagerness for the cultivation of intelligence. In the modern world, broadly speaking, opportunity is a matter of parental circumstance. Boys of a certain social status may assume that they will pass from the secondary school to the university. Boys whose parents are, broadly, manual workers will in the vast majority of cases be inevitably destined to manual work also. There is no reason to decry either the value or the dignity of manual work; but there is every reason to examine the social adequacy of a system which does not at every point associate the best training available with those whose qualities most fit them to benefit by that training. We do not want—possibly we cannot afford—to prolong the period of education unduly. But no State has established conditions of reasonable adequacy until the period of education is sufficiently long, first, to ensure that the citizen knows how to use his mind, and second, that those of special capacity are given that further training which prevents the wastage of their talent.

No one can deny that this wastage to-day is enormous. Any student of the results of adult education in Europe will have realised how great is the reservoir of talent we leave unused until it is too late. The sacrifices to-day involved when the average manual worker seeks the adequate education of his children are sacrifices we have no right to demand. Often enough, the training of one child is built upon the conviction of others to a life of unremitting toil. The circumstances which those who live by intellectual work know to be essential to its performance are, as a matter of definition almost, denied to the vast majority of the population. And since citizenship is largely a matter of the use of trained intelligence, it is obvious, accordingly, that its substance is denied to all save a fraction of the community. Our business, therefore, is to assure such an education to all as will make every vocation, however humble, one that does not debar those who follow it from the life of intelligence. That certainly means an extension of the period within which the earning of one's living is impossible. It means also that even after the earning period has commenced there are full opportunities for the devotion of leisure to intellectual ends. It means, thirdly, that those who devote themselves to the business of teaching represent the best minds at the service of the community. In the modern State the teacher has a responsibility far greater than that which devolves upon any other citizen; and unless he teaches from a full mind and a full heart he cannot release the forces which education has in leash.

Nothing in all this denies the probability that mental qualities are inherited and that, other things being equal, the children of able parents will be abler than the children of average parents. But it does deny the equation, characteristic of the modern State, between ability and material position. The average trade-union leader cannot afford to send his sons to the university; but the ability of the average trade-union leader is probably not inferior to that of the average banker or the average bishop. Where, that is to say, the inequalities of our system are not due to natural causes, there is a clear case for their remedy. Nor can we hope to discover the existence of capacity unless our system provides for its discovery. It may do so to-day in the case of the rich; assuredly it does not do so in the case of the poor. And it is urgent to remember that, important as nature may be, it requires an adequate nurture if it is to function satisfactorily. The present inequalities are not referable to principle. We have therefore to define the outlines of such a system as build the inequalities we admit upon the needs of society. At present they most largely arise from the impact of the property system upon the structure of the State. But what is reflected by the property system is less ability to serve the community than ability to gain economic power without reference to the quality of wants supplied.

The provision of adequate opportunity is, therefore, one of the basic conditions of equality, and it is mainly founded upon the training we offer to citizens. For the power that ultimately counts in society is the power to utilise knowledge; and disparities of education result, above all, in disparities in the ability to use that power. I am not pleading for equality of function. I am pleading only for the obvious truth that without education a man is not so circumstanced that he knows how to make the best of himself and that therefore, for him, the purpose of society is, *ab initio,* frustrated. Once men are in that situation where they can know themselves, the use they make of their opportunities becomes subject to principles of which equality is only one.

But if we agree, as I have argued earlier, that a democratic State regards its members as equally entitled to happiness, it follows that such differences as exist must not be differences inexplicable in terms of reason. Distinctions of wealth or status must be distinctions to which all men can attain and they must be required by the common welfare. If a State permits the existence of an hereditary aristocracy it must be because it is capable of proof that an hereditary aristocracy multiplies the chances of each man's realising his best self. If we are to have an economic system in which the luxury of a few is paralleled by the misery of the many, it must be because the common welfare requires that luxury. In each case the proposition is open to historical disproof. An hereditary aristocracy is bound, sooner or later, to use its political power to general disadvantage, unless, like the peerage of France, it has ceased to be anything but a faded memory. A State divided into a small number of rich and a large number of poor will always develop a government manipulated by the rich to protect the amenities represented by their property. It therefore follows that the inequalities of any social system are justified only as it can be demonstrated that the level of service they procure is obviously higher because of their existence. It is obvious that a general must have larger powers than a private because, thereby, the purpose of an army is more likely to be fulfilled. It is obvious that a statesman in office must be so remunerated that he is not oppressed by narrow material cares; and that might well involve placing him in a higher financial rank than a bootmaker or a shop assistant. In each case the measure of difference is conceived in social terms. It is set in a principle which is demonstrably rational. It is fitting the circumstances of function to the environment of which it has need.

Such a view admits, at least as a matter of theory, of fairly simple statement in institutional terms. The urgent claims of all must be met before we can meet the particular claims of some. The differences in the social or economic position of men can only be admitted after a minimum basis of civilisation is attained by the community as a whole. That minimum basis must admit of my realising the implications of personality. Above that level, the advantages of the situation I occupy must be advantages necessary to the performance of a social function. The advantages I enjoy must be the result of my own effort, because they are the return to me for my own services, and I am clearly not entitled to enjoy them as the result of someone else's services. One man is not entitled to a house of twenty rooms until all people are adequately housed; and one man, even in that environment, is not entitled to a house of twenty rooms because his father was a great advocate or a large industrialist. The things that are due to me are the rights I must enjoy in order to be a citizen, and the differential advantages which society adjudges inherent in the particular occupation I follow. We may, in other words, have Belgravias, if their existence is a necessary condition of social welfare; but we are not entitled to have Belgravias until we have secured the impossibility of Poplar's existence.

If all this is true, equality is most largely a problem in proportions. There is an aspect in which the things without which life is meaningless must be accessible to all without distinction in degree or kind. All men must eat and drink and obtain shelter. But those needs are, in their turn, proportionate to what they do. My wants are my claims to find a harmony of impulses. I do not want the same harmony if I am a miner as I shall want if I am a surgeon. But the system which obtains must not satisfy the claims of the surgeon at the expense of the miner's claims. My urgent needs are not less urgent than the needs of any other person, and they are entitled to equal satisfaction. Once urgency is satisfied superfluity becomes a problem of so fixing the return to service that each man can perform his function with the maximum return to society as a whole.

In this aspect, the problem of proportions is largely an economic problem. It is a question of the methods we use to determine the claim of each citizen upon the social dividend, and of the environment which surrounds the application of those methods. There have been famous answers to this problem. We have been told that response should be made in terms of need, or in terms of contribution; it has been insisted that identity of response is alone adequate. Of these solutions that which would reward me by what I do for society is certainly the least satisfactory. For it is impossible in any genuine way to measure service. We cannot say what Newton or Lister, Shakespeare or Robert Owen were "worth" to their fellow-citizens. We cannot measure the contribution of a banker against the contribution of a bricklayer. Often enough, as in the case of Galileo, for example, we may not be able to see how vast in truth the contribution is. Nor, it may be argued, is the communistic solution adequate. For, in the first place, there is no total identity of needs between men; nor is their effort so equal as to merit an identical return. The communistic principle is adequate up to the point where human urgencies are in question; it is not adequate after that point. And it is adequate only so far as its application wins the result of a deliberate effort on the part of those whose needs are satisfied to do work of civic quality. And since to do work of civic quality involves differentiation of function, it is, I think, clear that when the primary needs of all men are met, the differences they encounter must be differences their function requires; requirement involving always the context of social benefit.

But this, it will be argued, is to assume sufficiency. It implies that there is in fact enough to go round, whereas we know that the productivity of men does not suffice for their wants. What we ought rather to do is to allow the free play of capacity to win response to its need and let those prosper who show the power to triumph in the race. The answer involved in this attitude is far less simple than it seems. If the State exists for social good, "capacity" can only mean capacity to add to social good. It is not in the least certain that the exercise of talent in a society like our own does in fact result in social benefit. Capacity, in short, must run in the leading-strings of principle. It must be excited to the end our institutions have in view. And since that end is the achievement of happiness for each individual, it seems obvious that we must, if the margin be insufficient, suffer equally by its insufficiencies. We can never, therefore, as a matter of principle, justify the existence of differences until the point is reached when the primary claims of men win a full response. I have no right to cake if my neighbour, because of that right, is compelled to go without bread. Any social organisation from which this basis is absent by denying equality denies all that gives meaning to the personality of men.

Equality, therefore, involves up to the margin of sufficiency identity of response to primary needs. And that is what is meant by justice. We are rendering to each man his own by giving him what enables him to be a man. We are, of course, therein protecting the weak and limiting the power of the strong. We so act because the common welfare includes the welfare of the weak as well as of the strong. Grant, as we may well grant, that this involves a payment by society to men and women who limp after its vanguard, the quality of the State depends on its regarding their lives as worth preserving. To act otherwise is to regard them not as persons, but as instruments. It is to deny that their personality constitutes a claim. It is deliberately to weight institutions against a section of the community. If they are to harmonise their impulses in the effort after happiness, such bias is inadmissible. For it is utilising their service not for their own well-being, but for the well-being of others. That is essentially the definition of slavery. . . .

Broadly, I am urging that great inequalities of wealth make impossible the attainment of freedom. It means the dictation of the physical and mental circumstances which surround the less fortunate. It means the control of the engines of government to their detriment. The influence of the great corporations upon the legislative system of the United States is only a supreme example of that control. Hardly less deleterious is the way in which it controls the intellectual environment it encounters. It is able to weight the educational system in its interest. It is able, by the rewards it offers, to affect the propertyless brain-worker to its service. Since the judiciary will be largely selected from its paid advocates, legal decisions will largely reflect the lessons of its experience. Even the Churches will preach a gospel which is permeated by their dependence upon the support of the wealthy.

Political equality, therefore, is never real unless it is accompanied by virtual economic equality; political power, otherwise, is bound to be the handmaid of economic power. The recognition of this dependence is in the main due to the explanation of historic evolution, and it is, indeed, almost as old as the birth of scientific politics. Aristotle pointed out the equation between democracy and the rule of the poor, between oligarchy and the rule of the rich. The struggle to remedy economic disparity is the key to Roman history; it is at the root of English agrarian discontent. It underlies the sermons of John Ball, the *Utopia* of More, the *Oceana* of Harrington. The early history of socialism is most largely the record of a perception that the concentration of property other than labour-power in a few hands is fatal to the purpose of the State. It was that perception which Marx, in the *Communist Manifesto*, made the foundation of the most formidable political philosophy in the modern world. For though the materialistic interpretation of history is an over-emphasis of one link in the chain of causation, it is the link most intimately related to the experience of ordinary men. It is overwhelmingly right in its insistence that either the State must dominate property, or property will dominate the State.

For, as Madison wrote, "the only durable source of faction is property." But it is obvious that to base the differences between men on a contest for economic wealth is to destroy the possibility of a well-ordered commonwealth. It is to excite all the qualities in men —envy, arrogance, hatred, vanity—which prevent the emergence of social unity. It is to emphasise a competition based on their separation, instead of a competition based upon their mutual interest. As soon as we postulate approximate equality of wealth, our methods of social organisation enable us to respond to men's needs in terms of the substance of those needs. We are the more bound to this effort immediately we admit the logic of universal suffrage. For to confide to the mass of men the control of ultimate political power is broadly to admit that the agencies of the State must be utilised to respond to their needs. They involve, if they are to be satisfied, such a distribution of influence over authority as will balance fairly the incidence of its results among the members of society. It means, that is, that I must adjust my scale of wants to social welfare as that is organised in terms of a valuation which equally weights the primary needs of citizens; and that valuation remains ineffective if my power is a function not of my personality, but of my property.

But virtual equality in economic power means more than approximate equality of wealth. It means that the authority which exerts that power must be subject to the rules of democratic governance. It means the abrogation of unfettered and irresponsible will in the industrial world. It involves building decisions on principles which can be explained, and the relation of those principles to the service any given industry is seeking to render. The authority of a medical officer who orders the isolation of an infected house is intelligible; he is relating his powers to the preservation of public health. But the authority of an employer is not intelligible except in terms of self-interested motives. His demands cannot be scrutinised. They are not referable to his capacity for his post. They are not relevant to the well being of his servants. If a worker refuses to adulterate the product made by an employer, he may suffer dismissal. He may be penalised if he refuses to falsify his accounts, even when the sufferer by that falsification is the public revenue the burden of which he himself partially bears. There is, that is to say, all the difference in the world between an authority which grows naturally out of functions which are set consistently in a public context, and an authority which, equally consistently, is the outcome of private and irresponsible will.

The existence of this latter type is fatal to the civic implications of equality. It poisons industrial relations. It makes the position of master and servant one of waiting upon the threshold of war. Above all, it is intolerable wherever the function involved is one where continuity of service is essential to the life of the community. That industries like coal and electric power, transport and banking, the supply of meat and the provision of houses, should be left to the hazards of private enterprise will appear as unthinkable to a future generation as it is unthinkable to our own that the army of the State should be left to private hands. They must be subject to rules as rigorous as those which govern medicine, simply because they are not less vital to the national life. That does not mean direct operation by government as the inevitable alternative. It means the planning of constitutions for essential industries; and the possible types of constitutions are as various in industry as elsewhere.

(1925)

R. H. Tawney

57.

(1880-   )

R. H. Tawney, English economist and author of *Religion and the Rise of Capitalism,* offers in the following selection an analysis and vigorous defense of equality.

from Equality

Psychologists tell us that the way to overcome a complex is not to suppress it, but to treat it frankly, and uncover its foundations. It is perhaps worth while, therefore, to consider more closely our national habit of taking extreme inequality for granted, and our national attachment to arrangements which separate different social groups, not merely in the matter of income, but in respect of their environment, their opportunities of personal development and education, and even the qualities of mind and character which it is thought proper should be encouraged in them.

What a community requires, as the word itself suggests, is a common culture, because, without it, it is not a community at all. And evidently it requires it in a special degree at a moment of transition like the present, when circumstances confront it with the necessity of giving a new orientation to its economic life, because it is in such circumstances that the need for co-operation, and for the mutual confidence and tolerance upon which co-operation depends, is particularly pressing. But a common culture cannot be created merely by desiring it. It rests upon economic foundations. It is incompatible with the existence of too violent a contrast between the economic standards and educational opportunities of different classes, for such a contrast has as its result, not a common culture, but servility or resentment, on the one hand, and patronage or arrogance, on the other. It involves, in short, a large measure of economic equality— not necessarily, indeed, in respect of the pecuniary incomes of individuals, but of environment, of habits of life, of access to education and the means of civilization, of security and independence, and of the social consideration which equality in these matters usually carries with it.

And who does not know that to approach the question of economic equality is to enter a region haunted, not, indeed, "by hobgoblins, satyrs, and dragons of the pit," yet by a host of hardly less formidable terrors—"doleful voices and rushings to and fro," and the giant with a grim and surly voice, who shows pilgrims the skulls of those whom he has already despatched, and threatens to tear them also in pieces, and who, unlike Bunyan's giant, does not even fall into fits on sunshiny days, since in his territory the sun does not shine, and, even if it did, he would be protected against the weaknesses that beset mere theological ogres by the inflexible iron of his economic principles? Who does not recognize, when the words are mentioned, that there is an immediate stiffening against them in the minds of the great mass of his fellow-countrymen, and that, while in France and Scandinavia, and even in parts of the United States, there is, at least, an initial sympathy for the conception, and a disposition to be proud of such economic equality as exists, in England the instinctive feeling is one, not of sympathy, but of apprehension and repulsion, as though economic equality were a matter upon which it were not in good taste to touch? And who does not feel that, as a consequence of this attitude, though their practice is, as always, better than their principles, Englishmen approach the subject with minds that are rarely more than half open? They do not welcome the idea, and then consider whether, and by what means, the difficulties in the way of its realization, which are serious enough, can be overcome. They recite the difficulties with melancholy, and sometimes with exultant, satisfaction, because on quite other grounds—grounds of history, and social nervousness, and a traditional belief that advantages which are shared cease to be advantages at all, as though, when everybody is somebody, nobody will be anybody—they are determined to reject the idea.

So, when the question is raised whether some attempt to establish greater economic equality may not be desirable, there is a sound of what Bunyan called "doleful voices and rushings to and fro." They rear, and snort, and paw the air, and affirm with one accord that the suggestion is at once wicked and impracticable. Lord Birkenhead, for example, declared that the idea that men are equal is "a poisonous doctrine," and wrung his hands at the thought of the "glittering prizes" of life being diminished in value; and Mr. Garvin, with his eye for the dangers of the moment, and the temptations to which his fellow-countrymen are most prone to succumb, warns us against the spirit that seeks the dead level and ignores the inequality of human endowments; and Sir Ernest Benn writes that economic equality is "a scientific impossibility," because Professor Pareto has shown, he says, that "if the logarithms of income sizes be charted on a horizontal scale, and the logarithms of the number of persons having an income of a particular size or over be charted on a vertical scale, then the resulting observational points will lie approximately along a straight line," and that, if only this were more generally known, the poor, like the wicked, would cease from troubling; and Sir Herbert Austin implores us to "cease teaching that all men are equal and entitled to an equal share of the common wealth," and "enrich the men who make sacrifices justifying enrichment," and "leave the others in their contentment, rather than try to mould material that was never intended to withstand the fires of refinement"; and Dean Inge complains, in an address at Oxford, with a view, perhaps, to mitigating the class feeling which he rightly deplores, that "the Government is taking the pick of the working classes and educating them at the expense of the ratepayers to enable them to take the bread out of the mouths of the sons of professional men," and that this process, since it injures "the upper middle classes," who are "the cream of the community," must ultimately be injurious to the nation as a whole. . . .

A wise man once observed that, when an argument leads to an *impasse,* it is advisable to re-examine the premises from which it started. It is possible that the dilemma is not, after all, quite so hopeless as at first sight it appears to be. Rightly understood, Pareto's law is a suggestive generalization; and the biological differences between different individuals are a phenomenon of great interest and significance; and Dean Inge is, doubtless, more than justified in thinking that the working classes, like other classes, are no better than they should be, and in telling them so with the apostolic fervour which he so abundantly commands. It is the natural disposition of clever and learned people to attack the difficult and recondite aspects of topics which are under discussion, because to such people the other aspects seem too obvious and elementary to deserve attention. The more difficult aspects of human relations, however, though doubtless the most interesting to nimble minds, are not always the most important. . . .

It is probable that it is these simpler and more elementary considerations that have been in the minds of those who have thought that a society was most likely to enjoy happiness and good will, and to turn both its human and material resources to the best account, if it cultivated as far as possible an equalitarian temper, and sought by its institutions to increase equality. It is obvious, indeed, that, as things are to-day, no redistribution of wealth would bring general affluence, and that statisticians are within their rights in making merry with the idea that the equalization of incomes would make everyone rich. But, though riches are a good, it is not certain, nevertheless, that they are the only good; and because greater production, which is concerned with the commodities to be consumed, is clearly important, it does not follow that greater equality, which is concerned with the relations between the human beings who consume them, is not important also. An improvement in these relations, such as would be fostered, it is generally agreed, by a diminution of sharp contrasts of economic condition, is not to be desired primarily as a means of putting more money into the pockets of those who have too little, though that result is, doubtless, to be welcomed; on the contrary, if it is desirable to put more money into their pockets, the reason is primarily that such a course may be one means, among others, to a much-needed improvement in human relations. If riches are an economic good, and are the proper object of economic effort, equality may, nevertheless, be a social good, and be made no less properly the object of social effort. And there is nothing illogical or fantastic in desiring two good objects rather than one, unless, as in this case is sometimes asserted, but has hardly yet been conclusively proved, the objects in question are incompatible with each other.

It is obvious, again, that the word "Equality" possesses more than one meaning, and that the controversies surrounding it arise partly, at least, because the same term is employed with different connotations. Thus it may either purport to state a fact, or convey the expression of an ethical judgment. On the one hand, it may affirm that men are, on the whole, very similar in their natural endowments of character and intelligence. On the other hand, it may assert that, while they differ profoundly as individuals in capacity and character, they are equally entitled as human beings to consideration and respect, and that the well-being of a society is likely to be increased if it so plans its organization that, whether their powers are great or small, all its members may be equally enabled to make the best of such powers as they possess.

If made in the first sense, the assertion of human equality is clearly untenable. It is a piece of mythology against which irresistible evidence has been accumulated by biologists and psychologists. . . .

It is difficult for even the most sanguine of assemblies to retain for more than one meeting the belief that Providence has bestowed an equal measure of intelligence upon all its members. When the Americans declared it to be a self-evident truth that all men are created equal, they were thinking less, perhaps, of the admirable racial qualities of the inhabitants of the New World than of their political and economic relations with the Old, and would have remained unconvinced that those relations should continue even in the face of proofs of biological inferiority. When the French, whose attachment to the equalitarian idea roused the same horror a century and a quarter ago as that of the Russians does to-day, and who have had more success than the Russians in disseminating it, set that idea side by side with liberty and fraternity as the motto of a new world, they did not mean that all men are equally intelligent or equally virtuous, any more than that they are equally tall or equally fat, but that the unity of their national life should no longer be torn to pieces by obsolete property rights and meaningless juristic distinctions. . . .

Few men have been more acutely sensitive than Mill to the importance of encouraging the widest possible diversities of mind and taste. In arguing that "the best state for human nature is that in which, while no one is poor, no one desires to be richer," and urging that social policy should be directed to increasing equality, he did not intend to convey that it should suppress varieties of individual genius and character, but that it was only in a society marked by a large measure of economic equality that such varieties were likely to find their full expression and due meed of appreciation. Theologians have not, as a rule, been disposed to ignore the fact that there are diversities of gifts and degree above degree. When they tell us that all men are equal in the eyes of God, what they mean, it is to be presumed, is what Jeremy Taylor meant, when he wrote, in a book to-day too little read, that "if a man be exalted by reason of any excellence in his soul, he may please to remember that all souls are equal, and their differing operations are because their instrument is in better tune, their body is more healthful or better tempered; which is no more praise to him than it is that he was born in Italy." It is the truth expressed in the parable of the prodigal son, which clever people, like deans, sometimes seem to forget, but which it is specially necessary, perhaps, for such people to remember—the truth that it is absurd and degrading for men to make much of their intellectual and moral superiority to each other, and still more of their superiority in the arts which bring wealth and power, because, judged by their place in any universal scheme, they are all infinitely great or infinitely small. . . .

The equality which all these thinkers emphasize as desirable is not equality of capacity or attainment, but of circumstances, and institutions, and manner of life. The inequality which they deplore is not inequality of personal gifts, but of the social and economic environment. They are concerned, not with a biological phenomenon, but with a spiritual relation and the conduct to be based on it. Their view, in short, is that, because men are men, social institutions—property rights, and the organization of industry, and the system of public health and education—should be planned, as far as is possible, to emphasize and strengthen, not the class differences which divide, but the common humanity which unites, them.

Such a view of the life which is proper to human beings may, of course, be criticized, as it often has been. But to suppose that it can be criticized effectively by pointing to the width of the intellectual and moral differences which distinguish individuals from each other is a solecism, an *ignoratio elenchi*. It is true, of course, that such differences are important, and that the advance of psychology has enabled them to be measured with a new precision, with results which are valuable in making possible both a closer adaptation of educational methods to individual needs and a more intelligent selection of varying aptitudes for different tasks. But to recognize a specific difference is one thing; to pass a general judgment of superiority or inferiority, still more to favour the first and neglect the second, is quite another. The nightingale, it has been remarked, was placed in the fourth class at the fowl show. Which of a number of varying individuals is to be judged superior to the rest depends upon the criterion which is applied, and the criterion is a matter of ethical judgment, which will, if it is prudent, be tentative and provisional, since men's estimates of the relative desirability of initiative, decision, common sense, imagination, humility and sympathy appear, unfortunately, to differ, and the failures and fools—the Socrates and St. Francis—of one age are the sages and saints of another. Society would not be the worse, perhaps, if idiots like Dostoievsky's were somewhat less uncommon, and the condemnation passed on those who cause one of these little ones to offend was not limited to offenders against children whose mental ratio is in excess of eighty-five.

It is true, again, that human beings have, except as regards certain elementary, though still sadly neglected, matters of health and development, different requirements, and that these different requirements can be met satisfactorily only by varying forms of provision. But equality of provision is not identity of provision. It is to be achieved, not by treating different needs in the same way, but by devoting equal care to ensuring that they are met in the different ways most appropriate to them, as is done by a doctor who prescribes different regimens for different constitutions, or a teacher who develops different types of intelligence by different curricula. The more anxiously, indeed, a society endeavours to secure equality of consideration for all its members, the greater will be the differentiation of treatment which, when once their common human needs have been met, it accords to the special needs of different groups and individuals among them.

It is true, finally, that some men are inferior to others in respect of their intellectual endowments, and it is possible—though the truth of the possibility has not yet, perhaps, been satisfactorily established —that the same is true of certain classes. It does not, however, follow from this fact that such individuals or classes should receive less consideration than others, or should be treated as inferior in respect of such matters as legal status, or health, or economic arrangements, which are within the control of the community. . . .

Every one recognizes the absurdity of such an argument when it is applied to matters within their personal knowledge and professional competence. Every one realizes that, in order to justify inequalities of circumstance or opportunity by reference to differences of personal quality, it is necessary, as Professor Ginsberg observes, to show that the differences in question are relevant to the inequalities. Every one sees, for example, that it is not a valid argument against women's suffrage to urge, as used to be urged not so long ago, that women are physically weaker than men, since physical strength is not relevant to the question of the ability to exercise the franchise, or a valid argument in favour of slavery that some men are less intelligent than others, since it is not certain that slavery is the most suitable penalty for lack of intelligence.

Not every one, however, is so quick to detect the fallacy when it is expressed in general terms. It is still possible, for example, for one eminent statesman to ridicule the demand for a diminution of economic inequalities on the ground that every mother knows that her children are not equal, without reflecting whether it is the habit of mothers to lavish care on the strong and neglect the delicate; and for another to dismiss the suggestion that greater economic equality is desirable, for the reason, apparently, that men are naturally unequal. It is probable, however, that the first does not think that the fact that some children are born with good digestions, and others with bad, is a reason for supplying good food to the former and bad food to the latter, rather than for giving to both food which is equal in quality but different in kind, and that the second does not suppose that the natural inequality of men makes legal equality a contemptible principle. On the contrary, when ministers of the Crown responsible for the administration of justice to the nation, they both did their best, doubtless a very efficient best, to maintain legal equality, though in the eighteenth century statesmen of equal eminence in France and Germany, and in the nineteenth century influential thinkers in Russia and the United States, and, indeed, the ruling classes of Europe almost everywhere at a not very distant period, all were disposed to think that, since men are naturally unequal, the admission of a general equality of legal status would be the end of civilization.

Our modern statesmen do not agree with that view, for, thanks to the struggles of the past, they have inherited a tradition of legal equality, and, fortified by that tradition, they see that the fact that men are naturally unequal is not relevant to the question whether they should or should not be treated as equal before the law. But they have not inherited a tradition of economic equality, for that tradition has still to be created. So they do not see that the existence of differences of personal capacity and attainment is as irrelevant to the question whether it is desirable that the social environment and economic organization should be made more conducive to equality as it is to the question of equality before the law, which itself, as we have said, seemed just as monstrous a doctrine to conservative thinkers in the past as the suggestion of greater economic equality seems to them to-day.

And Sir Ernest Benn, who says that economic equality is a scientific impossibility, is quite unconscious, apparently, that, in some economic matters of the first importance—protection by the police against violence and theft, and the use of the roads, and the supply of water, and the provision of sewers and open spaces, and access to a minimum of education and medical attendance, all of which were once dependent on the ability of individuals to pay for them—all members of civilized communities are now secured equality irrespective of their personal attainments and individual economic resources, and that the only question is whether that movement shall be carried forward, or rather, since in fact it is carried forward year by year, how quickly society will decide to establish complete environmental equality in respect of the external conditions of health, and education, and economic security for all its members. So he behaves like the countryman who, on being for the first time introduced to a giraffe at a circus, exclaimed indignantly, "There ain't no such animal." He says that equality is a scientific impossibility, and draws a sharp line between the natural and, as he thinks, the healthy state of things, under which each individual provides all his requirements for himself, and the unnatural and morbid condition, under which the community, consisting of him and his fellows, provides some of them for him.

Such a line, however, is quite arbitrary, quite fanciful and artificial. Many services are supplied by collective effort to-day which in the recent past were supplied by individual effort or not supplied at all, and many more, it may be suspected, will be so supplied in the future. At any moment there are some needs which almost every one is agreed should be satisfied on equalitarian principles, and others which they are agreed should be met by individuals who purchase what their incomes enable them to pay for, and others, again, about the most suitable provision for which opinions differ. Society has not been prevented from seeking to establish equality in respect of the first by the fear that in so doing it may be perpetrating a scientific impossibility; nor will it be prevented from moving towards equality in respect of the second and third, if experience suggests that greater equality in these matters also would contribute to greater efficiency and to more general happiness. . . .

It is true, indeed, that even such equality, though the conditions on which it depends are largely within human control, will continue to elude us. The important thing, however, is not that it should be completely attained, but that it should be sincerely sought. What matters to the health of society is the objective towards which its face is set, and to suggest that it is immaterial in which direction it moves, because, whatever the direction, the goal must always elude it, is not scientific, but irrational. It is like using the impossibility of absolute cleanliness as a pretext for rolling in a manure heap, or denying the importance of honesty because no one can be wholly honest. It may well be the case that capricious inequalities are in some measure inevitable, in the sense that, like crime and disease, they are a malady which the most rigorous precautions cannot wholly overcome. But, when crime is known as crime, and disease as disease, the ravages of both are circumscribed by the mere fact that they are recognized for what they are, and described by their proper names, not by flattering euphemisms. And a society which is convinced that inequality is an evil need not be alarmed because the evil is one which cannot wholly be subdued. In recognizing the poison it will have armed itself with an antidote. It will have deprived inequality of its sting by stripping it of its esteem.

(1931)

E. F. Carritt

58.

(1876-   )

E. F. Carritt, English philosopher, offers comments on equality in his penetrating little book, *Morals and Politics*.

from Morals and Politics

My purpose has been to show in the first place that no tenable political philosophy can deny the reality of obligations and responsibilities, and secondarily that an obligation to obey the laws of our state is not a special obligation, but only derivative from and dependent on obligations to our fellow men. In other words, we think it is our duty to obey or to support any authority or society when and only when we think that by so doing we can affect other men as we ought. I have not claimed to give any exhaustive or systematic list of our responsibilities to other men. In detail that would plainly depend upon our condition and theirs and upon the relations already existing between us. But it might be possible to enumerate certain types of responsibility to our fellows or of claims that they have on us, and in fact I have said that they have claims to freedom, to justice, and to opportunities of happiness. If there are these claims, they may conflict. It was pointed out by Aristotle that *justice* is a word used in two senses. In the wider, it is the name for any obligation to others, so that, if we ought on some occasion to try to make them free or happy, we act unjustly when we do not. But it is also used as the name of one responsibility among others; so that it is said that, though we 'ought' (i.e. have a responsibility) to be beneficent, we 'ought' to be just first (i.e. have a greater responsibility, or perhaps a duty). The simplest examples of justice in this narrower sense are the claim on us to keep our bargains, and the claim of the labourer to his hire. Both these appear to be claims to preferential treatment. Yet Aristotle also remarked that justice is a kind of equality, and it is with equality that political justice has often been thought to be especially concerned. The idea that equal distribution is a more fundamental form of justice than the rewarding of desert, as if desert only justified exceptional deviations from equal treatment, was perhaps expressed by Locke, when he said that the fruit of the earth was given men in common, that is, to be divided equally, until some began to mix their labour with it. Men think they have a claim to equal means of satisfaction until some reason arises to the contrary, that is, until some stronger claim is exhibited. If water is short and you and I are both thirsty, we think prima facie that we ought to share and share alike. These are often the most striking facts in the situation, or the first to be known. If it turns out that you are the more industrious in fetching it, or that you will have to do all the hunting, which is thirsty work, or if you get a fever, the case is altered. It is hard to see in what sense the claim of men, as men, to equal shares is more primary or fundamental than their claims to greater shares on the ground of greater need, greater desert, or greater utility; certainly the former should often give way to the latter. The fact that it is a constant claim, while its rivals are various and occasional, is probably what is meant by calling it 'natural.'

But when we speak of political equality we mean equality in the distribution not only of opportunities for getting satisfactions (including freedom), but rather of political power or the opportunity of affecting the laws under which we live. And the question is raised whether the latter is a thing men have a claim to in itself or only because and so far as it is the sole security for the former. I think we must reply that so far as men desire political power for its own sake, independently of whether it will secure their equality in freedom and in opportunities for getting the other things they desire, they have a claim to an equal distribution of it, though of course this claim may be overridden by stronger claims of others to other things incompatible with it.

The claim to equality, *ceteris paribus,* is, I think, always recognized. Utilitarians have strained their system to breaking-point in the effort to include it. God has been praised as no respecter of persons. Kant spoke of duty as a law because law, at least within the limits it has laid down, treats all men as equals, and our duty is to act in a way we could 'will' all men to act. Those who have defended institutions which artificially produce or perpetuate inequalities have always felt bound to offer utilitarian reasons, good or bad, in justification for neglecting what they thereby admit is a claim to equality. I do not remember seeing or hearing inequality among men commended for its own sake, though the religious consciousness has thought that that men's wickedness made it necessary and we have seen Bosanquet palliating it as belonging only to the world of claims and counterclaims.

(1935)

Otto Klineberg
(1899-   )

59.

Otto Klineberg, social psychologist at Columbia University, has investigated racial problems and the relations between anthropology and psychology.

from Race Differences

In the field of racial psychology no other problem has attracted so much attention as the question of the inherent intellectual superiority of certain races over others. This problem . . . has been approached in a great many different ways, but usually with so much obvious bias as to make the scientifically minded student very sceptical of the conclusions. With the development of the first intelligence scales by Binet and their use in the quantitative measurement of individual differences, it was felt that perhaps an instrument had finally been devised which would make it possible to study with complete objectivity the relative ability of various races. Terman, one of the early authorities in this field, expressed the opinion that the Binet scale was a true test of native intelligence, relatively free of the disturbing influences of nurture and background. If this were so, the difficult problem of racial differences in intelligence might be solved as soon as a sufficiently large body of data could be accumulated.

The data are now available. The number of studies in this field has multiplied rapidly, especially under the impetus of the testing undertaken during the World War, and the relevant bibliography is extensive. The largest proportion of these investigations has been made in America, and the results have shown that racial and national groups differ markedly from one another.

Negroes in general appear to do poorly. Pintner estimates that in the various studies of Negro children by means of the Binet, the I. Q. ranges from 83 to 99, with an average around 90. With group tests Negroes rank still lower, with a range in I. Q. from 58 to 92, and an average of only 76. Negro recruits during the war were definitely inferior; their average mental age was calculated to be 10.4 years, as compared with 13.1 years for the White draft.

In the case of the American Indian, the I. Q.'s are also low, the majority being between 70 and 90. Mexicans do only slightly better. Chinese and Japanese, on the other hand, show relatively little inferiority to the Whites, the I. Q.'s ranging from 85 to 114, with an average only slightly below 100.

Among European immigrant groups, Italians have in general made a poor showing. In a series of studies their I. Q.'s ranged from 76 to 100, with an average about 87. Poles do equally poorly and in the Army tests were even slightly below the Italians. Immigrants from northwestern Europe have in general been more successful, and the demonstration by the Army psychologists that in the test results the immigrants from Great Britain, Holland, Germany and the Scandinavian countries were superior to others has been corroborated by more recent studies.

If we had absolute faith in tests of intelligence, we should have to regard this evidence of racial differences as conclusive. In recent years, however, more work has been done on the tests themselves, and little by little the conviction has grown that Terman's statement was an exaggeration, and that environmental factors cannot be ignored in any valid interpretation of these results. There may still be some controversy as to the extent to which these factors enter, but material has accumulated which leaves no doubt that they play an important part. In a recent critical survey, Garrett and Schneck write that "the examiner must always remember that comparisons are permissible only when environmental differences are absent, or at least negligible." . . .

. . . This chapter will rather be concerned with a critical discussion of some of the environmental, or non-racial, factors affecting the results, and individual studies will be cited only where they help to clarify the argument.

One preliminary caution is necessary. The problem of heredity versus environment, nature versus nurture, as it is here being considered, does not refer to individual, but to group, differences. This needs to be kept clearly in mind. It may be decided, for example, that heredity does not account for the observed intellectual differences between Negroes and Whites, and that the conditions of the environment are alone responsible. It would not follow that heredity did not enter into individual differences. There would still be room for wide variability within the Negro or within the White group, part of which at least could be explained only by the superiority or inferiority of individual or family germ plasm. The fact that persons living in almost the same environmental conditions will still differ widely from one another in intelligence, and the fact that identical twins living in very different environments will yet resemble each other closely, argue strongly in favor of an hereditary basis for part of the differences in intelligence between individuals and family lines. The problem of group differences, however, cannot be so easily dismissed. . . .

Many studies testify to the close correspondence between standing in the tests and the social and economic status of the groups tested. This was revealed in the study made by the Army testers, and it has been amply verified by subsequent investigations in England, France, Germany and Japan, as well as in the United States. There are marked differences, not only between adults in various occupational levels, but also between their children, the professional and moneyed classes ranking higher than skilled and unskilled laborers. . . .

The obvious difficulty in the interpretation of these findings is the question as to what is cause and what is effect; whether people are in the upper economic levels because they are more intelligent, or whether they do better on the tests because of their superior opportunities. The answer to this question is of great significance in the problem of racial differences. Most of the groups who rank low in the tests, for example, the Negro, the Mexican, the Italian, come largely from the lowest economic levels; if economic status affects test scores to any extent, they are very definitely handicapped in a comparative study.

Intelligence may be regarded as the cause of economic status only if opportunities are equal and competition is entirely free. Even within a relatively homogeneous, native-born White American population, this is not altogether true; the handicaps are not evenly distributed. In the case of the Negro, however, the difficulties in his way are so great that any inference from industrial status to intelligence is completely unwarranted. The kind of competition the Negro has to face in his search for a job has been carefully described by Johnson, Feldman, and Spero and Harris, who leave no doubt as to the additional handicaps he must overcome. The same is true, though not to so great an extent, of some foreign-born White groups, who tend to enter the occupations at the lowest economic level, emerging from these only after a generation. That their economic inferiority is only temporary is made clear by a report of the U. S. Immigration Commission, which indicates that although at the start the immigrants have much lower occupations than the native-born, in the second generation the majority rise to the average native-born level. Until we can be certain that the same opportunities have been given to the Negro and the Italian as to the native-born White, any direct comparison of average test scores will be meaningless. . . .

. . . There is no doubt of the rather close correspondence between amount of education and standing in the tests. This was first demon-

strated clearly by the Army testers . . . A number of studies followed
with similar results. . . .

It has sometimes been urged that amount of education is an effect,
rather than a cause, of intelligence, the more intelligent children stay-
ing longer at school and doing better in their school work. This is
certainly true in part, but there is no doubt that opportunity, as determined mainly by economic status, also enters. In addition, there is
direct evidence that schooling is important in determining the level
of the I. Q. . . .

These studies [by Barrett and Koch, Wellman, and others] make it
clear that merely equating two groups for school grade and assuming
that therefore their training has been substantially identical can hardly
be justified. Four years of schooling in a southern rural Negro school
are certainly not equivalent to four years in a White school in New
York or Chicago. It would be difficult to overemphasize the frequent
discrepancy in per capita expenditures, in equipment and facilities, in
the training of the teachers and in the length of the school term. In
spite of this, many of the comparisons upon which the conclusions
regarding racial differences are based involve groups whose schooling
is equally disparate. The study by Foreman has demonstrated a close
correspondence between scores on achievement tests and expenditures
for the schooling of Negro children in a number of southern rural communities. It would be interesting to repeat this study with tests of
intelligence. In any case, there seems to be little doubt that the inadequate schooling of the average southern Negro child may also be
regarded as playing an important part in test performance. . . .

Although it is true . . . that Negroes rank below Whites in most intelligence test studies, it must also be kept in mind that Negro groups
may differ markedly from one another, and that they are by no means
invariably inferior. It is well known, for example, that during the war
the Army testers found Negro recruits from the North far superior to
Negroes from the South, and, in the case of certain of the northern
states, superior also to southern Whites. This is shown in Table 23.

SOUTHERN WHITES AND NORTHERN NEGROES, BY STATES
ARMY RECRUITS

WHITES		NEGROES	
State	Median Score	State	Median Score
Mississippi	41.25	Pennsylvania	42.00
Kentucky	41.50	New York	45.02
Arkansas	41.55	Illinois	47.35
Georgia	42.12	Ohio	49.50

It was suggested at the time that one of two factors might account for these results: 1, the superior environment of the northern Negro, or 2, a selective migration of the more intelligent Negroes from South to North. The Army testers did not decide between these alternatives.

More recent studies, for the most part conducted upon children rather than upon adults, have in general corroborated these findings. There is on the average a difference of about seven points in the I. Q. of northern and southern Negro children. Usually the northern Negroes are still below the White norm, but in some studies they show no inferiority whatsoever. Clark, for example, gave the National Intelligence Test to 500 Negro elementary school children in five schools in Los Angeles, and obtained a median I. Q. of 104.7, which is slightly above that of the White children with whom they were compared. Peterson and Lanier gave a series of tests to twelve-year-old White and Negro boys in three different cities, Nashville, Chicago and New York. They found in general that whereas in Nashville there was a marked superiority of White over Negro boys, in Chicago this was not nearly so great, and in New York it disappeared altogether. Their conclusion was that these results could best be explained on the theory that there had been a selective migration northward, and that New York in particular had attracted an especially intelligent class of Negro migrants. Incidentally, they interpreted Clark's results in Los Angeles in a like manner.

This problem of selective migration appears to the writer to be crucial in the present status of Negro intelligence testing. If there is such a selection, the superiority of the New York and Los Angeles samples will prove nothing as to the intelligence of the average Negro; these groups will then be exceptions. If, on the other hand, there is no selective migration on the basis of intelligence, their superiority can mean only that an improved environment may raise the test scores of the Negro to the White level. In that case the whole argument for a racial difference as based on tests of intelligence will have no foundation.

A series of studies recently completed at Columbia University has been directed toward a solution of this problem. In one study the attempt was made to discover whether those Negroes who left the South for the North showed a measurable superiority in intelligence over those who stayed behind. For this purpose the school records in three southern cities, Birmingham, Nashville and Charleston (South Carolina), were examined carefully to see how the marks obtained by those

children who had migrated to the North compared with those who remained behind. The records for 1915-1930 were studied in this manner. When it was discovered that a particular Negro boy had left
Nashville, let us say, for New York or Chicago in 1927 after finishing
the fifth grade, the records were examined to determine where he had
ranked in comparison with the other members of his class. A simple
statistical formula was used for transmuting his rank into a score based
upon percentile position in the class, so that the ranks of all the children could be placed on a comparable basis. The destination of the
migrant was usually learned from the school authorities. In this way
over 500 cases were collected of migrants who were known to have gone
to one or another of the large northern cities, and the results were
analyzed for any indication of their superiority.

There was no evidence in favor of a selective migration. As it happened, the migrants from Charleston were a somewhat superior group;
those from Nashville were just about average; those from Birmingham
were definitely below. The migrants as a group were almost exactly at
the average of the whole Negro school population in these three southern cities. Whatever the selective factors in migration may be, they
appear to differ markedly for the different communities. To the extent
that school marks are a measure of ability, the use of the blanket
phrase "selective migration" is obviously unwarranted, as it is by no
means invariably the superior persons who leave. . . .

So far then, we have no right to assume that the superiority of
northern Negroes is due to selection. On the other hand, we have very
direct evidence of the degree to which the northern environment may
affect the test performance of southern-born Negro children. In our
series of studies over 3000 Negro school children in Harlem in New
York City were tested, the measures including a number of different
linguistic and performance tests—the Stanford-Binet, the National Intelligence Test, Otis Intermediate, Pintner-Paterson, Minnesota Form
Board. In each study the children examined were of the same sex, the
same age, attended the same or similar schools in Harlem, were all
southern-born and of approximately the same social and economic
status. They differed as far as could be ascertained only in one important respect, namely, the number of years during which they had
been living in New York. In each case they were compared with a
New-York-born group which was taken as the standard.

It was argued that if the superiority of the northern over the
southern Negroes is entirely due to selective migration, the length of
residence in New York City should make no appreciable difference in

the test scores, since all the migrants have presumably been selected for high intelligence. If, however, the environment has an effect, this should show itself in a gradual improvement in the test scores at least roughly proportionate to the length of time during which the superior environment has had a chance to operate. It was felt, therefore, that this procedure might make it possible to choose on strictly experimental grounds between the two alternatives.

The results vary slightly in the different studies, but almost without exception they agree in showing that the lowest scores are obtained by the groups which have most recently arrived from the South. There is a close though by no means perfect relationship between test score and length of residence in New York. . . .

There appears to be no doubt that an improvement in the environment, with all that that implies, can do a great deal to raise the intelligence test scores. Interestingly enough, this improvement seems to take place most markedly in the first five or six years; those children who have lived in New York for a longer period seem to show little further advancement. The subjects in these studies were all ten- and twelve-year-old children; and the results probably mean that when the school years have been spent entirely in New York City, the environmental opportunities may be said to have been equalized. It should be added that with the performance tests this result is not so clear, and that the environmental effect appears largely to be restricted, as far as these studies go, to tests with a definite linguistic component.

Two further checks were applied to this material. In one of the studies, anthropometric measurements were taken in order to determine whether the various migrating groups differed from one another in their possession of Negroid characteristics. It was found that the New-York-born group was a little less Negroid than those born in the South, but there was no difference between the groups corresponding to their length of residence in New York. This factor therefore can obviously not account for the observed differences in intelligence. In the second place, the question was asked whether there was any indication that the quality of the migrants was deteriorating, and that this fact rather than the change in the environment might account for the better showing of the earlier migrants. This was studied by comparing in two successive years two groups of twelve-year-old boys who had lived in New York the same length of time. The results showed that almost invariably the later migrants were superior. There is therefore no indication of a deterioration in the quality of the more recent migrants, and the correspondence between test score and length of residence in

New York seems to be due to the influence of the better environment. . . .

Even in the northern cities the Negro children are usually below the White norms, although Clark's study in Los Angeles and Peterson's and Lanier's in New York showed no such inferiority. The real test of Negro-White equality as far as intelligence tests are concerned can be met only by a study in a region in which Negroes suffer no discrimination whatsoever and enjoy exactly the same educational and economic opportunities. Such a region is difficult to find, although there may be an approximation to it in Martinique or Brazil. . . . It is safe to say that as the environment of the Negro approximates more and more closely that of the White, his inferiority tends to disappear.

It is the writer's opinion that this is where the problem of Negro intelligence now stands. The direct comparison between Negroes and Whites will always remain a doubtful procedure because of the impossibility of controlling the various factors which may influence the results. Intelligence tests may therefore not be used as measures of group differences in native ability, though they may be used profitably as measures of accomplishment. When comparisons are made within the same race or group, it can be demonstrated that there are very marked differences depending upon variations in background. These differences may be satisfactorily explained, therefore, without recourse to the hypothesis of innate racial differences in mental ability.

(1935)

U. S. Supreme Court

Norris v. Alabama

(1935)

60.

In the Norris v. Alabama or second "Scottsboro" case the U. S. Supreme Court found that Negroes had been excluded from juries because of their race, and held that their rights to equal protection under the law (14th Amendment) had again been violated.

NORRIS v. ALABAMA, Supreme Court of the U. S. (Certiorari to the Supreme Court of Alabama) 294 U. S. 587

OPINION OF THE COURT

MR. CHIEF JUSTICE HUGHES delivered the opinion of the Court.

Petitioner, Clarence Norris, is one of nine Negro boys who were indicted in March, 1931, in Jackson County, Alabama, for the crime of rape. On being brought to trial in that county, eight were convicted. The Supreme Court of Alabama reversed the conviction of one of these and affirmed that of seven, including Norris. This Court reversed the judgments of conviction upon the ground that the defendants had been denied due process of law in that the trial court had failed in the light of the circumstances disclosed, and of the inability of the defendants at that time to obtain counsel, to make an effective appointment of counsel to aid them in preparing and presenting their defense. *Powell* v. *Alabama*, 287 U.S. 45.

After the remand, a motion for change of venue was granted and the cases were transferred to Morgan County. Norris was brought to trial in November, 1933. At the outset, a motion was made on his behalf to quash the indictment upon the ground of the exclusion of Negroes from juries in Jackson County where the indictment was found. A motion was also made to quash the trial *venire* in Morgan County upon the ground of the exclusion of Negroes from juries in that county. In relation to each county, the charge was of long continued, systematic and arbitrary exclusion of qualified Negro citizens from service on juries, solely because of their race and color, in violation of the Constitution of the United States. The State joined issue on this charge and after hearing the evidence, which we shall presently review, the trial judge denied both motions, and exception was taken. The trial then proceeded and resulted in the conviction of Norris, who was sentenced to death. On appeal, the Supreme Court of the State considered and decided the federal question which Norris had raised, and affirmed the judgment. 229 Ala. 226; 156 So. 556. We granted a writ of certiorari. 293 U.S. 552.

First. There is no controversy as to the constitutional principle involved. That principle, long since declared, was not challenged, but was expressly recognized, by the Supreme Court of the State. Summing up precisely the effect of earlier decisions, this Court thus stated the principle in *Carter* v. *Texas,* 177 U.S. 442, 447, in relation to exclusion from service on grand juries: "Whenever by any action of a State, whether through its legislature, through its courts, or through its executive or administrative officers, all persons of the African race are excluded, solely because of their race or color, from serving as grand jurors in the criminal prosecution of a person of the African race, the equal protection of the laws is denied to him, contrary to the Fourteenth Amendment of the Constitution of the United States. . . ."

The question is of the application of this established principle to the facts disclosed by the record. That the question is one of fact does not relieve us of the duty to determine whether in truth a federal right has been denied. When a federal right has been specially set up and claimed in a state court, it is our province to inquire not merely whether it was denied in express terms but also whether it was denied in substance and effect. If this requires an examination of evidence, that examination must be made. Otherwise, review by this Court would fail of its purpose in safeguarding constitutional rights. Thus, whenever a conclusion of law of a state court as to a federal right and findings of fact are so intermingled that the latter control the former, it is incumbent upon us to analyze the facts in order that the appropriate enforcement of the federal right may be assured. . . .

Second. The evidence on the motion to quash the indictment. In 1930, the total population of Jackson County, where the indictment was found, was 36,881, of whom 2688 were Negroes. The male population over twenty-one years of age numbered 8801, and of these, 666 were Negroes.

The qualifications of jurors were thus prescribed by the state statute (Alabama Code, 1923, § 8603): "The jury commission shall place on the jury roll and in the jury box the names of all male citizens of the county who are generally reputed to be honest and intelligent men, and are esteemed in the community for their integrity, good character and sound judgment, but no person must be selected who is under twenty-one or over sixty-five years of age, or, who is an habitual drunkard, or who, being afflicted with a permanent disease or physical weakness is unfit to discharge the duties of a juror, or who cannot read English, or who has ever been convicted of any offense involving moral turpitude. If a person cannot read English and has all the other qualifications prescribed herein and is a freeholder or householder, his name may be placed on the jury roll and in the jury box." See Gen. Acts, Alabama, 1931, No. 47, p. 59.

Defendant adduced evidence to support the charge of unconstitutional discrimination in the actual administration of the statute in Jackson County. The testimony, as the state court said, tended to show that "in a long number of years no Negro had been called for jury service in that county." It appeared that no Negro had served on any grand or petit jury in that county within the memory of witnesses who had lived there all their lives. Testimony to that effect was given by men whose ages ran from fifty to seventy-six years. Their testimony was uncontradicted. It was supported by the testimony of officials. . . .

That testimony in itself made out a *prima facie* case of the denial of the equal protection which the Constitution guarantees. . . . The case thus made was supplemented by direct testimony that specified Negroes, thirty or more in number, were qualified for jury service. Among these were Negroes who were members of school boards, or trustees, of colored schools, and property owners and householders. It also appeared that Negroes from that county had been called for jury service in the federal court. Several of those who were thus described as qualified were witnesses. . . .

The question arose whether names of Negroes were in fact on the jury roll. The books containing the jury roll for Jackson County for the year 1930-31 were produced. . . . On the pages of this roll appeared the names of six Negroes. They were entered, respectively, at the end of the precinct lists which were alphabetically arranged. The genuineness of these entries was disputed. It appeared that after the jury roll in question had been made up, and after the new jury commission had taken office, one of the new commissioners directed the new clerk to draw lines after the names which had been placed on the roll by the preceding commission. These lines, on the pages under consideration, were red lines, and the clerk of the old commission testified that they were not put in by him. The entries made by the new clerk, for the new jury roll, were below these lines.

The names of the six Negroes were in each instance written immediately above the red lines. An expert of long experience testified that these names were superimposed upon the red lines, that is, that they were written after the lines had been drawn. The expert was not cross-examined and no testimony was introduced to contradict him. In denying the motion to quash, the trial judge expressed the view that he would not "be authorized to presume that somebody had committed a crime" or to presume that the jury board "had been unfaithful to their duties and allowed the books to be tampered with." His conclusion was that names of Negroes were on the jury roll.

We think that the evidence did not justify that conclusion. The Supreme Court of the State did not sustain it. . . .

. . . As we have seen, there was testimony, not overborne or discredited, that there were in fact Negroes in the county qualified for jury service. That testimony was direct and specific. After eliminating those persons as to whom there was some evidence of lack of qualifications, a considerable number of others remained. The fact that the testimony as to these persons, fully identified, was not challenged by evidence appropriately direct, cannot be brushed aside. There is no ground for an assumption that the names of these Negroes were not on the preliminary list. The inference to be drawn from the testimony is that they were on that preliminary list, and were designated on that list as the names of Negroes, and that they were not placed on the jury roll. There was thus presented a test of the practice of the commissioners. Something more than mere general asseverations was required. Why were these names excluded from the jury roll? Was it because of the lack of statutory qualifications? Were the qualifications of Negroes actually and properly considered?

The testimony of the commissioner on this crucial question puts the case in a strong light. That testimony leads to the conclusion that these or other Negroes were not excluded on account of age, or lack of esteem in the community for integrity and judgment, or because of disease or want of any other qualification. The commissioner's answer to specific inquiry upon this point was that Negroes were "never discussed." . . .

We are of the opinion that the evidence required a different result from that reached in the state court. We think that the evidence that for a generation or longer no Negro had been called for service on any jury in Jackson County, that there were Negroes qualified for jury service, that according to the practice of the jury commission their names would normally appear on the preliminary list of male citizens of the requisite age but that no names of Negroes were placed on the jury roll, and the testimony with respect to the lack of appropriate consideration of the qualifications of Negroes, established the discrimination which the Constitution forbids. The motion to quash the indictment upon that ground should have been granted. . . .

In *Neal* v. *Delaware, supra* [103 U.S. 370], decided over fifty years ago, this Court observed that it was a "violent presumption," in which the state court had there indulged, that the uniform exclusion of Negroes from juries, during a period of many years, was solely because, in the judgment of the officers, charged with the selection of grand and petit jurors, fairly exercised, "the black race in Delaware were utterly disqualified by want of intelligence, experience, or moral integrity, to sit on juries." Such a presumption at the present time would be no less violent with respect to the exclusion of the Negroes of Morgan County. And, upon the proof contained in the record now before us, a conclusion that their continuous and total exclusion from juries was because there were none possessing the requisite qualifications, cannot be sustained.

We are concerned only with the federal question which we have discussed, and in view of the denial of the federal right suitably asserted, the judgment must be reversed and the cause remanded for further proceedings not inconsistent with this opinion.

Reversed.

(1935)

61

John Dewey
(1859-1952)

John Dewey, distinguished American philosopher and educator, recognized democracy as a basic source of ethical value.

from "Democracy and Educational Administration"

Belief in equality is an element of the democratic credo. It is not, however, belief in equality of natural endowments. Those who proclaimed the idea of equality did not suppose they were enunciating a psychological doctrine, but a legal and political one. All individuals are entitled to equality of treatment by law and in its administration. Each one is affected equally in quality if not in quantity by the institutions under which he lives and has an equal right to express his judgment, although the weight of his judgment may not be equal in amount when it enters into the pooled result to that of others. In short, each one is equally an individual and entitled to equal opportunity of development of his own capacities, be they large or small in range. Moreover, each has needs of his own, as significant to him as those of others are to them. The very fact of natural and psychological inequality is all the more reason for establishment by law of equality of opportunity, since otherwise the former becomes a means of oppression of the less gifted.

While what we call intelligence [may] be distributed in unequal amounts, it is the democratic faith that it is sufficiently general so that each individual has something to contribute, whose value can be assessed only as [it] enters into the final pooled intelligence constituted by the contributions of all. Every authoritarian scheme, on the contrary, assumes that its value may be assessed by some *prior* principle, if not of family and birth or race and color or possession of material wealth, then by the position and rank a person occupies in the existing social scheme. The democratic faith in equality is the faith that each individual shall have the chance and opportunity to contribute whatever he is capable of contributing and that the value of his contribution be decided by its place and function in the organized total of similar contributions, not on the basis of prior status of any kind whatever.

(1937)

Walter T. Stace

(1886-   )

W. T. Stace, former British civil servant in Ceylon and Emeritus Professor of Philosophy at Princeton, analyzes equality in the light of basic moral conceptions.

62.

from The Concept of Morals

Justice, then, is a simple idea. And it may be defined as *the recognition* (I mean, of course, the recognition in practical action, not merely theoretical or intellectual recognition) *of the intrinsic equality of all persons as persons.* Another way of stating the same idea is to say that it is the recognition of the truth *that I = I,* i.e., that every I is intrinsically, or as an I, equal to every other I.

Actually, of course, men are unequal in all kinds of different ways—in ability, in goodness, in the extent and character of their needs, in the nature of their surrounding circumstances. But all these differences are *extrinsic,* that is, they do not arise from the essentials of the persons as persons, but from the fact that each person is this or that particular sort of person. One man is hungry, another sated (difference of needs). One is good, another bad (difference of merits or deserts). One is stupid, another clever (difference of ability). One is fortunate, another unfortunate (difference of surrounding circumstances). But all these differences are extrinsic, because none of them is of the essence of personality. To be a person, a man need not be hungry. And he need not be sated. And so of the other differences. None of them are essential to being a person. None of them are intrinsic to personality.

Now justice does not deny any of these extrinsic differences between persons. Nor does it deny that persons must be treated differently on the basis of their extrinsic differences. It does not deny, for example, that a hungry man may justly be given more than a sated person, nor that a good man may deserve more than a bad man. It can fully admit that both needs and deserts should be taken into account in the distribution of satisfactions. What it does deny, however, is that there ought ever to be any difference of treatment between different persons *except* on the basis of extrinsic differences of circumstances, character, or what not. It denies that there ought to be any different treatment of different persons simply as persons. It says that *intrinsically* all persons are equal.

This, it might be said, is self-evident, and therefore pointless, since there *are* no differences between persons other than extrinsic differences. According to the account just given, all differences whatever between persons are extrinsic, and no such things as intrinsic differences exist at all. And this would indeed be a very good way of expressing the principle of justice. The principle simply states that there are no intrinsic differences between persons. This, in fact, is the same as saying that they are all intrinsically equal. And since this arises from the mere definition of extrinsic, it is a pointless analytic proposition without content. No one could possibly deny it, and therefore there can be no point in asserting it.

And yet people do deny it—in their *actions*, if not theoretically and intellectually. *Practically* to deny it is in fact the root of all injustice. And we can best see this, and see at the same time the point of the principle, if we take for examination that particular type of justice which we have called altruism. Suppose that there is a question how certain satisfactions are to be divided between me and my neighbour. And suppose that I alone have the power to decide this question. I can take all, or give all, or divide as I please. This is the sort of situation which tests whether a man is selfish or unselfish, just or unjust. Now justice does not necessarily ordain that I ought to make an equal division. If all our respective needs, deserts, and other relevant circumstances were identical, then the just division would be an equal division. But if either my needs or my deserts are greater than my neighbour's, I may be acting justly and with perfectly proper altruism if I assign to myself more than I do to him. Injustice and selfishness will only arise if I give myself more, not on the basis of any extrinsic differences, but *because I am attaching to my own personality an intrinsically higher value than I attach to his.* I am unjust and selfish if I give myself more, on no proper grounds such as deserts or needs, but simply because *I am I.* I am then forgetting or denying that he is also an I and, simply as such, is entitled to as much as I am. The root of all selfishness, and indeed in the end the root of all evil, lies in the fact that each man tends to prefer himself simply because he is himself, and apart from any question of needs or deserts or any other circumstances. This is the denial of justice. And justice simply means the principle that, apart from such special needs, deserts, qualities, circumstances, all men are entitled to the same treatment. Intrinsically— and the word intrinsically simply means "apart from such special needs, deserts, qualities, circumstances"—all persons are of equal value and are entitled to identical treatment.

This principle is embodied in jurisprudence in the maxim that all men are equal before the law. This is not a denial of the obvious differences and inequalities which exist among men. Nor does the law divide up things equally between all men. It takes account of extrinsic differences, and bases upon them its differences of treatment. But it insists that, apart from these extrinsic differences, no differences of treatment are justified. It insists that no one can claim *privilege,* none can claim that, apart from special superiorities in his deserts, his abilities, or his circumstances, he is entitled to more consideration than other people. The equality of all men before the law is thus the juridical expression of the philosophical principle of the intrinsic equality of all persons as persons.

Another way of expressing the same idea is to say that justice is *impartiality.*

(1937)

U. S. Supreme Court

Missouri ex rel. Gaines v. Canada

63.

(1938)

In this case the Supreme Court decided that the State of Missouri's obligation to accord equal educational facilities could not be met by providing the petitioner with tuition in a law school in another state.

MISSOURI ex rel. GAINES v. CANADA, REGISTRAR OF THE UNIVERSITY OF MISSOURI, et al., Supreme Court of the U. S. (Certiorari to the Supreme Court of Missouri) 305 U. S. 337

OPINION OF THE COURT

Mr. Chief Justice Hughes delivered the opinion of the Court.

Petitioner Lloyd Gaines, a Negro, was refused admission to the School of Law at the State University of Missouri. Asserting that this refusal constituted a denial by the State of the equal protection of the laws in violation of the Fourteenth Amendment of the Federal Constitution, petitioner brought this action for mandamus to compel the curators of the University to admit him. On final hearing, an alternative writ was quashed and a peremptory writ was denied by the Circuit Court. The Supreme Court of the State affirmed the judgment. 113 S.W. 2d 783. We granted certiorari, October 10, 1938.

Petitioner is a citizen of Missouri. In August, 1935, he was graduated with the degree of Bachelor of Arts at the Lincoln University, an institution maintained by the State of Missouri for the higher education of Negroes. That University has no law school. Upon the filing of his application for admission to the law school of the University of Missouri, the registrar advised him to communicate with the president of Lincoln University and the latter directed petitioner's attention to § 9622 of the Revised Statutes of Missouri. . . .

Petitioner was advised to apply to the State Superintendent of Schools for aid under that statute. It was admitted on the trial that petitioner's "work and credits at the Lincoln University would qualify him for admission to the School of Law of the University of Missouri if he were found otherwise eligible." He was refused admission upon the ground that it was "contrary to the constitution, laws and public policy of the State to admit a Negro as a student in the University of

Missouri." It appears that there are schools of law in connection with the state universities of four adjacent States, Kansas, Nebraska, Iowa and Illinois, where nonresident Negroes are admitted. . . .

. . . While there is no express constitutional provision requiring that the white and Negro races be separated for the purpose of higher education, the state court on a comprehensive review of the state statutes held that it was intended to separate the white and Negro races for that purpose also. Referring in particular to Lincoln University, the court deemed it to be clear "that the Legislature intended to bring the Lincoln University up to the standard of the University of Missouri, and give to the whites and Negroes an equal opportunity for higher education—the whites at the University of Missouri, and the Negroes at Lincoln University." Further, the court concluded that the provisions of § 9622 . . . to the effect that Negro residents "may attend the university of any adjacent State with their tuition paid, pending the full development of Lincoln University," made it evident "that the Legislature did not intend that Negroes and whites should attend the same university in this State." In that view it necessarily followed that the curators of the University of Missouri acted in accordance with the policy of the State in denying petitioner admission to its School of Law upon the sole ground of his race.

In answering petitioner's contention that this discrimination constituted a denial of his constitutional right, the state court has fully recognized the obligation of the State to provide Negroes with advantages for higher education substantially equal to the advantages afforded to white students. The State has sought to fulfill that obligation by furnishing equal facilities in separate schools, a method the validity of which has been sustained by our decisions. . . .

The state court stresses the advantages that are afforded by the law schools of the adjacent States,—Kansas, Nebraska, Iowa and Illinois,—which admit non-resident Negroes. The court considered that these were schools of high standing where one desiring to practice law in Missouri can get "as sound, comprehensive, valuable legal education" as in the University of Missouri; that the system of education in the former is the same as that in the latter and is designed to give the students a basis for the practice of law in any State where the Anglo-American system of law obtains; that the law school of the University of Missouri does not specialize in Missouri law and that the course of study and the case books used in the five schools are substantially identical. Petitioner insists that for one intending to practice in Missouri there are special advantages in attending a law school there, both in relation to the opportunities for the particular study of Missouri law and for the observation of the local courts, and also in view of the prestige of the Missouri law school among the citizens of the State, his prospective clients. Proceeding with its examination of relative advantages, the state court found that the difference in distances to be traveled afforded no substantial ground of complaint and that there was an adequate appropriation to meet the full tuition fees which petitioner would have to pay.

We think that these matters are beside the point. The basic consideration is not as to what sort of opportunities other States provide, or whether they are as good as those in Missouri, but as to what opportunities Missouri itself furnishes to white students and denies to Negroes solely upon the ground of color. The admissibility of laws separating the races in the enjoyment of privileges afforded by the State rests wholly upon the equality of the privileges which the laws give to the separated groups within the State. The question here is not of a duty of the State to supply legal training, or of the quality of the training which it does supply, but of its duty when it provides such training to furnish it to the residents of the State upon the basis of an equality of right. By the operation of the laws of Missouri a privilege has been created for white law students which is denied to Negroes by reason of their race. The white resident is afforded legal education within the State; the Negro resident having the same qualifications is refused it there and must go outside the State to obtain it. That is a denial of the equality of legal right to the enjoyment of the privilege which the State has set up, and the provision for the payment of tuition fees in another State does not remove the discrimination. . . .

We do not find that the decision of the state court turns on any procedural question. The action was for mandamus, but it does not appear that the remedy would have been deemed inappropriate if the asserted federal right had been sustained. In that situation the remedy by mandamus was found to be a proper one in *University of Maryland* v. *Murray, supra* [169 Md. 478]. In the instant case, the state court did note that petitioner had not applied to the management of Lincoln University for legal training. But, as we have said, the state court did not rule that it would have been the duty of the curators to grant such an application, but on the contrary took the view, as we understand it, that the curators were entitled under the state law to refuse such an application and in its stead to provide for petitioner's tuition in an adjacent State. That conclusion presented the federal question as to the constitutional adequacy of such a provision while equal opportunity for legal training within the State was not furnished, and this federal question the state court entertained and passed upon. We must conclude that in so doing the court denied the federal right which petitioner set up and the question as to the correctness of that decision is before us. We are of the opinion that the ruling was error, and that petitioner was entitled to be admitted to the law school of the State University in the absence of other and proper provision for his legal training within the State.

The judgment of the Supreme Court of Missouri is reversed and the cause is remanded for further proceedings not inconsistent with this opinion.

Reversed.

(1938)

Jacques Maritain

64. (1882-   )

French neo-Thomistic philosopher and Catholic liberal reveals here his interest in the application of Christian ethics to contemporary problems.

from Ransoming the Time

The equality in nature among men consists of their concrete communion in the mystery of the human species; it does not lie in an idea, it is hidden in the heart of the individual and of the concrete, in the roots of the substance of each man. Obscure because residing on the level of substance and its root energies, primordial because it is bound up with the very sources of being, human equality reveals itself, like the nearness of our neighbour, to every one who practices it; indeed it is identical with that proximity of all to each, and of each to all. If you treat a man as a man, that is to say if you respect and love the secret he carries within him and the good of which he is capable, to that extent do you make effective in yourself his closeness in nature to and his equality or unity in nature with yourself. It is the natural love of the human being for his own kind which reveals and makes real the unity of species among men. As long as love does not call it forth, that unity slumbers in a metaphysical retreat where we can perceive it only as an abstraction.

In the common experience of misery, in the common sorrow of great catastrophes, in humiliation and distress, under the blows of the executioner or the bombs of total war, in concentration camps, in the hovels of starving people in great cities, in any common *necessity,* the doors of solitude open and man recognizes man. Man also recognizes man when the sweetness of a great joy or of a great love for an instant clears his eyes. Whenever he does a service to his fellow men or is helped by them, whenever he shares the same elementary actions and the same elementary emotions, whenever he truly considers his neighbour, the simplest action discovers for him, both in others and in himself, the common resources and the common goodness—primitive, rudimentary, wounded, unconscious and repressed—of human nature. At once the realness of equality and community in nature is revealed to him as a very precious thing, an unknown marvel, a fundamental basis of existence, more important than all the differences and inequalities superimposed upon it. When he will have returned to his routine pleasures, he will have forgotten this discovery.

The authentic instinct of equality in nature, which naturally underlies and strengthens the fragile conception that our heedless intelligence can gain of this same equality when we retain that realist perspective which I have endeavoured to describe, is no secondary tendency like pride or envy, no matter how deep-seated it is within us; it is a primary instinct, the instinct of communication founded on a common membership in the same specific whole. The realist conception of equality in nature is an inheritance of the judeo-christian tradition; it is a natural prerequisite for Christian thought and life. Just as there is in every being a natural love for God above all else, without which charity would not serve to perfect nature but to destroy it, so also, however it may be weakened by sin, there must be in man a natural love for his own kind without which the love of the gospel for men of every race and every condition would be contrary to nature rather than its exaltation. How should we all be called upon thus to love one another in God if we were not all equal in our condition and specific dignity as rational creatures?

Christianity confirms and emphasizes the concrete sense of equality in nature by affirming its historical and genealogical character, and by teaching that here we are concerned with a blood relationship, properly so-called, all men being descended from the same original parents, and being brothers in Adam before they are brothers in Christ. Heirs of the same sin and the same weaknesses, but heirs also of the same original greatness, all created in the image of God and all called to the same supernatural dignity as adopted sons of God, and to coheirship with Christ the Saviour, all redeemed by the same life-giving Blood, and thus destined to become equals of the angels in heaven, what Christian can look upon man with the demented gaze of racist pride? The *unity of mankind* is at the basis of Christianity. Pius XII asserts it from the eminence of the chair of Peter, when he condemns, as the first of the pernicious errors so widespread today, "The forgetting of that law of human solidarity and charity, required and imposed as much *by the community of origin and by the equality of rational nature among all men*, to whatever people they may belong, as by the sacrifice of redemption offered up by Jesus Christ. . . ." After having recalled to mind the insight which Saint Paul gives us on this matter, the Pope adds, "Marvellous insight which makes us contemplate the human race in the unity of its origin in God; in the unity of its nature similarly composed in all men of a material body and a spiritual and

immortal soul; in the unity of its immediate end and of its mission in
the world; in the unity of its dwelling place—the earth, the goods of
which all men, by natural right, can utilize to sustain and develop life;
in the unity of its supernatural end—God Himself, toward whom all
should strive; in the unity of the means to attain this end; . . . in the
unity of its relation to the Son of God; . . . in the unity of its redemption worked for all men by Christ."

It is because the Christian conception of life is based upon so concrete, broad, and fruitful a certainty of the equality and community in
nature between men that it, at the same time, insists so forcefully on
the orderings and hierarchies which spring and should spring from the
very heart of this essential community, and on the particular inequalities which they necessarily involve. For in the world of man as in the
world of creation, there can be no concourse or communication, no life
or movement without differentiation, no differentiation without inequalities.

Christianity fearlessly asserts the necessity of these inequalities; it
respects them, furthers them, favours them, for it knows that as long
as they remain normal—that is as long as the human will, by a kind of
perversion, does not undertake to make them serve as means of exclusion rather than of communication and make them crush the essential equality and the primordial community which they presuppose—
the inequalities, which lend variety to human life and intensify the
richness of life's encounters, in no way injure the dignities which befit
the unity of mankind and the rights which are grounded on this unity.
On the contrary, these inequalities make such a unity all the more
manifest. Every man is a man in his very essence, but no man is man in
essence, that is, exhausts in himself all the riches of the various perfections of which human-kind is capable. In this sense all the diversity of
perfections and virtues distributed through the generations of men in
space and time is but a varied participation in the common and in-
exhaustible potentialities of man.

The term *unity of mankind* is the Christian name, and the truest
name, of the equality in nature between men. It helps us to purify
the idea of that equality from all erroneous associations and implications, whether they arise from a geometric imagination or from a
passion for levelling. An arithmetic equality between two numbers
excludes all inequality between them, but equality in nature between
men, or the unity of human nature, for its full flowering demands
individual inequalities. To affirm the equality in nature between men

is for idealist egalitarianism to wish that all inequality among them should disappear. To affirm the equality in nature between men, or the unity of human nature, is for Christian realism to wish that those fruitful inequalities, whereby the multitude of individuals participates in the common treasure of humanity, should develop themselves. Egalitarian idealism interprets the word equality on a plane surface; realism interprets it with the dimension of depth as well. Not only should one conceive of equality as something fundamental from which arises an infinite number of differences, but equality itself is a profound thing—organic, intensive, and qualitative. Let us not say that one man is as good as another; that is a nihilistic formula which acquires real meaning only from deep religious pessimism (vanitas vanitatum, omnis homo mendax). Let us say that in a man are, virtualiter, all men. The Son of Man who "knows what there is within man" perceives in each man all men.

Thus we must assert both that equality in essence which unites men in rational nature and those natural individual inequalities which arise from this very unity or equality. But from this very fact we also recognize that it is equality which is primordial, and inequalities which are secondary. Because, speaking absolutely, the community of essence is of greater importance than individual differences; the root is more important than the branches.

The Church recently gave brilliant testimony to this primacy of equality in nature over derivative inequalities when on October 28, 1939, on the feast of Christ the King and while Europe was going into a period of convulsions which would make us lose hope for her if we had not hope in God, the Pope consecrated over the tomb of Saint Peter twelve bishops belonging to the most diverse peoples and groups of peoples, several of whom were men of colour. "Those who enter the Church, whatever may be their origin and their language," said he on this occasion, "must know that they have an equal right as sons in the house of the Lord, wherein reign the law and peace of Christ." But if this equality in the Church is established upon baptism and the grace of divine adoption, who can fail to see that it necessarily presupposes a similar fundamental equality in the order of nature? The exercise of episcopal government brings into play natural gifts and virtues as well as infused gifts. And here we have white men, according to the regions where they happen to live, who can be governed on the road to their eternal destiny by bishops of the yellow or black race, just as yellow or black men can be governed by bishops of the white race.

With regard to social life it is important at the outset to note that there too, and for the same reasons indicated above, there are and must be equality and inequalities; and that inequalities—which are normal, consubstantial with social life, flourishing everywhere— are and must be secondary. Equality is primary, inasmuch as it relates (as equality pure and simple) to the fundamental rights and common dignity of human beings, and (as equality of proportion) to justice.

Indeed, among all peoples that which is thus secondary, the inequalities, most often conceals that which is primary, not only because in general inequalities exist everywhere and are the more apparent, but doubtless also because in the social order men have always made much of inequalities, in themselves fragile and of human origin, by means of marks and insignia, manifestations of power and trappings of fear, thus trying to solidify and stabilize them. It remains true that, whatever may be the forms of a given society and the inequalities they involve, it is not only a denial of the Evangelical virtues, but in the natural order itself a baseness, an offence against creation, to treat as an *inferior man* a man belonging to some inferior part of the social structure, to make him conceive his inferior social condition as an inferiority of essence. To do this is to place in a relationship of effective prevarication both him who scorns and him who is scorned. If a man is of an inferior social condition, he is there not by virtue of one of those pseudo-essential necessities clarified in the first part of this chapter. Far from relegating him once and for all to his condition, it is only right to honour in him the powers and potentialities of human nature, thanks to which he might have found himself in a higher position if he had been born in some other cradle, or if the fortunes of life had offered him other opportunities, or if he had taken better advantage of those in fact offered him.

Ever since the New Law brought on earth liberated and energized the natural movement of history—in the very depths of the conflict occasioned by its opposing forces, which themselves became energized —this natural movement has not tended to iron out social inequalities; it has tended rather to bring them back to their proper proportions and to their secondary character with respect to common human dignity. To speak more generally, and concerning the demands of inequality as well as of equality, it can be said that, in the toilsome development of mankind and of reason, in proportion as the normal aspirations of the human personality succeed, under whatever given conditions, in more or less perfectly achieving reality, to the same extent the natural law—taken not as an abstract code but in its historical growth, which is itself natural—tends progressively to make explicit the potential requirements contained within its principles, and the positive law tends in its own sphere to open itself more to the influences of nature.

Certain social inequalities result from natural inequalities or are required by them. It is just that that part which by innate or acquired superiority renders more services to the whole should receive more in return. It is also just or equitable that individuals should receive in proportion not to their needs or desires, which tend to become infinite, but to the necessities of their life and development, the means for putting to use their natural gifts. In this sense the more a man has, the more he should receive. The same care that men bestow upon their rare plants or their most beautiful stallions they do not bestow upon the superior persons who are an honour to their own species. This is in itself an offence against nature; even though men's awkwardness is such that it is better for genius not to receive their care.

Other social inequalities, however, are themselves of social origin. It is important to concentrate our attention on these typically social inequalities, of which Pascal liked to point out both the importance and the whimsicality and which egalitarianism least understands. It is from the needs proper to the internal differentiation of the social body, indeed, not from the natural merits of the individuals who happen to be embodied in one or another of its parts, that arise the inequalities in duties and advantages attached to these parts. An imbecile king remains the king. The *orders* of the Old Régime may have given way to the *classes* (in the strict sense of the word) of our present régime, and these in their turn may give way to "bodies" having varied statuses. Always will some inequalities of intrinsically social origin bear witness to the inconquerable originality and vitality which belong to social life as such. It is clear, on the other hand, that such inequalities turn into a perversion of political life and into barbarism if bewildered men wish to erect them into a state of social servitude for the human groups assumed to be inferior.

Social equality itself, in so far as it merits the name, has also a value which is properly and truly social. Although it is based upon unity and equality in nature, it is not to be confused with it; it is rather an expression or development thereof in the social order. This is first of all that equality, recognized and sanctioned by society, in those rights—so hard to specify but none the less real—which we call the fundamental rights of the human person: the right to exist, to keep one's body whole, to found a family (itself assured the enjoyment of its liberties); the right of association, the right to the private ownership of material goods, the right to seek those good things through which a rational creature may perfect himself, the right to travel toward eternal life along the road one's conscience acknowledges as designated by God. It is also that equality in the respect which human dignity requires that social customs show to all men, by treating them all as men, not as things. Then again, it is "political equality, equality of all before the law, whether it represses or protects, the making available to all citizens of public employment." The institution of these last three equalities by the temporal power is derived, as the late Cardinal Verdier wrote, from the "evangelical streams released by Christ throughout the world." It is, finally, that equal condition as coheirs of the effort of all, in accordance with which all should in so far as possible participate "free of charge" in the elementary goods needed for human life.

This social equality is thus, in its own way and like equality in nature, not a surface thing, but lies deep; and it includes essential differences, not only in degrees and modes, but in its basis in the law. I have said that this equality, with its differing forms and degrees, has, as the term "social equality" sufficiently indicates, a proper and real social value. Let it be added that it possesses this in a different way from the social inequalities, in this sense that, taken all in all, the inequalities proceed from society more than from nature, whereas social equality proceeds from nature more than from society. It is by virtue either of the exigencies or of the wishes of human nature that, taking into account the different degrees I have pointed out in the domain of natural law, common law, or positive law, social equality assumes in society the proper and real social value about which I have spoken. The fundamental rights of the human person are in themselves anterior to civil society, and the equality of these rights has social value only in so far as society recognizes and sanctions them in its own order. The other kinds of equality, although they derive from nature as their principle, as does society itself, rise up progressively in the midst of society, like a social flowering forth or fructifying of the equality of nature. In any case social equality is not a condition of existence set by "nature" for "all men," like

their arms and legs or the colour of their eyes, which social life, unexpectedly coming into being, needs thereafter only to protect, as
Jean-Jacques Rousseau would have it. Social equality is a condition
of existence which, whether in its various degrees it be postulated
or desired more or less imperiously by nature, achieves reality in society. "All men" are not born in this effective condition of existence.
The members of a sufficiently developed civil community obtain it
from the community through natural law or through positive law,
either by virtue of being men (if it is a question of the fundamental
rights of the person) or, if it is a question of other kinds of equality,
by virtue of being citizens.

In itself, and when its nature is not vitiated by absolute egalitarianism, the multiform social equality which we have been discussing
favours the development of natural inequalities, because in opening to each a greater number of possibilities, it favours at the same
time differences in growth and in development. And on the other
hand it requires that these natural inequalities be compensated for
by a process of organic redistribution, by virtue of which the weak
and the less favoured share in the benefits which the social whole
owes to others.

Similarly, in so far as the true character and the true rôle of social equality are effectively recognized, this social equality, serving
as a seemingly natural ground for social inequalities of structure and
function, gives them more intrinsic stability than the artifices of
constraint can give; yet on the other hand it requires that these social inequalities be compensated for in two ways: first, by the fact
that the conditions to which they correspond be not closed but open
(open for the circulation of elements which come from other levels);
and second, by the fact that in each one of these conditions individuals may enjoy a state of life that is truly human and may really be
able to strive (I do not say easily, because without obstacles to over-
ride there is no progress for us) for the fullness of human development.

If what I have said concerning the indestructible originality of
the social life and its proper differentiations is just, it is an illusion to
wish that all may have at the start strictly identical opportunities to
mount to the highest degrees in social life. (From the very fact that
every one is bound up in a differing social fabric, the initial opportunities of one differ from those of another; and then again it
is naïve indeed to believe that the reward of a good life should
consist in a change of social level.) But it is proper that the highest

social conditions should not of themselves be closed to any one, and even more important, it is proper that in whatever *social* structure men are involved, they should have the same opportunities to achieve —each one according to his effort and his condition—their *human* fullness, those fruits of wisdom and human virtue whose savour is not identical, but similarly good in each, whether he spends his life in working the earth, in philosophizing or in governing the State. Thus, such notions as that of equality of opportunity or equality of conditions, which egalitarianism would make chimerical, become true and proper if they are understood in the sense not of an equality pure and simple, but of a *proportional* equality.

This *equality of proportion* plays a capital rôle in the temporal community. What Proudhon and the great egalitarianists did not understand was that in the domain of relations between the social whole and its parts, such a proportional equality is justice itself. Having respect for the differences, and hence the concrete inequalities, associated with the carrying on of personal life in the midst of society—equality, by the very fact that it does not relate to an abstract Man-in-himself, but to concrete persons, in a certain fashion seeks to move over into the sphere of these very inequalities. It then becomes the equality of proportion that characterizes distributive justice, which latter deals with each in accordance with his merits. And thus, pervading and reconciling all inequalities, justice to a certain extent restores equality, thereby making civic friendship possible. For, as Thomas Aquinas put it, "friendship is a certain union or society of friends, which cannot exist among persons remote from one another, but has as its prerequisite that they have access to equality. Hence it pertains to friendship equally to use the equality which has been previously established; but it pertains to justice to lead unequals to equality. When this equality has achieved reality, the task of justice is performed. Thus equality is a final end as regards justice, but a principle as regards friendship." Finally, if equality lies at the root and inequality rests in the branches, it is a new kind of equality which, by virtue of justice, friendship, and human compassion and by virtue of the communication they provoke, is realized in the fruit.

It is well to insist upon this last statement, and elaborate its implications. Because social life, while postulated by nature, is the work of reason and virtue and implies, however opposed it may be, a movement of progressive conquest of man over nature and over himself, social equality is not something ready-made; it implies in itself a certain dynamism. Like liberty, it is itself an end to struggle for, and with difficulty, and at the price of a constant tension of the energies of the spirit. If, by postulates of nature, it is, in its most general forms, basic and primary, social equality is yet only a seed which must develop and which works in the direction of fruition. It requires not only the exercise of distributive justice in the temporal community; it requires as wide a measure as possible of free participation by all in the necessary good things, material and spiritual, and that redistribution to persons of the common good of which we spoke above. It requires the progress of social justice; the organic development of institutions of law; the participation, in more and more extensive degrees, of persons as such in political life; the transition to conditions which would really offer to each an equal opportunity (equal in the proportional sense) to bring his gifts to fruit, and which would permit the formation of an aristocracy born of personal work, that pays back the good effects of its labour for common use; the sharing more and more by all in the benefits of culture and the mind, and in that inner liberty which is given by mastery over self and knowledge of the truth.

The civilization which we have before our eyes has sought these things, but because it sought them in the wrong way it has often found their very opposites. Doubtless the illiterate craftsmen of medieval France participated more in the commonwealth of the mind than do the middle classes of today, to whom such rare technical marvels as the movies and the radio, used in disastrous fashion, as far as the masses are concerned, provide the delights of a scattered mind and the uniformity of emptiness. I am well aware of all this. Nor do I think that being illiterate is a good thing in itself. We must then renew ourselves, and we must undertake to seek the good in the good way. Such a leaven of equality as has been disseminated by pseudo-Christian egalitarianism has filled the world with unhealthy fermentations; but there is another leaven of equality which is a leaven of justice and is a proper stimulant of human history, and which tends to raise the human mass toward a way of life more truly human, wherein inequalities are not suppressed, but compensated, and subordinated to that high equality of the common use of the good things which nourish and exalt our rational nature. In sum, the error has been to seek equality in a regression toward the basis set up by "nature," and in a levelling down to this base. It should be sought in a progressive movement toward the end which is composed of the good things of rational life becoming in so far as possible and

in various degrees accessible to all, and this, thanks to the very inequalities themselves, by justice and fraternal friendship turned away
from seeking domination and toward helpfulness and cooperation.

The equality I have been discussing should be called *Christian
equality,* not only because it issues from the judeo-christian tradition
and conforms with the Christian conception of life, but also because,
if it were not for the influence of the Christian leaven injected into
secular history, and if it were not for the added stimulus, which in
its own sphere temporal civilization receives from Christian energies, this equality could not succeed in coming to pass. As there is a
flowering of the natural law which can be attained only with the
help of the virtues of the New Law, there is also a human flowering,
a real humanism of civil life which can be attained only with the
help of these virtues.

The rôle played by the irrational instincts and tendencies is major
in the political life of men. To make possible the existence of a
political life in which the dynamism of equality works in the right direction, the habits and customs which spring from the Christian virtues in the human mass must therein tame the irrational with reason
and develop right instincts. For the development among men of a real
sense of equality without egalitarianism and of that civic love, which
is not a gift of nature but an heroic conquest of reason and liberty,
in this temporal order which is the very home of conflicts, of weaknesses and of the sins of the world, the sap of the gospel, the sense
of supernatural equality of those called to a divine life, the sense
of brotherly charity must permeate this temporal order to give it life
and lift it up. "Wherever prevails a religion other than ours," wrote
Joseph de Maistre, "slavery is the rule, and wherever that religion
is weakened, the nation becomes, in exact proportion, less jealous
of the general liberty. . . . Government alone cannot govern; it requires either slavery, which diminishes the number of the wills operative within the State, or divine energy, which, by a kind of spiritual
grafting process, destroys the natural violence of those wills and enables them to act together without harming each other."

(1941)

Ralph Barton Perry

65.

(1876-1957)

R. B. Perry, American philosopher and for more than forty years a teacher at Harvard, reassesses and interprets the significant role of Puritanism in American life, in the book from which this discussion of equality is taken.

from Puritanism and Democracy

The declaration that men are born not only free but "equal" has been the butt of an extraordinary amount of labored and irrelevant wit, such as this of Calhoun's: "Taking the proposition literally, there is not a word of truth in it. It begins with, 'all men are born,' which is utterly untrue. Men are not born. Infants are born. They grow to be men." John Adams and others have from time to time made the profound and, as they have seemed to think, annihilating discovery that no two objects are "perfectly alike." Even contemporary writers occasionally indulge in these hollow polemical victories. But it is a safe maxim never to impute to doctrines which have played a great role in history meanings which must have been palpably absurd to their own contemporaries. The eighteenth-century exponents of equality knew as well as Calhoun and Adams or more modern critics that men are endowed by nature with unequal capacity, as they are endowed with unequal stature, strength, fingerprints, or cephalic indices. The equality of which they spoke drew its meaning, not from a mere disregard of facts, but from a group of ideas which had their roots in Greek and Hebrew antiquity and their proof in the moral, political, and religious philosophy of the age.

The equalitarian doctrine can be summarily expounded. It was not an assertion that the several individual members of the human race are *as a matter of fact in all respects* alike; but that they *are and ought to be* alike in *certain* respects; and that these likenesses have a great deal to do with the aims of organized society.

In the first place, all men are equally men—which means not that they possess human attributes in the same degree, but that they possess the same attributes in some degree. All members of an audience, whether they sit in boxes or in the pit, possess the same type of skeleton, the same organs, and the same physiological functions. Whether a man is born in a hovel or in a palace, the reproductive process is

273

the same; whether a man works in a private office on Wall Street or in a coal mine in Pennsylvania, he draws his energy from the combustion of food, and gives off carbon dioxide. But the generic sameness of men is not confined to these baser anatomical and physiological levels; they possess the same psychological traits, from the simpler reflexes of coughing and sneezing to the so-called higher processes of memory and thought. All men experience pleasure and pain, hunger and thirst, fear and anger, love and hate, joy and despair. All men recollect their past, anticipate their future, and perceive their present. All men exercise in some degree the activities of generalization and inference. This fact may be summarily expressed either in naturalistic or in religious terms. All men belong to the same species in the hierarchy of evolution; or all men are created in the same image of God.

What is true of the constitution of man is true also of his life-cycle, and his fundamental relationships to his fellow men and to his physical environment. All men are born, grow old, and die. They traverse the same ardors of youth, the same sobrieties of middle age, and the same scleroses of senescence. All men inhabit the same planet, are exposed to its alternations of season and weather, and are dependent on its resources. All men have parents, and most men have brothers and sisters and children. All men have neighbors, with whom they must establish terms of reasonable accord. All men suffer from the necessity, or enjoy the opportunity, of living with their fellows. They all have one life to live, face the same inevitable death, and hear the same crack of doom.

Owing to many causes, men are disposed to forget or ignore these indisputable facts. Generic sameness tends to be eclipsed by differences of individual and class. Equalitarianism exhorts us to reverse this tendency: to be reverently disposed toward the commonplace, and to be astonished by what is taken for granted. . . .

According to the way of thinking characteristic of the eighteenth century, the notable differences between man and man, such as that between king and subject, noble and commoner, priest and layman, or rich and poor, are products of organized society. This idea led to the habit of abstracting from organized society, and from the differences which it has created. Men were imaginatively divested of institutional accretions—their trappings, powers, and privileges; and when thus denuded and reduced to the ranks they looked strangely alike. The doctrine that equality is "natural" was a way of saying that the more palpable and invidious inequalities are artificial.

That which is artificial can be unmade, and the purpose of social change was thus conceived as the restoration of a primitive equality. But, as was the case with the conception of "nature" in all its applications, this retrospective manner of speaking concealed the essence of the matter. Fundamentally, nature signified what men *could* be and *ought* to be, rather than what they *had* been. When man's past came to be better known, the state of nature was transferred from the past to the future, and conceived as an attainable and valid ideal rather than as a historical beginning.

Man's equality of endowment came thus to be conceived in terms of a sameness of potentiality rather than of attainment, and faith in human nature assumed the form of a belief in his educability. This faith was still extravagant, but the locus of its extravagance was shifted. It became an excessively optimistic view, not of what men are or have been, but of what they are capable of becoming when the frustrations and malformations due to human institutions are corrected. Given the air and the sun and the moisture which they require, all individuals of the species are capable, it was believed, of the same flowering. The error now lay in underestimating the inborn differences which predetermine the limits of growth.

The biological emphasis on inherited traits and the psychological emphasis on inherited aptitude and intelligence belong to a later age from that in which American democracy was born, and their acceptance modifies one of its premises. But democracy accepts innate limitations reluctantly. It gives to every man the benefit of the doubt, and the doubt is so far justified as to make the gift significant. The rival claims of heredity and environment are still disputed, and no final adjudication of them is yet in sight.

Anti-democratic social philosophies justify inequalitarian institutions, as Aristotle once justified slavery. It is claimed that the inequalities of power and privilege in organized society are a mere projection of the native and ineradicable inequalities of its members. Men get what they are fit for, and what they are fit for will in the long run determine their happiness. This theory affords a suspiciously convenient justification for those who are most favored by the existing system, as did the puritan theory that power and privilege are the just earnings of virtue. Reformers are accused of making humble people discontented with a lot which corresponds to their inborn capacity and provides the only kind of happiness of which they are capable.

The democratic social philosophy, on the other hand, emphasizes the degree to which mental and moral traits are an effect of the social environment, and proposes that this environment shall be made as auspicious as possible. The extreme hereditarian position is, in the present state of the question, as dogmatic as the doctrine of equal potentiality. Even the commonly accepted opinion of the relative superiority of races is a product of pride and vested interest rather than of science. The least that can be said for the equalitarian view is that it is the more generous and fruitful of two dogmatisms between which science allows an option.

Insofar as native differences of capacity are admitted, there is a tendency in democracy to conceive them as differences of vocation rather than of merit or dignity. And if the idea of generic equality tends to be superseded by the idea of equal opportunity, which affirms only that each man shall be enabled to raise his attainment to the limit of his capacity, this is still accompanied by the belief that such capacity is high. Democracy retains, if only as a regulative principle of social organization, an elixir of hopefulness. For what men attain is, in part, an effect of their belief in themselves and of the confident expectation of others.

Generic equality, then, is the idea that beneath the clothes they wear, and the status or occupation which organized society has bestowed upon them, all men are men, with the same faculties, the same needs and aspirations, the same destiny, and similar potentialities of development. Granting that the reservations are more evident to ourselves than to our fathers, this is still true. No one will deny it, once the question is raised in this form.

Why is this unquestionable fact so neglected that it has to be proclaimed? The founders of democracy were right not only in affirming the fact, but in their explanation of its neglect. The generic sameness of men is overlaid with surface differences. Men wear clothes and insignia, and they wear them on the outside of their persons where they are most in evidence. Every man has a station in life into which he is born, or to which he attains. This station is in part a matter of space and time. A man's spatio-temporal location distributes other men along radii of proximity; his neighbors are near, and others are distant. Those who are near can be seen easily, while those at a distance require the straining of the eye or an unnatural exercise of the faculty of imagination. But his station is also functional, consisting in the role he plays in the drama of life, and determining the relations in which he stands to his fellow actors.

These differences of station are not only more palpable but more interesting. Attention is fastened, not upon the common physiognomy of man, but upon those differences of feature, emphasis, and expression which distinguish the individual face with which one may claim acquaintance. And the functional differences that divide men are of commanding importance, in the sense of practical urgency. One's transactions are not with mankind, but with distinct individuals, or limited groups of individuals. Having an aching tooth, it is more important to consider a dentist as such than to reflect that he is a man, like oneself. The worker's struggle for existence forces upon his attention the difference between those who own capital and those who, like himself, depend upon the wages which the capitalist dispenses.

Man's generic sameness tending thus to be ignored, what is the means of heightening it and investing it with feeling? It might be supposed that modern science in its application to man would have provided such a means. Biology, anthropology, and psychology concern themselves with structures, functions, and laws common to all men. But the scientist, while he is interested in man, is not in his scientific capacity interested in men. Nor is it sufficient merely to acquire perspective. It is true that distance tends to render individual differences unnoticeable. To the European, all Chinese or even Orientals tend to 'look alike.' From an astronomical distance all men, as earth-dwellers, present an aspect of sameness that subordinates the uniqueness of genius and the significance of historic events. But it is also true that distance extinguishes interest in individuals. If human suffering occurs at a sufficient distance, it produces apathy; the suffering or the death of a few thousand, more or less, signifies little.

Neither science nor distance will create equalitarianism, which is an interest in individual men, combined with a recognition of their sameness. It is an appreciation of their common value. It is not a perception or a judgment, but a sentiment. . . .

The maxim of equal opportunity owes its place in the American creed not only to the alleged personal and social benefits of competition, but also to the assumption that, since all men are endowed with the same faculties of reason and conscience, and since natural resources are abundant, the effect of equal opportunity will be to raise all men to *approximately* the same high level of attainment. The fact is that equality of opportunity is at best a secondary principle, subordinate to the principle of the maximum possible benefit to all individuals. There is no ethical axiom to the effect that individuals are entitled only to what they have earned or achieved for themselves. As between the maxims "Each man should be rewarded in proportion to his service" and "To each according to his needs," the ethics of universalistic individualism is clearly on the side of the latter. Ethically speaking, there is no limit to the benefit which the state should confer on its members save its power to confer such benefits.

The competitive system in its ordinary economic sense has its own peculiar limitations. Even though it be admitted that economic goods are promoted by the system of laissez faire, it does not follow that this system is equally favorable to the so-called creative goods of art and science, "where to divide is not to take away." To covet excellence in art and science does not imply that one shall outstrip or deprive others, but that one shall judge oneself by some standard of perfection. It may well be that the state can best promote goods of this sort by furnishing qualified individuals with the requisite means, education, and leisure, thus relieving them from the pressure and the preoccupations of competitive struggle. Whatever in this sphere of life it can do is what it ought to do, without respect to any prejudice in favor of independent livelihood.

But the secondary character of equal opportunity is best demonstrated by stressing the fact that any free competitive struggle predetermines the attributes of the successful contestant. Its freedom is relative to the rules, the rules define the form of the achievement, and the form of the achievement favors those who possess the corresponding form of capacity. All orderly competitions encourage something. Competition for wealth puts a premium upon the qualities of acquisitiveness. This may or may not be desirable; in any case, it is important to recognize its negative as well as its positive implications. Insofar as society as a whole is cast into the form of the traditional laissez-faire capitalism, it sanctions greed and guile as well as industry and invention.

It is important, furthermore, that if the race is to be "fair," the contestants should be at all times free from handicaps other than the ineradicable handicaps of native aptitude. But since the economic struggle is a continuing struggle of families and groups, the individual in some measure inherits the gains or losses of his antecedents; and he finds himself not at the start of a race where all are abreast, but at some later stage where the contestants are already spread in a column of advancement.

Public education is an attempt to remove this handicap of birth.

It does so only to a limited degree. It may provide the individual of the younger generation with free "tuition," or even give him "room and board," but it cannot discount the effects of the domestic environment. It cannot free the son of poor parents from the pressure of livelihood, or the lack of "spending money," or the social ignominy of caste. So long as there are marked differences which surround the individual during his early years and create advantages and disadvantages of "background," it cannot be said that the contestants in the economic struggle are equal. The individual also finds himself competing, not with other individuals, but with durable and centrally controlled aggregations of corporate wealth. It is this which is fundamentally accountable for the socialistic strain in modern social thought. Professor Tawney says:

> In the absence of measures which prevent the exploitation of groups in a weak economic position by those in a strong, and make the external conditions of health and civilization a common possession, the phrase equality of opportunity is obviously a jest, to be described as amusing or heartless according to taste. It is the impertinent courtesy of an invitation offered to unwelcome guests, in the certainty that circumstances will prevent them from accepting it.

At any stage of the contest, furthermore, the individual finds himself permanently favored or handicapped by his gains or losses up to that time. He runs only one race. Suppose him to be a man whose powers mature late, or who is the victim of accidental misfortune, or whose aptitudes lie elsewhere than in the economic struggle for existence. He enters the race at an early age, and being outdistanced, can never from henceforth compete on equal terms with his fellows.

Much has been said of the value of struggle as a school of character. But this school is commonly judged by those who succeed in graduating—little is heard of those who fail. The experience of adversity is benign to those who triumph over adversity. To those who fail, especially if they believe that their failure has been due to no fault of their own, adversity is often a cause of bitterness and moral dissolution. As the struggle for existence becomes more desperate, the number of moral casualties increases and the number of victors declines.

It never has been and never will be possible for a democratic state to avoid bestowing gratuities on its people with a view to promoting the equality of their competitive positions. It owes to all individuals as much of further positive good as it can dispense. It owes this in the sense that this is the reason for its being. In setting the terms of competition it assumes responsibility for the effect of those terms on the individuals who compete. It is obliged to make the terms of the race fair in substance and not merely in name; but it is no less obliged to consider the effect of the race upon the contestants, both upon those who win and upon those who lose. It has a duty, furthermore, toward the creation and distribution of those goods which flourish best under non-competitive conditions. These considerations amply justify measures which democratic states have in fact undertaken: to provide facilities for individual development, to correct the abuses of competition, to foster the arts and sciences, to protect the standard of living, to succor the ill, the poor, or the unemployed, and to redistribute wealth.

Gross inequalities of wealth tend, furthermore, to destroy that spirit of fraternity and of mutual respect which we have yet to consider, and which constitutes the spirit and flavor of a democratic society. "Where conditions are such," as Professor Tawney says, "that two-thirds of the wealth is owned by one per cent of the population, the ownership of property is more properly regarded as the badge of a class than as the attribute of a society." Democracy defeats its own purpose if it merely substitutes for a hierarchy of birth, or of ecclesiastical or political privilege, a hierarchy based on the advantages and the disadvantages of accumulated wealth, or the degree of economic opportunity which its members enjoy. Said James Fitzjames Stephen:

> Equality, like liberty, appears to me to be a big name for a small thing . . . Upon the whole, I think that what little can be truly said of equality is that as a fact human beings are not equal; that in their dealings with each other they ought to recognize real inequalities where they exist as much as substantial equality where it exists. That they are equally prone to exaggerate real distinctions, which is vanity, and to deny their existence, which is envy.

But this is not "a small thing." The writer of these words commits the opposite and more serious error of making little of much—of making nothing of what is in a sense everything. For from these mixed equalities and inequalities and from the attitude taken toward them is compounded the very essence of social life.

(1944)

Gunnar Myrdal

(1898-   )

66. Gunnar Myrdal, Swedish economist, sociologist, and public official, directed for the Carnegie Corporation (1938-1942) a large-scale study of the problems of the American Negro. An interpretive report of the findings of the study appeared under the title, *An American Dilemma,* from which the following selection is taken.

---

from An American Dilemma

Emancipation loosened the bonds on Negro slaves and allowed them to leave their masters. The majority of freedmen seems to have done some loitering as a symbolic act and in order to test out the new freedom. Reconstruction temporarily gave civil rights, suffrage, and even some access to public office. It also marked the heroic beginning of the Negroes' efforts to acquire the rudiments of education.

There is no doubt that Congress intended to give the Negroes "social equality" in public life to a substantial degree. The Civil Rights Bill of 1875, which, in many ways, represented the culmination of the federal Reconstruction legislation, was explicit in declaring that all persons within the jurisdiction of the United States should be entitled to the full and equal enjoyment of the accommodations, advantages, facilities, and privileges of inns, public conveyances on land and water, theaters, and other places of public amusement; subject only to the conditions and limitations established by law, and applicable alike to citizens of every race and color, regardless of previous condition of servitude. The federal courts were given exclusive jurisdiction over offenses against this statute. Stephenson observes in *Race Distinctions in American Law* that "Congress apparently intended to secure not only equal but identical accommodations in all public places for Negroes and Caucasians."

During Congressional Reconstruction some Southern states inserted clauses in their constitutions or in special laws intended to establish the rights of Negroes to share on equal terms in the accommodations of public establishments and conveyances. Louisiana and South Carolina went so far as to require mixed schools. From contemporary accounts of life in the South during Reconstruction, it is evident, however, that Negroes met considerable segregation and

281

discrimination even during these few years of legal equality. It is also apparent that nothing irritated the majority of white Southerners so much as the attempts of Congress and the Reconstruction governments to remove social discrimination from public life.

After Restoration of "white supremacy" the doctrine that the Negroes should be "kept in their place" became the regional creed. When the Supreme Court in 1883 declared the Civil Rights Bill of 1875 unconstitutional in so far as it referred to acts of social discrimination by individuals—endorsing even in this field the political compromise between the white North and South—the way was left open for the Jim Crow legislation of the Southern states and municipalities. For a quarter of a century this system of statutes and regulations—separating the two groups in schools, on railroad cars and on street cars, in hotels and restaurants, in parks and playgrounds, in theaters and public meeting places—continued to grow, with the explicit purpose of diminishing, as far as was practicable and possible, the social contacts between whites and Negroes in the region.

We do not know much about the effects of the Jim Crow legislation. American sociologists, following the Sumner tradition of holding legislation to be inconsequential, are likely to underrate these effects. Southern Negroes tell quite a different story. From their own experiences in different parts of the South they have told me how the Jim Crow statutes were effective means of tightening and freezing—in many cases of instigating—segregation and discrimination. They have given a picture of how the Negroes were pushed out from voting and officeholding by means of the disfranchisement legislation which swept like a tide over the Southern states during the period from 1875 to 1910. In so far as it concerns the decline in political, civic, and social status of the Negro people in the Southern states, the Restoration of white supremacy in the late 'seventies—according to these informants—was not a final and consummated revolution but *the beginning of a protracted process which lasted until nearly the First World War. During this process the white pressure continuously increased, and the Negroes were continuously pushed backward.* Some older white informants have related much the same story.

Before the Jim Crow legislation there is also said to have been a tendency on the part of white people to treat Negroes somewhat differently depending upon their class and education. This tendency was broken by the laws which applied to *all* Negroes. The legislation thus solidified the caste line and minimized the importance of class differences in the Negro group. This particular effect was probably the more crucial in the formation of the present caste system, since class differentiation within the Negro group continued and, in fact, gained momentum. As we shall find, a tendency is discernible again, in recent decades, to apply the segregation rules with some discretion to Negroes of different class status. If a similar trend was well under way before the Jim Crow laws, those laws must have postponed this particular social process for one or two generations.

While the federal Civil Rights Bill of 1875 was declared unconstitutional, the Reconstruction Amendments to the Constitution—which provided that the Negroes are to enjoy full citizenship in the United States, that they are entitled to "equal benefit of all laws," and that "no state shall make or enforce any law which shall abridge the privileges and immunities of citizens of the United States"—could not be so easily disposed of. The Southern whites, therefore, in passing their various segregation laws to legalize social discrimination, had to manufacture a legal fiction of the same type as we have already met in the preceding discussion on politics and justice. The legal term for this trick in the social field, expressed or implied in most of the Jim Crow statutes, is "separate, but equal." That is, Negroes were to get equal accommodations, but separate from the whites. It is evident, however, and rarely denied, that there is practically no single instance of segregation in the South which has not been utilized for a significant discrimination. The great difference in quality of service for the two groups in the segregated set-ups for transportation and education is merely the most obvious example of how segregation is an excuse for discrimination. Again the Southern white man is in the moral dilemma of having to frame his laws in terms of equality and to defend them before the Supreme Court—and before his own better conscience, which is tied to the American Creed—while knowing all the time that in reality his laws do not give equality to Negroes, and that he does not want them to do so.

The formal adherence to equality in the American Creed, expressed by the Constitution and in the laws, is, however, even in the field of social relations, far from being without practical importance. Spokesmen for the white South, not only recently but in the very period when the segregation policy was first being legitimatized, have strongly upheld the principle that segregation should not be used for discrimination. Henry W. Grady, for instance, scorned the "fanatics and doctrinaires who hold that separation is discrimination," emphasized that "separation is not offensive to either race" and exclaimed:

... the whites and blacks must walk in separate paths in the South. As near as may be, these paths should be made equal— but separate they must be now and always. This means separate schools, separate churches, *separate accommodations everywhere —but equal accommodations where the same money is charged, or where the State provides for the citizen.*

Further, the legal adherence to the principle of equality gives the Southern liberal a vantage point in his work to improve the status of the Negroes and race relations. Last, but not least, it gives the Negro people a firm legal basis for their fight against social segregation and discrimination. Since the two are inseparable, the fight against inequality challenges the whole segregation system. The National Association for the Advancement of Colored People has had, from the very beginning, the constitutional provisions for equality as its sword and shield. Potentially the Negro is strong. He has, in his demands upon white Americans, the fundamental law of the land on his side. He has even the better conscience of his white compatriots themselves. He knows it; and the white American knows it, too.

(1944)

Robert Redfield
(1897-1958)

67.

Robert Redfield, who was chairman of the Department of Anthropology at the University of Chicago and a recognized authority on the ethnology of Yucatan and Guatemala, delivered the following selection as an address before the American Association of Collegiate Registrars.

from "Race and Religion in Selective Admission"

The institutions of higher learning of this country practice racial or religious discrimination in violation of a major principle of our national life. The truth of this general fact will not be seriously contested, although in any particular institution the discrimination there practiced may be denied, ignored or justified. I am today concerned with the justifications offered in defense of the practice of these discriminations in enrolling students. With those who deny or ignore that discrimination exists one cannot usefully discuss the principles of conduct involved. In large part, however, the practices are defended as wise or as necessary. It is these defenses that have my attention today. I bring them before you for examination, in the hope that discussion of them may help to clarify the duty and the opportunity of colleges and universities in meeting a common problem.

That the problem is common may not at once appear. Jews and Negroes are the two groups that notoriously experience discrimination, and the situations of the two may appear more different than similar. The relative difficulties of the Negro in obtaining a higher education form only a small part of his disadvantages and arise from a great system of institutions and attitudes rooted particularly in the history of our country, which relegate him to a position as a sort of half-citizen, or citizen with only secondary rights. The discriminations from which the Jew suffers are derived from prejudices ancient and world-wide; his social and educational advancement is as great as is that of the white gentile; and the obstacles to his enrollment or employment created by colleges and universities constitute one of the chief injustices of which he is conscious.

The Jew and the Negro are perhaps not always aware that each is engaged in the other's cause. Indeed, the different attitudes occasionally taken by Jew and Negro as to the application of a quota suggest viewpoints diametrically opposed. The Jew regards the quota as an unjust limitation on his right to compete in education and in the professions with non-Jews. On the other hand, some Negro leaders ask that Negroes be included in this association, in that committee or agency or other group, in proportion to their numbers in the national or local community. For the Negro, often denied any admission at all to a public group, the argument of proportionate representation offers an opening toward the improvement of his situation. For the Jew, the application of a quota prevents him from bettering his position in free competition. Whether or not the quota is defensible in either case is something to be considered later in this paper.

The differences as between North and South also obscure the common character of the problem. In the North the Negro is excluded, or his admission is made difficult, without the support of the law. But in seventeen states the denial of admission of Negro citizens to the principal institutions of higher learning is obedient to law as well as to custom. How can the colleges and universities take any single position with regard to racial discrimination in education when a great subcommunity of the nation has made segregation, in a multitude of details of community life, a legal requirement? Do the colleges of the South then share with those of the North any common responsibility in the matter?

One may point out that one of the differences between North and South in regard to racial and religious discrimination makes each region the victim of discrimination practiced in the other. On the whole the Negro finds it less difficult to get a good higher education in the North than in the South, especially education in some of the professions, and therefore southern Negroes who have the means to do so go North for higher education. In some southern institutions, on the other hand, discrimination against the Jew, especially in medical schools, is less severe than it is in many northern institutions, and therefore some northern Jews go south for such higher education. In this way each major American region bears a burden of higher education which is thrust upon it by the greater discrimination practiced by institutions in the other region. Perhaps this fact alone provides a basis for consideration of the problem as common and national.

With regard to another ethnic group of students, the adventures in discrimination experienced by our colleges and universities in recent years did not divide into patterns along the Mason and Dixon line. I refer to United States citizens of Japanese parentage. Here, during the war, the obstacles to enrollment differed greatly from one institution to another, but not according to the location of the institution in the North or in the South. Some colleges and universities showed more courage than others in admitting such students at a time when the Japanese-Americans were unjustly excluded as a group from participation in the national life. Some small colleges, especially some with church leadership, were bold in admitting Japanese-Americans against opposition in their local communities. Others—and some of the largest and most independent universities were included in this number—seemed positively eager to use the ambiguous and changing pronouncements of the War Department as to enrollment of Nisei students as a cover for their own disposition to discriminate. The large institution with war contracts to carry out and military officers close at hand often offered little resistance to advices that Nisei be excluded from its campus. Certain results were absurd. An administrative officer found himself denying admission as a student to some young Americans with Japanese parents, and perhaps on the same day signing a form appointing to the teaching faculty some Japanese alien hired to teach the Japanese language to soldiers of our army. The point in mind here is that the problems of discriminations in education raised by the removal and dispersion of Americans of Japanese origin were nationwide, and presented to all of us in common terms the basic issues of ethnic discrimination in American education.

That the problem is in fact the same problem in all parts of the country and with regard to all minority groups appears from a mere statement of the principle of our national life and from recognition of discrimination as discrimination, no matter how explained locally.

The principle is simply that nothing granted one citizen is to be denied another by reason solely of his membership in a racial or religious group. Every fundamental American document has stated this principle, and no judicial decision, no great public pronouncement, has denied it. The inherent equality of all men with respect to the fundamental human rights declared in 1776 makes no exception against men of any particular racial or religious group. The Constitution contains no provision which would authorize racial or religious discrimination, and the Fourteenth and Fifteenth Amendments were enacted in order to preserve this equality, as against discriminatory legislation of the States, for Negro citizens. Moreover, the principle of equality of all individuals, no matter what their religious or racial character, has in recent years become explicit and fundamental in the nascent international community. If any one document today approximates expression of the conscience of mankind, it is the Charter of the

United Nations Organization. In signing this document, our own country has pledged itself to promote respect for human rights and for the fundamental freedoms without distinction of race. Article Thirteen, defining the powers of the General Assembly, provides that the Assembly shall make studies and recommendations to promote "international co-operation in the . . . educational . . . field(s)" and to assist "in the realization of human rights and fundamental freedoms for all without distinction as to race. . . ." Thus the right to education is recognized as a fundamental human right which is to be enjoyed by all without distinction as to race. A principle early enunciated in the United States of America has become a principle of international co-operation; the failure of the United States to realize its own principle within is own borders can then hardly be a matter for Americans to ignore.

It will be pointed out, however, that in many States of the union separate education for Negroes and for Whites is provided by law and that it is the duty of the college or university to obey the law. That, of course, is true. But it does not follow that it is the duty of the college or university to stand silent before educational discrimination. It is notorious that educational facilities offered Negroes are inferior to those provided for Whites. The Gaines decision is now eight years old, but it will not be claimed that Negroes find ready for them everywhere state institutions of higher learning and professional training equal to those open to Whites. The law of the State may require an institution to segregate Negroes from Whites; it does not require it to do nothing about bringing about equality of educational opportunity. Decisions of the Supreme Court have given legal recognition to local practices of segregation, but they have not made racial or religious discrimination lawful. It is the duty of every citizen to work to overcome such discrimination.

Moreover, the law does not require that citizens do not change the law. Let it be remembered that there is no national pronouncement adopting racial segregation as a national measure. Let it be recalled that Congress once adopted a federal civil rights statute and is free to do so again. Let it also be admitted that the decisions of the Supreme Court which make racial segregation legal rest on arguments of questionable validity, that the constitutionality of segregation has never been fully argued in terms of the broad social consequences to the nation of these practices, and finally that, with the growing dependence for survival of all of us on the rapid development of a world community in which the principle of racial and religious equality has already found vigorous expression—then will it not follow that any citizen whose conscience so directs has an obligation to examine the bases and consequences of segregation in education and to call for a reversal of local practice and legislation? And if a world community is really required for survival, is it proper that the interests and traditions of one part of the country, when in conflict with a fundamental national principle, should stand in the way of the paramount interests of the whole?

To these questions someone may reply that whatever may be the conviction and the duty of the individual citizen, it is not the business of a college or university to question race discrimination or racial segregation in education. It will be said that education is the sole business of the college, and education and research the sole businesses of the university, and that neither education nor research includes questioning the accepted decisions of the community as to the relations between the races, let alone trying to change them. It will further be said that single acts that fly in the face of the prevailing attitudes of the community do not change the attitudes of the community and therefore are not to be attempted. The first argument says that the college or university has no responsibility, or no right, to change the prevailing attitudes of its community; the second, that it is helpless to do so. Both arguments involve assumptions as to the relation of single acts to community attitudes. Both involve assumptions as to the role and responsibility of institutions of higher learning in the national life. Conclusions as to these assumptions lead to conclusions on the questions at issue.

I take the second argument first. Is it true that the institution of higher learning is helpless to act to reduce discrimination if the attitudes of the community approve of the discrimination? I say it is not helpless. The assumption may be questioned that law and administration are no more than expressions of the mores. It may rather be asserted that the relation between law and administration on the one hand and the mores on the other is a reciprocal relation. Legislation and administration express the mores, but it is also true that they make the mores. A courageous act by a legislature or by an administrator, whether in a public or a private institution, that is consistent with the national principle of equality as among men, changes the mores to make them by some degree more nearly consistent with the principle. The mores are not extra-human pressures, like the weight of the atmosphere or the pull of gravity. They are not something external to the wishes and sentiments of men. They *are* the wishes and the sentiments of men (so far as imbued by a sense of rightness), and men change their wishes and their sentiments in response to what other men do and in response to what they themselves do. If one man or one institution takes a public position against racial prejudice so as to make effective an equality as among racial groups that was before denied, that act gives encouragement to all others whose attitudes inclined toward equality and justice but who were held from acting in accordance with their inclination by uncertainty or timidity or other causes. As a result, some of these will now act on their convictions; others will then be in their turn encouraged, and commit themselves to justice rather than injustice by performing just acts. And, as men tend to believe in the rightness of what they do, having done what is just, attitudes of these men will have changed toward racial and religious equality and away from prejudice and injustice, and so the center of gravity of the attitudes of the whole community will have shifted. On the other hand, an administrative decision to exclude citizens from a college, or from some facility of that college, or to limit the opportunity of students to enroll in the college because of racial or religious origin, results in moving the mores of the community in the opposite direction. An unjust act makes men complacent about their own unjust attitudes. We have seen the operation of this principle in the case of the Japanese-Americans in the recent war years. There is, I think, little doubt that the act of the national government in removing all persons from the Pacific Coast whose ancestry was Japanese, on that sole basis of selection, hardened the attitudes of a part of our people against their fellow citizens of Japanese ancestry. The important act of their own government, in seizing and so stigmatizing as possibly disloyal all persons of a certain ancestry seemed to give a formal and general approval to the prejudices of many Americans. Perhaps the act was made possible not only by the war but also by pre-existing anti-Oriental prejudice in some quarters, but on the other hand the act increased and widened the prejudice.

The point has been recently well argued with respect to legislation by Carey McWilliams. He has assembled impressive evidence to show that in California prejudice against the Chinese and later against the Japanese was a creation of the agitation of small groups with special interests. Some special groups with a special interest, perhaps in a vested economic advantage, perhaps merely in professional super-Americanism, would agitate for passage of a law restricting the freedom of the Oriental. Once enacted, its existence helped deepen and generalize the prejudice. Similarly, it was not the mores of the whole community, but the special interests of the railway unions that excluded Negroes from jobs as trainmen and foremen—jobs custom had permitted them to fill for fifty years before the exclusion policy was adopted. In part, then, the mores follow legislative and administrative acts. McWilliams also argues that the legalization of segregation between Negro and White in the South has intensified racial prejudice, and quotes the prediction of that eminent Kentuckian, Justice Harlan, who dissented in the important *Plessy* case in which the segregation of the races in common carriers was upheld: "What can more certainly arouse race hatred, what more certainly create and perpetuate a feeling of distrust between these races than state enactments, which, in fact, proceed upon the grounds that colored citizens are so inferior and degraded that they cannot be allowed to sit in public coaches occupied by white citizens."

What can more certainly arouse race hatred, what more certainly create a feeling of distrust between racial or religious groups than rules of schools or colleges which proceed upon the grounds that citizens of one racial or religious origin are so inferior—or so dangerously competent in free competition—that they cannot be allowed to attend or to attend in numbers proportionate to their scholastic competence, institutions of higher learning controlled by white gentiles? It seems to me that the reasoning offered by Justice Harlan has great force for those of us who make or administer the rules of admission of colleges and universities. The responsibility for the general consequences to our national community of acts of discrimination in schools and colleges cannot be escaped by a claim that what we do is necessarily a reflection of public attitudes and cannot itself make the public attitudes. The acts of colleges and universities have that same effect upon the mores which have the decisions of national and State governments. Indeed, within the field of education they have much more effect. Colleges and universities are the principal organs of society that function as to education; they are the laboratories and the forums and the assemblies in which those of the community most concerned with education experiment, and make decisions, and the people respond to these decisions, changing their own attitudes in accordance. Whether we like it or not, our every act of discrimination or of equal treatment as between ethnic groups is an influence upon the general attitudes of the community. If we act so as to bring about just treatment of all citizens, the people of our community will, on the whole, tend to uphold that justice; if we act unjustly, then men will be helped to excuse their unjust attitudes. We are not helpless to reduce discrimination in the community.

If the policies and practices of the college or university inevitably tend to influence the community toward justice or away from it, the responsibility of the college or the university is clear. It is to lead toward justice. The colleges and universities must discharge a responsibility they cannot escape. The university especially, in this view, is an institution of moral leadership in the community. The university is not a mere agency of the general public opinion. I reject the view that it is the simple duty of a university to bring together teachers and scholars concerned, each separately, with teaching and studying what each wishes to study or is hired to teach. A university is put there by society not that each of its professors shall pursue his own interests but that there shall be a better society. The freedom of academic people does not have its final end in the relative freedom from interference enjoyed by the professors. Knowledge is to be sought and to be taught for the common good. The very privileges of academic people, and the special opportunities to study and to reflect which they enjoy, give the university a role of leadership in the common effort which it would be stupid to ignore and cowardly to refuse. What the college or university does within matters subject to its control is presumably what, on the basis of the special opportunities of its members to think about the matter, it believes to be right. If it excludes students whom the law permits it to admit, because of the racial or religious origin of the students, presumably that is what it believes to be right. If it puts any limitation on the free association of citizens to meet under its auspices or on their freedom to discuss public questions, including the question of segregation itself, then presumably it regards this action as a right action. But our national society has not as a whole said that either of these actions is right. If the university does either of these things it leads away from, not toward, the direction of the common effort.

The society we have said we want to be is a society in which the dignity and worth of the individual is a central good, and in which every individual is judged only by qualities which are personal to him and is denied no opportunity because of his race or religion. The many prevailing exceptions to the realization of such a society are admitted to be exceptions, even when they are justified. In the opinion of most Americans they should disappear. The university, more than any other institution, is the transmitter and refiner of our heritage. Freedom and equality are parts of that heritage, and in the university, itself a community in which what is thought is inevitably interdependent with what is done, the clarification of the problems of achieving freedom and equality cannot be carried on apart from action within that community that will tend to achieve freedom and equality. To argue that the university, or the college, must take no step toward racial and religious equality until the attitudes of the people outside have caught up with the spirit of the action is to deny the function of education. For who is to work to change these attitudes in the direction of the declared common ideal if it be not educators? If an institution of higher learning, within matters in its power, does not take every measure to make our society more nearly what it has declared it wishes to be, it has failed a responsibility. The rest of society has a right to ask if it has a good excuse for its failure.

To exclude citizens from opportunities to education legally open to them because of the applicants' race or religion is such a failure. To limit the number or proportion of students of any race, nationality or religion in the total enrollment, is failure also. The consequences of excluding all Negroes or all Jews or all Catholics are bad, but at least the action is clear, and raises without confusion the issue of racial or religious discrimination. The application of a racial or religious quota is in two respects more serious in its consequences than is total exclusion. In most cases the quota (or the informal procedures whereby the number of Jews, Negroes, Catholics or Italians is restricted without the fixing of a definite numerical limit) is invisible; its operations occur in private offices and in informal discussions, and the practice is not admitted or perhaps even recognized. In other cases the limited restriction of students of some minority group is defended by arguments which have specious plausibility. It is said, in effect, that the limitation of educational opportunity on a racial or national or religious basis is done in order to realize good ends. The ends which it is said to serve are three. In this last part of my remarks I will consider if these ends are indeed good, if they are served by application of a quota, and if they conflict with even greater ends.

The educational quota is sometimes defended on the grounds that to have a good society there must be such a limitation. This justification is commonly heard in professional schools. It is argued that there should be no more Jewish doctors or, maybe, Catholic lawyers in a community than would correspond with the proportion of Jewish or Catholic citizens in the community. This argument assumes that Jewish doctors should take only Jewish patients or that Catholic clients should look only to Catholic lawyers for legal aid. The United States of America was not founded on such a principle. It has never been assumed that this country should be composed of self-sufficient ethnic or religious groups, each providing all the services required of that sub-community from among its own members. Only in the case of the Negro has such a semi-separate ethnic group developed, and the result there is the plainest of all inconsistences with our national ideal. (Even in this case, where segregation is most strongly established, there are communities in the North where Negro teachers teach white pupils and communities in the South where Negro doctors treat white patients.) The quota, or *numerus clausus,* is no characteristically American device; it is well known in Europe; and we have lately seen to what horrors it leads. To apply the quota on the ground that the specialists in the nation should have ethnic origins corresponding to the numbers of such groups in the population is to deny the American assumption that men of all religious and all ethnic origins may come to acquire the capacities for carrying on the common life. That men of all religions have this capacity is not often denied today. That men of certain racial origins lack the capacity is asserted often enough, but no anthropologist of any repute reaches that conclusion. The capacities to carry on the activities and responsibilities of the citizen, the doctor, the lawyer or the educated man are as common and as general among the representatives of one ethnic group as of any other. To insist that specialists shall be limited by ethnic quotas is to deny the truth that human nature and intelligence are present in all ethnic groups.

A second justification for the quota is based on consideration of, not the general community, but the college or the university itself. Restriction of enrollment on an ethnic basis is defended as necessary to preserve a quality of the college community: the college must remain "Christian" or "non-urban" or must, still more vaguely and generally, "remain the kind of college it has always been." This argument is defective in at least two respects. In the first place it is not to be accepted without question that every college and every university ought to remain what it has always been. Institutions must change as society changes; our society has, on the whole, tended to realize, in a series of slow steps, the inclusive and democratic principles on which it was established. Even educational institutions that are accustomed to the preservation of one particular strain out of the manifold cultural heritage of America may find, on thinking it over, that it is to the interests of the learning and education they serve to widen their ethnic and cultural representation. They may, simply, do a better job by so doing. In the second place, even assuming the end a good end, the application of a quota in racial or religious terms, as a means to preserve the face and habits of the institution itself, is inappropriate because it is not adapted to the end sought and improper because it violates a more important principle. To limit the number of Jews, because they are Jews, is to assume that certain qualities of mind, character or manners are present in every Jew. This is not far from the principle of collective responsibility for crime. And besides, it isn't so. If we assume that proper qualifications for admission to a college or university include more than evidence of sufficient ability to learn, all additional qualifications, like the qualifications of educational preparation and intelligence, can and should be tested for each individual applicant, as an individual. It denies the principle of responsibility of the individual for his own acts only to seek to realize those qualifications in a student body by attributing them to a student because of his ethnic origin.

No, the arguments for the educational quota are shown to be unworthy of respect by incontrovertible facts. It is never applied consistently, and it is never applied against the ethnic or religious group of the people who apply it. The administrator of the dental school who restricts the number of Jews admitted to ten per cent of the students never insists that another ten per cent of the students be Negroes. Never do we hear a demand that "Germans be limited in breweries, Catholics in municipal administration, Poles in symphony orchestras, Irishmen in fire departments and police forces, and whites in well-paying jobs of all sorts." These words are those of Yves Simon, who goes on to declare that he will believe, "with Pascal, in the sincerity of witnesses who allow themselves to be martyred; . . . in the sincerity of the partisans of the *numerus clausus* when they demand that their principle be applied with a rigor fatal to their own interests. Until we see white workers demanding a limit on the number of white workers in well-paid positions, we shall refuse to believe that the advocates of the *numerus clausus* are really interested in the common good and in the harmonious distribution of the various parts of the community." The real reasons behind the application of ethnic quotas lie in the motive to preserve, for a privileged group, the competitive advantages its members enjoy, with respect to both jobs and prestige. When the competition gets hard, we hear a demand for the quota. Race or religion provides a criterion for excluding people of a group to which, one may be sure, the excluder does not belong.

There is yet a third argument offered in justification of limitation of enrollment on a religious or racial basis. With a comment on this third justification I will conclude. This third argument justifies restriction as a measure conducive to the welfare not of the general community and not of the college community but of the minority group itself. It is the argument stressed by President Hopkins in his famous letter written a year ago to Herman Shumlin about the limitation of enrollment of Jews in Dartmouth College. It is argued that the number of Jews admitted should be limited in order to prevent an increase in anti-Semitism. It is argued that it is not safe to admit Jews and non-Jews merely according to the capacities of the applicants as individuals, but that even competent Jews should be excluded after there are already so many Jews in the college that to admit more would result in more anti-Jewish sentiment than existed before. From this point of view the non-Jewish applier of ethnic discrimination does the Jew a service, for he prevents a "concentration" which would be "ill-advised."

This argument is often buttressed with reference to the concentration of the Jews in Germany before the rise of Nazism and statements that it was this concentration which laid a foundation for Hitler's work. Therefore, this argument runs, let the non-Jew, by excluding the Jew, protect him from the results of his efforts to find his place in society in equal competition with non-Jews.

What is to be said about this argument? It may be said that the concentration of Jews in Germany was not as it has been represented by Nazis or by those who have uncritically accepted Nazi representations. It may be asked if the greater association of Jews with non-Jews, or of members of any ethnic group with another always results in an increase of prejudice between them, or if it even usually has this result. But these are not the principal weaknesses in the argument for educational quotas which I am now considering. The trouble with the argument is not so much that it is false in fact but that it is in some part true in fact. It is in considerable part true that increase in success achieved by members of a group that has for long been the object of discrimination brings an increase of prejudice or even hatred against that group. The real weakness of the argument is that it is made by the wrong people. It might be open to the Jew to ask that fewer of his kind be caused to appear in areas where the Jew fears that an increase in his numbers might do him harm. But is it proper that members of the majority group should compel an unjust limitation of the numbers of members of the minority group, against the will of the minority, on the ground that the majority group is thereby protecting the minority from injustices or even violence that would be committed by the majority? Is there not something disingenuous in one, not a Jew, who contends that the Jew is his own worst enemy and that to keep him from injuring himself by pushing his case too far, he, the non-Jew, should limit the enrollment of Jews, when it is remembered that it will be the self-appointed protector's own group that will do the threatened damage to the Jew? There are occasions when we are compelled to take measures of this sort. If a man, innocent or guilty, is pursued by a mob bent on his destruction, the sheriff may rightly put into the safety of the jail the man who is pursued. But it is understood that this is a remedy of desperation. We know that it is the mob that should be jailed, and we jail the man only because we cannot jail the mob. But all such cases of protective custody are confessions of wrong done by the jailer, and all such cases carry the danger that the power exercised by the majority may be used against the minority in the real but hidden interest of the majority. To limit admission to the schools or the professions against the will of a minority is to admit one's own group to be the doer of the wrong which one claims to prevent, and the measure chosen therefore cannot be a measure that goes to the heart of the difficulty. In every such case, whatever be the nationality, the religion or the color of the group thus compelled to accept an injustice in what the dominant group says to be the interest of the group so treated—in every such case we may look into the underlying circumstances with some care. For, by limiting the minority one gives an unjust advantage, in the getting of jobs or the getting of an education, to himself, to his own group, and the honesty as well as the effectiveness of the measures one employs are open to challenge.

(1947)

68

Emil Brunner

(1889-   )

Emil Brunner, Swiss Protestant theologian at the University of
Zurich, analyzes equality in the light of the neo-orthodox interpretation of Christian history.

from Christianity and Civilization

The Christian knows that he has to serve justice, because it is the
principle of God's order; at the same time he knows that this service
of justice is not an ultimate and that respect for justice is never
sufficient as motive. This place is reserved to love. With the drawing of
this distinction there is already established an enormous difference
between the ancient and the Christian ideas of justice. For the former
justice is the highest, the unconditioned ideal, and service rendered to
the orders of justice is the supreme task of his life. He is incapable of
conceiving anything which surpasses and transcends the idea of the just
order of the world. Because his God is not above the world-order, his
ethics cannot rise above that principle which is the principle of ethical
order, namely justice. He does not know the God of love, therefore he
does not know that love which is above justice. The Christian, however, stands in relation to these orders of justice in the same way as he
stands within this earthly existence as such, namely as one who is looking forward to a better country that is a heavenly one, to the city
"whose builder and maker is God." The Christian knows that above
the demands of justice are always those of love—that he should not
merely treat his neighbour as a member of an order of justice, but also,
and above all, as a brother, as a man who, as a person called by God,
is more than any order of justice. Therefore he will try—and never
cease to try—to bring into the orders of justice an element which is
more than justice, although he knows that this love, surpassing justice,
can never fit into an order and can never be expressed in terms of
order and law, but only in terms of personal relationship.

The second difference concerns the content of the idea of justice,
and that means its relation to the idea of equality. In the Christian idea
of justice, also, equality has its supreme importance. All men are created by God equally in His image. They all share in this original dignity of person conferred by God. They all have the same essential
rights, based on this human dignity of God's creation. In this affirma-

tion of equality before God and of these original God-created rights, the Christian doctrine of justice comes close to the Stoic one. All the same, there is a distinction between the two of no small importance. The Christian idea of rights, in distinction to the Stoic, has its reference exclusively to man and never to God. Man has no rights over against God, being His creature and property; he lives entirely from God's grace and mercy. Rights he has only in so far as God gives them. Therefore the rights of man are under the same reservation which applies to the whole sphere of justice. They are always limited by the unconditional imperative of love. The Roman idea, *fiat justitia pereat mundus,* is unthinkable within the Christian context.

But, above all, the Christian idea of justice is different from that of antiquity in that it gives to the element of inequality or unlikeness its due place alongside that of equality. God has created all equally in His image, but He has not created them alike; on the contrary, He has created each one different from all the rest, with his own individuality. This corresponds to the personalism of the Biblical anthropology. The human personality is based on the personal call of God. That means that everyone is created in a unique act of creation, and therefore not according to a general pattern, but as a unique individuality. While the philosophers say: *principium individuationis est materia,* the Bible says: *principium individuationis est voluntas dei creatoris.* The differences between human beings are therefore not irrelevant, casual, immaterial, but just as much God's will and creation as the equality of personal dignity.

The elements of equality and unlikeness, however, do not stand on the same level. In Christ Jesus all differences, and therefore all individuality, become irrelevant. "There is neither Jew nor Greek, there is neither bond nor free, there is neither male nor female: for ye are all one in Christ Jesus." This is the eschatological, and therefore the final, point of view. It is within this earthly, preliminary existence that these differences are to be acknowledged and taken seriously. It is here that the preliminary principle of justice is valid. There shall be a time when justice gives way to love, when the law shall be superseded, when all the earthly conditions and limitations shall no longer exist. Then the individual differences will play no role, but till then they have to be acknowledged as God's will for this earthly existence. God has given to every one his own "face"; that is why unlikeness comes into the idea of justice.

Of course, the fact of the unlikeness of man was not unknown to the philosophers of antiquity, but from this fact they drew conclusions

which have to be repudiated from the point of view of Biblical
thought. They drew one of two conclusions. In older Greek philosophy,
as represented by Plato and Aristotle, the unlikeness of man is the
foundation of a different claim. The unlikeness is primarily understood
as a different participation in reason. Greeks have more reason than
the barbarians; men have more reason than women; the slaves have
none at all. They have to be treated accordingly; that means that the
difference of men limits their equality of dignity and rights. The later
Stoics have another view. Their conception of man is dominated by the
idea of equality and equal dignity in such a measure that they have no
interest at all in unlikeness. It seems to them something irrelevant,
casual, not worth taking seriously. That is to say, the principle of
equality encroaches upon unlikeness. It is the exact reverse of the older
view.

In Christian thought, however, the two elements of equality and
unlikeness are not in competition with each other and do not limit
each other, because they are on a different plane. Men are equal in
their relation to God, and therefore in their dignity. They are unlike in
their individuality, and therefore in their function in the created
world. There is but one and the same dignity for all, just as theirs is
only one and the same destiny whether they are men or women, children or adults, black or white, whether they are strong or weak, intelligent or dull. Their final destiny being the same, their personal dignity
cannot but be the same. All the same, the individual differences are
not negligible. What God has created cannot be irrelevant or negligible. The difference of individuality involves a difference of the function
within society.

Finally, the two elements—equality and unlikeness, equal dignity
and different function—are combined in such a way that both get their
full expression in the Christian idea of communion. Because men are
different from each other, they are also dependent on each other. Man
needs woman in order to be entirely man; woman needs man in order
to be entirely woman. This unlikeness points towards mutual completion and co-operation. Individuals are different, like the limbs of the
body, each one having its own function for which it is fitted by its
individuality. The difference of function necessarily creates a somewhat
hierarchical order in service, which again rests on the difference of individuality. According to his make-up, the one is fit for a subordinate,
the other for a superior position, the one for a more extraverted, the
other for a more introverted function. In this way the function of
woman in marriage and family is entirely different from that of man,

and the function of the children entirely different from that of the parents. This difference, or unlikeness, in kind and function is exactly the unity of the family as a community. It is so because this difference in no ways encroaches upon the equal dignity. Functional subordination has nothing whatever to do with lesser dignity or person. Society is thought of as a community of unlike individuals, who are bound to each other by the necessity of mutual completion and united by mutual respect for their equal dignity. We might call this idea an organic conception of society, but, in doing so, we must distinguish it clearly from that conception of organic unity which we find in a certain Romantic philosophy. For this Romantic organology lacks that element which is decisive within the Christian understanding of society, namely equality of personal dignity. Within Romantic thought the person is subordinated to the social whole by some kind of mystical principle of a *Gesamtpersönlichkeit*. The Romantic conception is totalitarian or collectivist, robbing human personality of its finality.

This, then, is the unique character of the Christian idea of society and of justice: that it combines the two principal elements of equality and unlikeness which everywhere else are in conflict with each other. It is this combination of the transcendental and the psychological, of the personal and the functional aspect, which gives the Christian idea of justice a flexibility, a dialectical subtlety, which no other has. It is neither egalitarian nor authoritarian, it is organic and, nonetheless, spiritual. It combines the naturalistic evaluation of different individuality and functional subordination with the most unconditional acknowledgment of the finality of every person. Now this combination of elements, and therefore this idea of justice which excludes both individualism and collectivism, authoritarianism and egalitarianism, is essentially and exclusively Christian. It is the Christian conception of divine creation—creation by the individual call of God to the universal destiny of all—which makes this possible and necessary. Apart from its basis in Christianity, this combination is possible only as a matter of chance without any inner necessity.

(1948)

69. Harry S. Truman
(1884-   )

Harry S. Truman, 32nd President of the United States, presents to the Congress in 1948 a Message on Civil Rights.

Message on Civil Rights

To the Congress of the United States:

In the state of the Union message on Jan. 7, 1948, I spoke of five great goals toward which we should strive in our constant effort to strengthen our democracy and improve the welfare of our people. The first of these is to secure fully our essential human rights. I am now presenting to the Congress my recommendations for legislation to carry us forward toward that goal.

This nation was founded by men and women who sought these shores that they might enjoy greater freedom and greater opportunity than they had known before. The founders of the United States proclaimed to the world the American belief that all men are created equal, and that Governments are instituted to secure the inalienable rights with which all men are endowed. In the Declaration of Independence and the Constitution of the United States, they eloquently expressed the aspirations of all mankind for equality and freedom.

These ideals inspired the peoples of other lands and their practical fulfillment made the United States the hope of the oppressed everywhere. Throughout our history men and women of all colors and creeds, of all races and religions, have come to this country to escape tyranny and discrimination. Millions strong, they have helped build this democratic nation and have constantly reinforced our devotion to the great ideals of liberty and equality.

AMERICAN FAITH SIMPLY STATED

With those who preceded them, they have helped to fashion and strengthen our American faith—a faith that can be simply stated:

We believe that all men are created equal and that they have the right to equal justice under law.

We believe that all men have the right to freedom of thought and of expression and the right to worship as they please.

We believe that all men are entitled to equal opportunities for jobs, for homes, for good health and for education.

We believe that all men should have a voice in their government and that government should protect, not usurp, the rights of the people.

These are the basic civil rights which are the source and the support of our democracy.

Today, the American people enjoy more freedom and opportunity than ever before. Never in our history has there been better reason to hope for the complete realization of the ideals of liberty and equality.

We shall not, however, finally achieve the ideals for which this nation was founded so long as any American suffers discrimination as a result of his race, or religion, or color, or the land of origin of his forefathers.

FLAGRANT VIOLATIONS STILL SEEN

Unfortunately, there still are examples—flagrant examples—of discrimination which are utterly contrary to our ideals. Not all groups of our population are free from the fear of violence. Not all groups are free to live and work where they please or to improve their conditions of life by their own efforts. Not all groups enjoy the full privileges of citizenship and participation in the government under which they live.

We cannot be satisfied until all our people have equal opportunities for jobs, for homes, for education, for health and for political expression, and until all our people have equal protection under the law.

One year ago I appointed a committee of fifteen distinguished Americans and asked them to appraise the condition of our civil rights and to recommend appropriate action by Federal, State and local governments.

The committee's appraisal has resulted in a frank and revealing report. This report emphasizes that our basic human freedoms are better cared for and more vigilantly defended than ever before. But it also makes clear that there is a serious gap between our ideals and some of our practices. This gap must be closed.

This will take the strong efforts of each of us individually, and all of us acting together through voluntary organizations and our governments.

RIGHTS BASED ON MUTUAL RESPECT

The protection of civil rights begins with the mutual respect for the rights of others which all of us should practice in our daily lives. Through organizations in every community in all parts of the country —we must continue to develop practical, workable arrangements for achieving greater tolerance and brotherhood.

The protection of civil rights is the duty of every government which derives its powers from the consent of the people. This is equally true of local, state and national governments. There is much that the states can and should do at this time to extend their protection of civil rights. Wherever the law enforcement measures of State and local governments are inadequate to discharge this primary function of government, these measures should be strengthened and improved.

The Federal Government has a clear duty to see that constitutional guarantees of individual liberties and of equal protection under the laws are not denied or abridged anywhere in our Union. That duty is shared by all three branches of the Government, but it can be fulfilled only if the Congress enacts modern, comprehensive civil rights laws, adequate to the needs of the day, and demonstrating our continuing faith in the free way of life.

PROGRAM SET FOR CONGRESS

I recommend, therefore, that the Congress enact legislation at this session directed toward the following specific objectives:

1. Establishing a permanent Commission on Civil Rights, a Joint Congressional Committee on Civil Rights, and a Civil Rights Division in the Department of Justice.

2. Strengthening existing civil rights statutes.

3. Providing Federal protection against lynching.

4. Protecting more adequately the right to vote.

5. Establishing a Fair Employment Practice Commission to prevent unfair discrimination in employment.

6. Prohibiting discrimination in interstate transportation facilities.

7. Providing home rule and suffrage in Presidential elections for the residents of the District of Columbia.

8. Providing statehood for Hawaii and Alaska **and a** greater measure of self-government for our island possessions.

9. Equalizing the opportunities for residents of the United States to become naturalized citizens.

10. Settling the evacuation claims of Japanese-Americans.

FOR BETTER FEDERAL SET-UP

As a first step, we must strengthen the organization of the Federal Government in order to enforce civil rights legislation more adequately and to watch over the state of our traditional liberties.

I recommend that the Congress establish a permanent Commission on Civil Rights, reporting to the President. The Commission should continuously review our civil rights policies and practices, study specific problems and make recommendations to the President at frequent intervals. It should work with other agencies of the Federal Government, with state and local governments and with private organizations.

I also suggest that the Congress establish a Joint Congressional Committee on Civil Rights. This committee should make a continuing study of legislative matters relating to civil rights and should consider means of improving respect for and enforcement of those rights.

These two bodies together should keep all of us continuously aware of the condition of civil rights in the United States and keep us alert to opportunities to improve their protection.

To provide for better enforcement of Federal civil rights laws, there will be established a Division of Civil Rights in the Department of Justice. I recommend that the Congress provide for an additional assistant Attorney General to supervise this division.

I recommend that the Congress amend and strengthen the existing provisions of Federal law which safeguard the right to vote and the right to safety and security of person and property. These provisions are the basis for our present civil rights enforcement program.

Section 51 of Title 18 of the United States Code, which now gives protection to citizens in the enjoyment of rights secured by the Constitution or Federal laws, needs to be strengthened in two respects. In its present form, this section protects persons only if they are citizens, and affords protection only against conspiracies by two or more persons.

This protection should be extended to all inhabitants of the United States. Whether or not they are citizens and should be afforded [protection] against infringement by persons acting individually, as well as in conspiracy.

Section 52 of Title 18 of the United States Code, which now gives general protection to individuals against the deprivation of Federally secured rights by public officers, has proved to be inadequate in some cases because of the generality of its language. An enumeration of the principal rights protected under this section is needed to make more definite and certain the protection which the section affords.

PROTECTION AGAINST LYNCHING

A specific Federal measure is needed to deal with the crime of lynching—against which I cannot speak too strongly.

It is a principle of our democracy, written into our Constitution, that every person accused of an offense against the law shall have a fair, orderly trial in an impartial court. We have made great progress towards this end, but I regret to say that lynching has not yet finally disappeared from our land. So long as one person walks in fear of lynching, we shall not have achieved equal justice under law.

I call upon the Congress to take decisive action against this crime.

PROTECTING RIGHT TO VOTE

Under the Constitution, the right of all properly qualified citizens to vote is beyond question.

Yet the exercise of this right is still subject to interference. Some individuals are prevented from voting by isolated acts of intimidation. Some whole groups are prevented by outmoded policies prevailing in certain states or communities.

We need stronger statutory protection of the right to vote. I urge the Congress to enact legislation forbidding interference by public officers or private persons with the right of qualified citizens to participate in primary, special and general elections in which Federal officers are to be chosen. This legislation should extend to elections for state as well as Federal officers in so far as interference with the right to vote results from discriminatory action by public officers based on race, color, or other unreasonable classification.

Requirements for the payment of poll taxes also interfere with the right to vote. There are still seven states which, by their Constitutions, place this barrier between their citizens and the ballot box. The American people would welcome voluntary action on the part of these states to remove this barrier.

Nevertheless, I believe the Congress should enact measures insuring that the right to vote in elections for Federal officers shall not be contingent upon the payment of taxes.

I wish to make it clear that the enactment of the measures I have recommended will in no sense result in Federal conduct of elections. They are designed to give qualified citizens Federal protection of their right to vote. The actual conduct of elections, as always, will remain the responsibility of state governments.

FAIR EMPLOYMENT PRACTICE BODY

We in the United States believe that all men are entitled to equality of opportunity. Racial, religious and other invidious forms of discrimination deprive the individual of an equal chance to develop and utilize his talents and to enjoy the rewards of his efforts.

Once more I repeat my request that the Congress enact fair employment practice legislation prohibiting discrimination in employment based on race, color, religion or national origin. The legislation should create a Fair Employment Practice Commission with authority to prevent discrimination by employers and labor unions, trade and professional associations and Government agencies and employment bureaus.

The degree of effectiveness which the wartime Fair Employment Practice Committee attained shows that it is possible to equalize job opportunity by Government action, and thus to eliminate the influence of prejudice in employment.

The channels of interstate commerce should be open to all Americans on a basis of complete equality. The Supreme Court has recently declared unconstitutional state laws requiring segregation on public carriers in interstate travel. Company regulations must not be allowed to replace institutional state laws. I urge the Congress to prohibit discrimination and segregration, in the use of interstate transportation facilities, by both public officers and the employees of private companies.

THE DISTRICT OF COLUMBIA

I am in full accord with the principle of local self-government for residents of the District of Columbia. In addition, I believe that the Constitution should be amended to extend suffrage in Presidential elections to the residents of the District.

The District of Columbia should be a true symbol of American freedom and democracy for our own people and for the people of the world. It is my earnest hope that the Congress will promptly give the citizens of the District of Columbia their own local, elective government.

They themselves can then deal with the inequalities arising from segregation in the schools and other public facilities and from racial barriers to places of public accommodation which now exist for one-third of the District's population.

The present inequalities in essential services are primarily a problem for the District itself, but they are also of great concern to the whole nation. Failing local corrective action in the near future, the Congress should enact a model civil rights law for the nation's capital.

TERRITORIES AND POSSESSIONS

The present political status of our territories and possessions impairs the enjoyment of civil rights by their residents.

I have in the past recommended legislation granting statehood to Alaska and Hawaii, and organic acts for Guam and American Samoa, including a grant of citizenship to the people of these Pacific islands. I repeat these recommendations.

Furthermore, the residents of the Virgin Islands should be granted an increasing measure of self-government and the people of Puerto Rico should be allowed to choose their form of government and their ultimate status with respect to the United States.

EQUALITY IN NATURALIZATION

All properly qualified legal residents of the United States should be allowed to become citizens without regard to race, color, religion or national origin.

The Congress has recently removed the bars which formerly prevented persons from China, India and the Philippines from becoming naturalized citizens. I urge the Congress to remove the remaining racial or nationality barriers which stand in the way of citizenship for some residents of our country.

During the last war more than 100,000 Japanese-Americans were evacuated from their homes in the Pacific States solely because of their racial origin. Many of these people suffered property and business losses as a result of this forced evacuation and through no fault of their own.

The Congress has before it legislation establishing a procedure by which claims based upon these losses can be promptly considered and settled. I trust that favorable action on this legislation will soon be taken.

The legislation I have recommended for enactment by the Congress at the present session is a minimum program if the Federal Government is to fulfill its obligation of insuring the Constitutional guarantees of individual liberties and of equal protection under the law.

Under the authority of existing law, the Executive Branch is taking every possible action to improve the enforcement of the Civil Rights Statutes and to eliminate discrimination in Federal employment, in providing Federal services and facilities, and in the Armed Forces.

I have already referred to the establishment of the Civil Rights Division of the Department of Justice. The Federal Bureau of Investigation will work closely with this new division in the investigation of Federal Civil Rights Cases. Specialized training is being given to the Bureau's agents so that they may render more effective service in this difficult field of law enforcement.

FOR EQUALITY IN ARMED FORCES

It is the settled policy of the United States Government that there shall be no discrimination in Federal employment or in providing Federal service and facilities. Steady progress has been made toward this objective in recent years. I shall shortly issue an Executive Order containing a comprehensive restatement of the Federal non-discrimination policy, together with appropriate measures to ensure compliance.

During the recent war and in the years since its close we have made much progress toward equality of opportunity in our Armed Services without regard to race, color, religion or national origin. I have instructed the Secretary of Defense to take steps to have the remaining instances of discrimination in the Armed Services eliminated as rapidly as possible. The personnel policies and practices of all the Services in this regard will be made consistent.

I have instructed the Secretary of the Army to investigate the status of civil rights in the Panama Canal Zone with a view to eliminating such discrimination as may exist there. If legislation is necessary, I shall make appropriate recommendations to the Congress.

The position of the United States in the world today makes it especially urgent that we adopt these measures to secure for all our people their essential rights.

The peoples of the world are faced with the choice of freedom or enslavement, a choice between a form of government which harnesses the State in the service of the individual and a form of government which chains the individual to the needs of the State.

WORKING FOR A FREE WORLD

We in the United States are working in company with other nations who share our desire for enduring world peace and who believe with us that, above all else, men must be free. We are striving to build a world family of nations—a world where men may live under governments of their own choosing and under laws of their own making.

As part of that endeavor, the Commission on Human Rights of the United Nations is now engaging in preparing an international bill of human rights by which the nations of the world may bind themselves by international covenant to give effect to basic human rights and fundamental freedoms. We have played a leading role in this undertaking designed to create a world order of law and justice fully protective of the rights and the dignity of the individual.

To be effective in these efforts, we must protect our civil rights so that by providing all our people with the maximum enjoyment of personal freedom and personal opportunity we shall be a stronger nation—stronger in our leadership, stronger in our moral position, stronger in the deeper satisfactions of a united citizenry.

We know that our democracy is not perfect. But we do know that it offers a fuller, freer, happier life to our people than any totalitarian nation has ever offered.

If we wish to inspire the peoples of the world whose freedom is in jeopardy, if we wish to restore hope to those who have already lost their civil liberties, if we wish to fulfill the promise that is ours, we must correct the remaining imperfections in our practice of democracy.

We know the way. We need only the will.

(1948)

Universal Declaration of Human Rights

70. (1948)

This is a statement drafted by the Commission on Human Rights, a division of the Economic and Social Council of the United Nations, which was adopted by the U. N. on December 10, 1948.

UNIVERSAL DECLARATION OF HUMAN RIGHTS

PREAMBLE

WHEREAS, recognition of the inherent dignity and of the equal and inalienable rights of all members of the human family is the foundation of freedom, justice and peace in the world; and

WHEREAS, disregard and contempt for human rights have resulted in barbarous acts which have outraged the conscience of mankind, and the advent of a world in which human beings shall enjoy freedom of speech and belief and freedom from fear and want has been proclaimed as the highest aspiration of the common people; and

WHEREAS, it is essential if man is not to be compelled to have recourse as a last resort to rebellion against tyranny and oppression that human rights should be protected by the rule of law; and

WHEREAS, it is essential to promote the development of friendly relations between nations; and

WHEREAS, the peoples of the United Nations have in the Charter reaffirmed their faith in fundamental human rights, in the dignity and worth of the human person and in the equal rights of men and women, and determined to promote social progress and better standards of life in larger freedom; and

WHEREAS, the member states have pledged themselves to achieve, in cooperation with the United Nations, the promotion of universal respect for and observance of human rights and fundamental freedoms; and

WHEREAS, a common understanding of these rights and freedoms is of the greatest importance for the full realization of this pledge,

Now, therefore,

THE GENERAL ASSEMBLY

PROCLAIMS this Declaration of Human Rights as a common standard of achievement for all peoples and all nations, to the end that every individual and every organ of society, keeping this declaration constantly in mind, shall strive by teaching and education to promote respect for these rights and freedoms and by progressive measures, national and international, to secure their universal and effective recognition and observance, both among the peoples of member states themselves and among the peoples of territories under their jurisdiction.

ARTICLE 1. All human beings are born free and equal, in dignity and rights. They are endowed with reason and conscience, and should act towards one another in a spirit of brotherhood.

ART. 2. Everyone is entitled to all the rights and freedoms set forth in this Declaration, without distinction of any kind, such as race, colour, sex, language, religion, political or other opinion, national or social origin, property, birth or other status.

Furthermore, no distinction shall be made on the basis of the political, jurisdictional or international status of the country or territory to which a person belongs, whether it be independent, trust, non-self-governing or under any other limitation of sovereignty.

ART. 3. Everyone has the right to life, liberty and security of person.

ART. 4. No one shall be held in slavery or servitude; slavery and the slave trade shall be prohibited in all their forms.

ART. 5. No one shall be subjected to torture or to cruel, inhuman or degrading treatment or punishment.

ART. 6. Everyone has the right to recognition everywhere as a person before the law.

ART. 7. All are equal before the law and are entitled without any discrimination to equal protection of the law. All are entitled to equal protection against any discrimination in violation of this declaration and against any incitement to such discrimination.

ART. 8. Everyone has the right to an effective remedy by the competent national tribunals for acts violating the fundamental rights granted him by the Constitution or by law.

ART. 9. No one shall be subjected to arbitrary arrest, detention or exile.

ART. 10. Everyone is entitled in full equality to a fair and public hearing by an independent and impartial tribunal, in the determination of his rights and obligations and of any criminal charge against him.

ART. 11. 1. Everyone with a penal offence has the right to be presumed innocent until proved guilty according to law in a public trial at which he has had all the guarantees necessary for his defence.

2. No one shall be held guilty of any penal offence on account of any act or omission which did not constitute a penal offence, under national or international law, at the time when it was committed. Nor shall a heavier penalty be imposed than the one that was applicable at the time the penal offence was committed.

ART. 12. No one shall be subjected to arbitrary interference with his privacy, family, home or correspondence, nor to attacks upon his honor and reputation. Everyone has the right to the protection of the law against such interference or attacks.

ART. 13. 1. Everyone has the right to freedom of movement and residence within the borders of each state.

2. Everyone has the right to leave any country, including his own, and to return to his country.

ART. 14. 1. Everyone has the right to seek and to enjoy in other countries asylum from persecution.

2. This right may not be invoked in the case of prosecutions genuinely arising from non-political crimes or from acts contrary to the purposes and principles of the United Nations.

ART. 15. 1. Everyone has the right to a nationality.

2. No one shall be arbitrarily deprived of his nationality nor denied the right to change his nationality.

ART. 16. 1. Men and women of full age, without any limitation due to race, nationality or religion, have the right to marry and to found a family. They are entitled to equal rights as to marriage, during marriage and at its dissolution.

2. Marriage shall be entered into only with the free and full consent of the intending spouses.

3. The family is the natural and fundamental group unit of society and is entitled to protection by society and the state.

ART. 17. 1. Everyone has the right to own property alone as well as in association with others.

2. No one shall be arbitrarily deprived of his property.

ART. 18. Everyone has the right to freedom of thought, conscience and religion; this right includes freedom to change his religion or belief, and freedom, either alone or in community with others and in public or private, to manifest his religion or belief in teaching, practice, worship and observance.

ART. 19. Everyone has the right to freedom of opinion and expression; this right includes freedom to hold opinions without interference and to seek, receive and impart information and ideas through any media and regardless of frontiers.

ART. 20. 1. Everyone has the right to freedom of peaceful assembly and association.

2. No one may be compelled to belong to an association.

ART. 21. 1. Everyone has the right to take part in the Government of his country, directly or through freely chosen representatives.

2. Everyone has the right of equal access to public service in his country.

3. The will of the people shall be the basis of the authority of Government; this will shall be expressed in periodic and genuine elections which shall be by universal and equal suffrage and shall be held by secret vote or by equivalent free voting procedures.

ART. 22. Everyone, as a member of society, has the right to social security and is entitled to the realization, through national effort and international cooperation and in accordance with the organization and resources of each state, of the economic, social and cultural rights indispensable for his dignity and the free development of his personality.

ART. 23. 1. Everyone has the right to work, to free choice of employment, to just and favorable conditions of work and to protection against unemployment.

2. Everyone, without discrimination, has the right to equal pay for equal work.

3. Everyone who works has the right to just and favorable remuneration, ensuring for himself and his family an existence worthy of human dignity, and supplemented, if necessary, by other means of social protection.

4. Everyone has the right to form and to join trade unions for the protection of his interests.

ART. 24. Everyone has the right to rest and leisure, including reasonable limitation of working hours and periodic holiday with pay.

ART. 25. 1. Everyone has the right to a standard of living adequate for the health and well-being of himself and of his family, including food, clothing, housing and medical care and necessary social services, and the right to security in the event of unemployment, sickness, disability, widowhood, old age or other lack of livelihood in circumstances beyond his control.

2. Motherhood and childhood are entitled to special care and assistance. All children, whether born in or out of wedlock, shall enjoy the same social protection.

Art. 26. 1. Everyone has the right to education. Education shall be free, at least in the elementary and fundamental stages. Elementary education shall be compulsory. Technical and professional education shall be made generally available, and higher education shall be equally accessible to all on the basis of merit.

2. Education shall be directed to the full development of the human personality and to the strengthening of respect for human rights and fundamental freedoms, it shall promote understanding, tolerance and friendship among all nations, racial or religious groups, and shall further the activities of the United Nations for the maintenance of peace.

3. Parents have a prior right to choose the kind of education that shall be given to their children.

Art. 27. 1. Everyone has the right freely to participate in the cultural life of the community, to enjoy the arts and to share in scientific advancement and its benefits.

2. Everyone has the right to the protection of the moral and material interests resulting from any scientific, literary or artistic production of which he is the author.

Art. 28. Everyone is entitled to a social and international order in which the rights and freedoms set forth in this declaration can be fully realized.

Art. 29. 1. Everyone has duties to the community in which alone the free and full development of his personality is possible.

2. In the exercise of his rights and freedoms, everyone shall be subject only to such limitations as are prescribed by law solely for the purpose of securing due recognition and respect for the rights and freedoms of others and of meeting the just requirements of morality, public order and the general welfare in a democratic society.

3. These rights and freedoms may in no case be exercised contrary to the purposes and principles of the United Nations.

Art. 30. Nothing in this Declaration may be interpreted as implying for any states, groups or persons, any right to engage in any activity or to perform any act aimed at the destruction of any of the rights and freedoms set forth herein.

(1948)

Reinhold Niebuhr

71.

(1892-   )

Reinhold Niebuhr, American theologian, social critic, and teacher of Christian ethics at Union Theological Seminary in New York, offers criticisms of the Catholic natural law interpretation of equality.

from Faith and History

The most frequent general principle of justice in the thought of modern as well as Stoic and Catholic proponents of natural law is the principle of equality. The dominant position of the principle of equality in all natural-law concepts is significant. Equality stands in a medial position between love and justice. If the obligation to love the neighbor as the self is to be reduced to rational calculation, the only guarantee of the fulfillment of the obligation is a grant to the neighbor which equals what the self claims for itself. Thus equality is love in terms of logic. But it is no longer love in the ecstatic dimension. For the principle of equality allows and requires that the self insist upon its own rights and interests in competition with the rights and interests of the other. Therefore equal justice is on the one hand the law of love in rational form and on the other hand something less than the law of love. The heedlessness of perfect love can not be present in the rational calculations of justice. The self's lack of concern for its own interests may have to be reintroduced into the calculations of justice, however, when and if it becomes apparent that all calculations of justice, however rational, tend to weight the standard of justice on the side of the one who defines the standard.

This existential defect in definitions of justice becomes apparent just as soon as it is recognized that equality is a guiding, but not an absolute, standard of justice. If, as in Marxism, equality is made into an absolute standard, it bears the ideological taint of the "lower" classes in society. They rightly resent unequal privileges but they wrongly fail to appreciate the necessity of inequality of function, without which no society could live. Undoubtedly the classes in society who perform the more important functions appropriate more privileges than the proper performance of function requires or deserves. Yet on the other hand the function does require some special privileges. It is possible and necessary to correct this ideological taint in

316

Marxist equalitarianism. An adequate social theory must do justice both to the spirit of equality and to the necessities of functional inequality. But such a social theory can not possibly have the validity of what is usually meant by "natural law." It will be filled with speculative judgements on just how much special privilege is required for the performance of certain functions in society. It will certainly contain as many ideological taints as any Marxist theory.

It must be obvious that, as one moves from the primary principle of justice to more detailed conclusions, judgements become more hazardous, and conclusions should be regarded as the fruit of social wisdom rather than of pure logic. Most of the propositions which are presented to us in the name of "natural law" are in fact in the category of what Aquinas defined as "secondary principles which . . . are certain detailed proximate conclusions drawn from first principles" and which he admitted to be subject to change. Others might well be placed on the even lower level of practical applications to particular problems about which Aquinas admits that "the more we descend toward the particular the more we encounter defects," for "in matters of action truth or practical rectitude is not the same for all."

The right to the possession of property as defined in Catholic natural-law theory is a good illustration of the defects of a too inflexible legalism. "Every man has by nature the right to possess property of his own," declares Leo XIII in the encyclical "On the Condition of the Working Man." Property is "natural," according to the theory, in both meanings of that word. "Natural" means, on the one hand, that man, as distinguished from animals, has both the ability and the inclination to appropriate instruments, goods and land and "make them his own." It is "natural," on the other hand, in the sense that reason justifies this extension of the power of the person as logically implied in his power over himself and because it contributes to social peace and justice since "we see that among those who hold anything in common and undivided ownership, strifes not infrequently arise" (Aquinas). The social wisdom of regarding property as a relatively effective institution of social peace and justice can not be challenged. It is a "remedy for sin" in the sense that it gives the person power to defend himself against the inclination of others to take advantage of him. It endows him with instruments for the proper performance of his function and grants him a measure of security in an insecure world. But both Catholic and Protestant social theory tended to make the right of property much too absolute. The wisdom of some of the early church Fathers was forgotten. They understood that the power of property could be an instrument of injustice as well as of justice; and that it could be the fruit of sin as well as remedy for sin.

These scruples of the early Fathers achieved a new relevance in an industrial age in which new and dynamic aggregates of economic power developed. They were too inordinate to come into the category of defensive power; and they obviously encouraged the temptation to injustice in men. For great inequalities of power always tempt the strong to take advantage of the weak. Resentment against rising injustices in an industrial society gave birth to a new and heretical religion of social redemption. According to this Marxist religion, property was the very root of sin in human nature; and its abolition would redeem society from sin, ushering in a utopian harmony of all interests and vitalities. This heretical religion blew the half of the truth which the early Fathers of the church had recognized (namely that property could be the fruit and bearer of sin) into a monstrous error.

The error should have been countered by a profound reconsideration of the whole problem of the relation of property to justice. Instead it was met by a hard and fast Christian legalism, proclaiming "eternal" principles of natural law, which daily experience continued to prove problematic and contingent, rather than eternal.

Even Pope Leo XIII, despite his interest in and understanding of the problems of justice in an industrial age, declared categorically that proposals for the socialization of property "are emphatically unjust because they would rob the lawful possessor, bring the state into a sphere not its own and cause complete confusion in the community."

Less than a century later the Vatican made a much more qualified judgement on the problem of property; for Pius XI declared: "It may well come about that the tenets of a mitigated socialism will no longer differ from those who seek to reform society according to Christian principles. For it is rightly contended that certain forms of property must be reserved to the state since they carry within them an opportunity for dominating, **too** great to be left to private individuals." The difference in accent between the two encyclicals can hardly be denied. Some rather tragic social history in western civilization accounts for the difference. One is tempted to speculate whether some of that history might have been avoided if the earlier encyclical had contained the wisdom of the second.

In any event the difference between them is not to be accounted for by a difference in the logic by which reason moves from primary to secondary principles of justice. It is a difference in social wisdom, determined by differences in social experience. The difference proves that the application of general principles of justice to particular situations includes not merely the application of general rules to particular instances and persons, but to particular epochs and to particular types of general institutions. The institution of "property" is not one but many. Property in land may mean the power of the landlord over the peasant and it may mean the security of the peasant in his own land. Property in industry may mean inordinate power; and it may mean the right of an inventive genius to profit from his inventions.

There are, in short, fewer specific principles of justice with "eternal" validity than is assumed in almost all theories of natural law.

Rules of justice do not follow in a "necessary manner" from some basic proposition of justice. They are the fruit of a rational survey of the whole field of human interests, of the structure of human life and of the causal sequences in human relations. They embody too many contingent elements and are subject to such inevitable distortion by interest and passion that they can not possibly be placed in the same category with the logical propositions of mathematics or the analytic propositions of science. They are the product of social wisdom and unwisdom. Reason itself is not the source of law, since it is not possible to prove the self's obligation to the neighbor by any rational analysis which does not assume the proposition it intends to prove. Yet reason works helpfully to define the obligation of love in the complexities of various types of human relations.

If the *Agape* of New Testament morality is the negation as well as the fulfillment of every private virtue, it is also the negation and the fulfillment of all structures and schemes of justice. It is their fulfillment in the sense that the heedlessness of perfect love is the source and end of all reciprocal relations in human existence, preventing them from degenerating into mere calculation of advantage. It is also the source of the principle of equality and may be a complement to it in all intimate and private relations.

Yet *Agape* stands in contradiction to all structures, schemes and systems of justice, insofar as all historic schemes of justice embody sinful elements, because they contain implicit rationalizations of special interests. This sinful corruption is as obvious in rational definitions of justice as in the positive laws of justice which are historically enacted in given states.

Thus a Christian morality, inspired by the spirit of the New Testament, must be as ready to challenge legalism as relativism.

Against relativists it must insist that no man or nation, no age or culture can arbitrarily define its own law. Against legalists it must insist that there is no virtue in law as such (Romans 7:7-25). It does not have the power within itself to compel obedience. All genuine obedience to law is derived from the grace of love, which is more than law. Neither does law have the virtue to define the interests of the self and the neighbor with precision, since there is no completely disinterested intelligence in history. If the faulty criteria of law are not corrected by love, law is always in danger of becoming the instrument of sin.

The Pauline admonition against legalism, "Stand fast therefore in the liberty wherewith Christ hath made us free, and be not entangled again in the yoke of bondage" (Galatians 5:1), is inspired not merely by a consideration of the moral defects in any specific system of law but by the limits of law as such. The admonition has been shockingly disregarded by most versions of the Christian faith. They have found some way of making law, whether derived from Scripture or from the supposed absolutes of reason, too binding. The only exception to this legalism is found in modern sentimental forms of Christianity which assume that the supremacy of the law of love makes it possible to dispense with subordinate laws of justice. It is not possible to dispense with them; but it is important to recognize the historically contingent elements in every formulation of the principles of justice.

It is specially important to reaffirm the New Testament spirit of freedom over law in our own day because the task of preserving justice in the rapidly shifting circumstances of a technical society and of preserving personal integrity under conditions of growing human power require that the spirit of love be freed of subservience to traditional codes. It is not wise to alter social customs and traditional restraints upon human expansiveness lightly. The more the historical root of social restraints is known, the greater must be the inclination to deal conservatively with any viable structure of the human community. But no historic structure or traditional restraint deserves the sanctity which is usually ascribed to it. A truly religious morality must appreciate the virtue of historic and traditional forms of justice against attack by abstract forms of rationalism; but it must at the same time subject every structure of justice, whether historically, rationally, or Scripturally validated, to constant scrutiny.

(1949)

U. S. Supreme Court

Brown et al. v. Board of Education et al.

72.

(1954)

In considering cases from four states, the Supreme Court ruled that segregation in public education is a denial of the equal protection of the laws guaranteed by the Fourteenth Amendment.

BROWN ET AL. v. BOARD OF EDUCATION OF TOPEKA ET AL., Supreme Court of the U. S. 347 U. S. 483

OPINION OF THE COURT

MR. CHIEF JUSTICE WARREN delivered the opinion of the Court.

These cases come to us from the States of Kansas, South Carolina, Virginia, and Delaware. They are premised on different facts and different local conditions, but a common legal question justifies their consideration together in this consolidated opinion.

In each of the cases, minors of the Negro race, through their legal representatives, seek the aid of the courts in obtaining admission to the public schools of their community on a nonsegregated basis. In each instance they had been denied admission to schools attended by white children under laws requiring or permitting segregation according to race. This segregation was alleged to deprive the plaintiffs of the equal protection of the laws under the Fourteenth Amendment. In each of the cases other than the Delaware case, a three-judge federal district court denied relief to the plaintiffs on the so-called "separate but equal" doctrine announced by this Court in *Plessy* v. *Ferguson*, 163 U.S. 537. Under that doctrine, equality of treatment is accorded when the races are provided substantially equal facilities, even though these facilities be separate. In the Delaware case, the Supreme Court of Delaware adhered to that doctrine, but ordered that the plaintiffs be admitted to the white schools because of their superiority to the Negro schools.

The plaintiffs contend that segregated public schools are not "equal" and cannot be made "equal," and that hence they are deprived of the equal protection of the laws. Because of the obvious importance of the question presented, the Court took jurisdiction.

Argument was heard in the 1952 Term, and reargument was heard this Term on certain questions propounded by the Court.

Reargument was largely devoted to the circumstances surrounding the adoption of the Fourteenth Amendment in 1868. It covered exhaustively consideration of the Amendment in Congress, ratification by the states, then existing practices in racial segregation, and the views of proponents and opponents of the Amendment. This discussion and our own investigation convince us that, although these sources cast some light, it is not enough to resolve the problem with which we are faced. At best, they are inconclusive. The most avid proponents of the post-War Amendments undoubtedly intended them to remove all legal distinctions among "all persons born or naturalized in the United States." Their opponents, just as certainly, were antagonistic to both the letter and the spirit of the Amendments and wished them to have the most limited effect. What others in Congress and the state legislatures had in mind cannot be determined with any degree of certainty.

An additional reason for the inconclusive nature of the Amendment's history, with respect to segregated schools, is the status of public education at that time. In the South, the movement toward free common schools, supported by general taxation, had not yet taken hold. Education of white children was largely in the hands of private groups. Education of Negroes was almost non-existent, and practically all of the race were illiterate. In fact, any education of Negroes was forbidden by law in some states. Today, in contrast, many Negroes have achieved outstanding success in the arts and sciences as well as in the business and professional world. It is true that public school education at the time of the Amendment had advanced further in the North, but the effect of the Amendment on Northern States was generally ignored in the congressional debates. Even in the North, the conditions of public education did not approximate those existing today. The curriculum was usually rudimentary; ungraded schools were common in rural areas; the school term was but three months a year in many states; and compulsory school attendance was virtually unknown. As a consequence, it is not surprising that there should be so little in the history of the Fourteenth Amendment relating to its intended effect on public education.

In the first cases in this Court construing the Fourteenth Amendment, decided shortly after its adoption, the Court interpreted it as proscribing all state-imposed discriminations against the Negro race. The doctrine of "separate but equal" did not make its appearance in this Court until 1896 in the case of *Plessy* v. *Ferguson, supra,* involving not education but transportation. American courts have since labored with the doctrine for over half a century. In this Court, there have been six cases involving the "separate but equal" doctrine in the field of public education. In *Cumming* v. *County Board of Education,* 175 U. S. 528, and *Gong Lum* v. *Rice,* 275 U. S. 78, the validity of the doctrine itself was not challenged. In more recent cases, all on the graduate school level, inequality was found in that specific benefits enjoyed by white students were denied to Negro students of the same educational qualifications. *Missouri ex rel. Gaines* v. *Canada,* 305 U. S. 337; *Sipuel* v. *Oklahoma,* 332 U. S. 631; *Sweatt* v. *Painter,* 339 U. S. 629; *McLaurin* v. *Oklahoma State Regents,* 339 U. S. 637. In none of these cases was it necessary to re-examine the doctrine to grant relief to the Negro plaintiff. And in *Sweatt* v. *Painter, supra,* the Court expressly reserved decision on the question whether *Plessy* v. *Ferguson* should be held inapplicable to public education.

In the instant cases, that question is directly presented. Here, unlike *Sweatt* v. *Painter,* there are findings below that the Negro and white schools involved have been equalized, or are being equalized, with respect to buildings, curricula, qualifications and salaries of teachers, and other "tangible" factors. Our decision, therefore, cannot turn on merely a comparison of these tangible factors in the Negro and white schools involved in each of the cases. We must look instead to the effect of segregation itself on public education.

In approaching this problem, we cannot turn the clock back to 1868 when the Amendment was adopted, or even to 1896 when *Plessy* v. *Ferguson* was written. We must consider public education in the light of its full development and its present place in American life throughout the Nation. Only in this way can it be determined if segregation in public schools deprives these plaintiffs of the equal protection of the laws.

Today, education is perhaps the most important function of state and local governments. Compulsory school attendance laws and the great expenditures for education both demonstrate our recognition of the importance of education to our democratic society. It is required in the performance of our most basic public responsibilities, even service in the armed forces. It is the very foundation of good citizenship. Today it is a principal instrument in awakening the child to cultural values, in preparing him for later professional training, and in helping him to adjust normally to his environment. In these days, it is doubtful that any child may reasonably be expected to succeed in life if he is denied the opportunity of an education. Such an opportunity, where the state has undertaken to provide it, is a right which must be made available to all on equal terms.

We come then to the question presented: Does segregation of children in public schools solely on the basis of race, even though the physical facilities and other "tangible" factors may be equal, deprive the children of the minority group of equal educational opportunities? We believe that it does.

In *Sweatt* v. *Painter, supra,* in finding that a segregated law school for Negroes could not provide them equal educational opportunities, this Court relied in large part on "those qualities which are incapable of objective measurement but which make for greatness in a law school." In *McLaurin* v. *Oklahoma State Regents, supra,* the Court, in requiring that a Negro admitted to a white graduate school be treated like all other students, again resorted to intangible considerations: ". . . his ability to study, to engage in discussions and exchange views with other students, and, in general, to learn his profession." Such considerations apply with added force to children in grade and high schools. To separate them from others of similar age and qualifications solely because of their race generates a feeling of inferiority as to their status in the community that may affect their hearts and minds in a way unlikely ever to be undone. The effect of this separation on their educational opportunities was well stated by a finding in the Kansas case by a court which nevertheless felt compelled to rule against the Negro plaintiffs:

> "Segregation of white and colored children in public schools has a detrimental effect upon the colored children. The impact is greater when it has the sanction of the law; for the policy of separating the races is usually interpreted as denoting the inferiority of the negro group. A sense of inferiority affects the motivation of a child to learn. Segregation with the sanction of law, therefore, has a tendency to [retard] the educational and mental development of negro children and to deprive them of some of the benefits they would receive in a racial[ly] integrated school system."

Whatever may have been the extent of psychological knowledge at the time of *Plessy* v. *Ferguson,* this finding is amply supported by modern authority. Any language in *Plessy* v. *Ferguson* contrary to this finding is rejected.

We conclude that in the field of public education the doctrine of "separate but equal" has no place. Separate educational facilities are inherently unequal. Therefore, we hold that the plaintiffs and others similarly situated for whom the actions have been brought are, by reason of the segregation complained of, deprived of the equal protection of the laws guaranteed by the Fourteenth Amendment. This disposition makes unnecessary any discussion whether such segregation also violates the Due Process Clause of the Fourteenth Amendment.

Because these are class actions, because of the wide applicability of this decision, and because of the great variety of local conditions, the formulation of decrees in these cases presents problems of considerable perplexity. On reargument, the consideration of appropriate relief was necessarily subordinated to the primary question—the constitutionality of segregation in public education. We have now announced that such segregation is a denial of the equal protection of the laws. In order that we may have the full assistance of the parties in formulating decrees, the cases will be restored to the docket, and the parties are requested to present further argument on Questions 4 and 5 previously propounded by the Court for the reargument of this Term. The Attorney General of the United States is again invited to participate. The Attorneys General of the states requiring or permitting segregation in public education will also be permitted to appear as *amici curiae* upon request to do so by September 15, 1954, and submission of briefs by October 1, 1954.

It is so ordered.

(1954)

73. Barrington Moore, Jr.

(1913-   )

The Senior Research Fellow at Harvard's Russian Research Center offers observations on the functions of egalitarianism.

from Notes on the Process of Acquiring Power

Where nativism and egalitarianism are combined in a charter myth, the egalitarian aspect often falls short of universal application. Sparta, living under the permanent emergency of a Helot revolt, constitutes a well-known example. There the equality prevailing in the ruling caste did not of course extend to the suppressed Helots. In nationalist movements, too, the conception of equality is ambiguous. During the early stages, admiration for the oppressor may occur along with a demand for equality with the dominant group. Both themes are very noticeable in Indian nationalism. Even the Nazis displayed some Anglophile sentiments, particularly admiration for the supposed cunning of the British aristocracy, regarded as the major reason for the German defeat in 1918. Later such admiration may turn to hate. One might summarize the characteristic stages of development in a series of slogans. First: "We ought to be equal to you, our oppressors!" Second: "We really are equal to you, our oppressors!" Third: "We are superior to you and everyone else, though in comparison to such unfortunates as you, we are equal among ourselves!" Thus for nativist movements the doctrine of equality serves two purposes. It furnishes the ground for denying the out-group's claim of superiority. And it emphasizes similarities within the in-group, in order to distinguish the in-group from the out-group.

Nativism represents a twisted or idealized affirmation of the existing order, so twisted as to be genuinely revolutionary. Nevertheless, in its more developed form of a fanatical religious or secular patriotism, nativism is always tied to a particular group. In Germany it may take the form of National Socialism, while in Japan it appears in the guise of a revival of the imperial cult. In India it becomes Hindu or Islamic communalism, and in the United States 200 per cent Americanism.

Egalitarianism, on the other hand, generally represents a rejection and negation of the existing order. This fact may account for what appears to be its greater capacity for xenophilia. English egalitarianism

326

once looked to the French Revolution, while the French revolutionists looked to republican Rome, the Greek tyrannicides, or to an imaginary state of nature. About equalitarian movements among American Negroes it has often been observed that their center of gravity lies outside the Negro caste, and that they take their standards of behavior from the American middle class.

In contrast to nativism, egalitarianism represents a universal, though utopian, principle for the ordering of social relationships. For this reason its appeal can readily transcend national and religious boundaries. During the initial stages of political upheaval, this universal quality may constitute one of the strategic advantages of Communism over nativist forms of authoritarian rule, especially in Asia. However, as the super-patriotism of latter-day Stalinism demonstrates, once an egalitarian revolution acquires a territorial base and a vested interest in a particular social order, it may acquire the traits we have noticed in nativism.

As a program in its own right, egalitarianism by definition calls for the replacement of the status quo by a society in which the prevailing inequalities will be leveled out or perhaps merely reversed. It may take either a secular or a religious form, an attempt at the active reconstruction of the world or a withdrawal from it. Even in the latter instance, as in monasticism in both its Asiatic and Western forms, it may achieve considerable secular power. However, since the acquisition of power requires the development of hierarchy and discipline at some point, an egalitarian movement starts off at an initial disadvantage in relation to its competitors. Sooner or later, if it is to be effective, it must compromise with its initial principles. Christianity required several centuries to reach this compromise, while Marxism, especially in its Leninist version, reached this stage very rapidly.

Thus the quest for power is justified in terms of some larger scheme of values. For the early stages of a movement, therefore, it is probably always correct to assert that power is an instrumental value, something that is sought not in its own right, but to obtain something else. Very rapidly, however, power tends to become an ultimate value. The very fact that power is such a vital instrument in the pursuit of many other values tends to transform it, in the course of its acquisition, from a mere instrument to an end in itself. The process may be clearly observed in the rise of the Papacy and in Russian Marxism, as well as in many other movements.

In addition to providing a justification for the search for power, the charter myth usually contains at least rudimentary rules for the allocation of authority within the power-seekers' own organization. As part of such rules there is also some explicit or implicit provision designating what persons may interpret the doctrine in the future. Still another very significant aspect of the charter myth is the definition of membership in the group.

(1955)

Maurice Zinkin

74.

(1915-   )

An economist and former member of the Indian Civil Service discusses the impact of the Western idea of equality on Asian societies.

from Development for Free Asia

If Asia is to develop, it requires the talent, the effort, the innovations, the willingness to change and the capacity to lead, of all its people, women as well as men, religious minorities as well as religious majorities, untouchables as well as touchables, poor as well as rich. Asia's societies must become equal instead of hierarchic. Success must matter more than birth. Yet the advance to equality involves also great risks. The old leadership may be destroyed before new leaders arise. The rich may cease to take risks before the poor have learnt that risks must be taken. And whilst equality once achieved is a great solvent of social tension, the quarrels on the way can lead all too easily to class war. Equality may be the only path up the mountain of riches; but it is a path beset by precipices on every side.

Ever since the French Revolution the desire for equality has been Europe's major political fact. In the last sixty or seventy years it has also become the dominant political fact in Asia.

The urge to be equal did not indeed begin with the French Revolution. It was asserted in the American Revolution, in the English Civil War, and by the sixteenth-century Anabaptists. It is perhaps in the long run an inevitable political consequence of the Christian belief that all men are brothers. Since all are equal in the eyes of God, it has always required a rather gymnastic form of philosophical reasoning to prove that men should not be equal in their own, so much lesser, eyes.

Only since the French Revolution, however, have all the political consequences of this revolutionary doctrine been ruthlessly drawn. Nineteenth-century European history is above all the story of the assertion of its equality by every group which had been suppressed, whether the suppressed group was religious or linguistic, national or economic, a sex or a class. Catholics, Nonconformists and Jews became the legal equals of Anglicans in England. Languages which had been beginning to die, like Slovene and Slovak in face of German and Magyar, were revived. Nationalities which had been thought forgotten or absorbed reasserted themselves, until the Irish became the key to English politics and the Hapsburgs spent their time fending off disintegration. The vote spread downwards from the large property owner to the small, and then to the man without any property at all. The institutions which defended the better-educated and the wealthier, like the English House of Lords or the Prussian system of Chambers, came under steadily more severe attack as the idea spread that every man has a right to a share in deciding his own political destiny, and that the right should no longer be confined to those with 'a stake in the country.' Under the influence of the Socialists from Owen to Proudhon, and still more of the Marxists, a large section of opinion began to argue that equality must mean not only political equality but also economic equality, or else the political equality itself would be unreal.

In country after country women began to stir and to demand the same rights as men. Finally, the society of Europe, until 1800 based almost entirely on class, has for the last 150 years been steadily dissolving its classes. The Communist countries have gone to extremes, first turning their class pyramid upside down and then creating a new class structure. But in countries like Norway and Sweden class distinction, except perhaps for differences in education, has almost disappeared; and for all Western countries the model is more and more the nearly classless society of the United States.

So short a summary necessarily does less than justice to the rich complication of Europe's recent history. No more is, however, perhaps necessary in order to use European history as a means of understanding what has been happening in Asia. Asia awakened to modern forms of political life only in the second half of the nineteenth century or later. 1867, the Restoration of the Emperor, might be an appropriate date for Japan, the early 1880s, Lord Ripon's viceroyalty, for India. Probably 1911, the Revolution against the Manchus, is the best date for China. The exact period is always arguable. One could, for example, push the Japanese date back to 1855, when the West first brought its force to bear on Japan, or push it forward to the 1890s, when Europe finally accepted Japan as a Western-style State.

Whatever particular dates are taken it is important that Asia's modern political life begins at a time when in Europe certain forms of equality were generally accepted as ideals, others were still being argued about, and none were yet applied. The acceptance of the ideas of religious, national, and political equality was widespread in the advanced countries of Europe by 1880; but it was still virtually impos-

sible for a Catholic or a Jew to be a Prussian General, the Magyars
showed no intention of giving any real political say to their Rumani-
ans or Slavs, and even the English agricultural labourer did not get
the vote until 1884. As for sex equality, class (or social) equality, and
economic equality, they were still in 1880 the ideas of an *avant
garde*. Shaw's *Pygmalion* has no point except in a society which takes
social inequality for granted, the British Labour movement did not
really begin till the 1890s, and John Stuart Mill was thought slightly
odd for advocating votes for women.

The Asian, as he became politically conscious, tended to accept
straightaway those ideals of equality which had been generally accepted in Europe, to accept rather more slowly those which were
accepted only by the European *avant garde* and to demand in all cases
that Europeans should be consistent in their ideas and apply them to
him as well as to themselves.

That does not mean that these ideas spread round Asia like wild-
fire. They could not be expected to, for in the form in which they were
to be politically important, they were European, not Asian, ideas,
though for some of them Asia had equivalents. Islam is classless, Chinese doctrine gave the people the right to revolt if the government was
bad, Hinduism and Buddhism are religiously completely tolerant.
These equivalents have sometimes made it much easier to accept particular Western ideas; the Indian secular state gets popular acceptance
because of Hindu tolerance; the Chinese Communists have been
helped by the respectability of revolution in China. But what has
mattered in Asian politics has mostly been not such Asian traditions,
but the various forms equality took in Western politics, perhaps because Asia has never had an organised political life in which the
ordinary citizen took part above the level of the village. Indigenous
Asian conceptions have occasionally been important for the resistance
against equality they have enabled privileged groups to put up. Islam
justifies the Pakistani Muslim in not treating Hindus quite as equals.
Caste made an overwhelmingly Brahmin leadership for long acceptable
in India. They have had no importance beyond that.

Because, therefore, the Western idea of equality had to be accepted
in its Western forms, its spread in Asia was very slow indeed. In order
to adopt a Western idea, a man must first be able to understand it. In
order to understand it he must know something of the cadre of concepts and institutions into which it fits. At the beginning, for the
first people who adopt the idea, this means a very high level of education indeed. They must be able to take themselves out of their own

world of ideas, and into a completely new one. That takes years, and great intellectual curiosity. Naturally it took over half a century from the British conquest of Bengal to the first great Westernizer, Ram Mohun Roy, another half century before Western ideas became commonplace even among the élite. Once, however, a Western idea does become commonplace among the élite, the process of absorbing it speeds up greatly, for the élite translates it into terms the rest of society can understand with relatively little effort and without having to understand the whole set of ideas of which the particular idea being translated forms only a part.

What the élite take over is therefore of crucial importance, for the rest of society does not go to the wellspring direct, but drinks from the élite's hands. What the élite has taken over has varied a good deal, but, with the exception of Japan, which is a rather special case, certain phenomena are common.

The idea of national equality has been accepted everywhere. There was a time when some people in Asia, like the lower classes in Europe, believed themselves inferior. That was the inevitable consequence of Europe's immense nineteenth-century bound ahead. But nobody likes considering himself inferior. Asians very soon learnt to use against Europe the European notion of the nation and its rights. This idea, more than any purely Asian reaction, has been behind the Asian nationalist movements, and it explains the passionate Asian suspicion of colonialism. It explains, too, why it is that the different layers of Asian society have normally become nationalist only when they have become Western educated, or at least susceptible to the influence of the Western educated. So deep has the idea of national equality gone that Asians do not even conduct their quarrels amongst themselves in terms of superiority and inferiority. The Japanese never thought of the Chinese, nor do the Pakistani think of the Indians, as inferiors in the way so many nineteenth-century Englishmen thought of the Irish, or so many twentieth-century Germans thought of Poles and Jews.

The idea of equality between religions required very little acceptance. It came naturally to the countries of Hindu or Buddhist tradition, which are most of Asia, and for a time it found some acceptance amongst Muslims too. Now, however, Islam is reacting against an idea so alien to it, and in Pakistan especially there is an insistence on some superiority for the Muslim. The most important effect of the idea of religious equality was not, however, as between religions, but within each religion itself. Islam was already a brotherhood; all that has happened there is that the sense of the value of that brotherhood has been strengthened. In Hinduism, however, the doctrine that all men are equal before God has proved the major solvent of caste, until today caste is defended by habit, or by the vague feeling that people of other castes are 'different,' or by the prejudices of grandmother, but is rarely defended philosophically, as an institution. Caste has, it is true, rather little Vedic sanction; but temple entry for untouchables, indeed the whole fierce campaign against untouchability, comes less from the feeling that caste is the result of a misinterpretation of the scriptures than from a now widespread sense that it is wrong to treat one man as religiously inferior to another.

The third idea which was generally accepted in nineteenth-century Europe, and is equally generally accepted in non-Communist twentieth-century Asia, is that of political equality. One person, one vote, is the usual rule of independent Asia; and there have been few attempts to complicate the issue with special representation for businessmen or landowners, property-owners or university graduates. Where some section of the community is disfranchised, as with most Indians in Ceylon, it is because they are alleged not to be citizens; where representation is gerrymandered against them, as with caste Hindus in Pakistan, it is because they are suspected of being disloyal citizens. And both phenomena are rare in the extreme. Equally, where there is special representation, as for teachers in Indian upper houses, it is a gesture of respect. It does not affect the seat of power.

Asia has thus accepted whole-heartedly the three forms of equality which were generally accepted, at least in theory, in nineteenth-century Europe. Asia has also tended to accept with less question than Europe itself the three forms of equality—sex equality, social equality, and economic equality—which were the subject of fierce controversy in nineteenth-century Europe. But, whereas national equality, religious equality and political equality are today in Asia on the whole facts, these three other forms of equality which require social as well as legislative changes to establish them, are still on the whole only aspirations. It is true that aspirations which are generally accepted come nearer and nearer to being facts with every decade in which they remain accepted; and this is happening in Asia. But each of these three has in general in Asia a considerable way to go.

Politically, sex equality is the rule. Women have the vote, and women are coming out into public life. There are women ministers, and women ambassadors, and women civil servants. Socially, it is not yet so general. In the Buddhist countries there is no difficulty. Women have always been virtually their men's equals. In Communist China, sex equality is being enforced as part of the Communist creed. In India, the Constitution lays down the equality of women, and Hindu law has been changed to prohibit polygamy, and to give women the rights of property, guardianship and divorce without which it is much harder for wives to be the equals of husbands, or daughters of sons. But it is still the exception for women to work, and a change in property rights for which the village woman has not herself clamoured may well take a generation to affect her position. In Pakistan and the countries of the Middle East, the battle against purdah and polygamy and the unilateral right to divorce of the husband goes slowly. Women do not always object to any of these three; purdah can be a protection, polygamy valued for its company; the husband's right to divorce may be used when it is the wife who wants the divorce. But all effectively prevent sex equality. No wife can be equal whose knowledge of the world depends upon her husband, or who is always afraid that too violent a disagreement may drive her husband to divorce or a second wife. On the other hand, in all the Islamic countries, the woman's property rights have always been very considerable. If she had the man's education and freedom, there would be no economic bar to her equality.

Social equality is, on the whole, more widespread in Asia than in Europe. In general, in Asia, every position is open to anybody who acquires the qualifications, and in practice equality is limited not by anybody's prejudices, but by the limitations of the educational systems, which make it difficult for many people to acquire the qualifications. Today in most of Asia it is not very important who a man's grandfather was. In the ex-colonial countries most of the positions of power and prestige are inevitably held by new men, for until recently they were held by foreigners; and in every country, even Japan, it was not the sons of great houses who learnt the new techniques which give position in the modern world, but middle and lower class boys. Samurai, not daimyo, ran Meiji Japan; the Indian Army is not officered with the sons of princes and great landowners. Lately, moreover, the great houses have in several countries been further diminished in importance by land reform and by their having supported the colonial power (in Japan the pre-war regime), while in the Communist countries, China and North Vietnam, to have had a grandfather is a sin to be expiated. The great landowner is indeed still a force in the Islamic countries, but there the social consequences are greatly mitigated by the classlessness of Islam. Even caste, which to the European eye often seems to be the class society at its most rigid, is in fact something very different, for it divides society into a series of sections within each of which class has much less force than in Europe. It is, for example, usually more important in deciding whether a man is suitable to become a connection by marriage to know whether he is a Brahman or a Mahratta than to know whether he is a High Court judge or a clerk.

A class structure is indeed beginning to form in Asia, based on Western education, power and money. There are senses in which generals, secretaries to Government and big industrialists rank well above sergeant-majors, clerks and shopkeepers. Whereas in Europe, however, it is customary for a man in a particular class to have his relations in or near that class, in Asia the general's cousins may very well be sergeants, or, more likely still, small peasants. Given time, the situation would doubtless stabilise itself into a class structure, as the general's sons and nephews become officers in their turn, and the village relations become increasingly remote. But the time is not being given. Equality of opportunity is being incorporated more and more into Asian institutions and there are not enough particularly good schools and highly educated mothers to give one whole range of children the advantages the children of the professional classes have in Europe. In twenty years' time it is likely that only Communist China with its party members and its privileged artists and technicians will be a class society.

Asia has, therefore, to face the demand for economic equality—the most important form of equality from the development point of view—without any of Europe's natural defences. Its countries either have no aristocracy, or their aristocracies no longer count. Asia's only approach to a Churchill or a de Gaulle was Pakistan's Liaquat Ali Khan; and he has had no successor. Asia also has no entrenched professional class, able to justify its position by its intelligence and hard work, and willing to use the hold it has on all society's main levers of power in order to defend itself. Asia's professionals are still individuals rather than a class; and these individuals are far more likely to feel guilty about being better-off than other people than to look upon themselves as the carriers of their society's civilisation entitled to a certain level of material ease as a pre-requisite for the proper fulfilment of their function.

In the ex-colonial countries there is yet another obstacle to any real resistance to the demand for economic equality. In the European countries which governed Asia, the demand for independence for the colonies was on the whole supported by the parties of the Left and re-

sisted by the parties of the Right. The Right's reasons were often idealistic; they believed European government was good for Asia. The Left's
reasons were sometimes material; they believed the possession of colonies made it easier for their own governing classes to exploit them.
With these niceties, however, the Asian seeking independence did not
concern himself. One side, as he saw it, told him that he was quite
capable of looking after himself, and that his backwardness was due to
his being exploited by others. The other side, as he understood them,
told him that, left to himself, he would descend into anarchy, and
that his backwardness was due to his own ignorance, unteachability,
and passion for procreation. Naturally, he did not hesitate much in
choosing his side; moreover, those who did hesitate, who were not quite
so sure that independence was a panacea, who fifty years ago were very
important, have been discredited by the mere fact that independence
has been achieved. Naturally, ex-colonial Asia is run mainly by men
of the Left or semi-Left. In India and Burma, for example, to be a
Socialist is *de rigueur* even for conservatives. Even in the countries
where it is not quite so necessary to be Socialist, like Pakistan or the
Philippines, there is no economic conservative doctrine, only a religious
one. Economic equality may in fact be resisted, but there is no theory
behind the resistance; and resistance without a theory tends in the long
run to be surprisingly weak.

Partly as a result of this lack of resistance, but also because of
Asia's poverty and the past great inequality of its incomes, economic
equality tends to mean levelling down, which is frequently bad for
development, rather than levelling up, which is always good for development. In the West, levelling down through progressive taxation,
death duties and the opening of all walks of life to talent, has been less
important than the levelling up achieved by improving education,
housing, health and above all the productivity of the poor. In the
United States and Scandinavia, the most economically equal of all
Western societies, the levelling has been overwhelmingly up. Levelling
up, however, is a slow process. It has been going on in the West certainly since 1870, in some countries longer still.

Asia cannot wait so long. It is true that it is doing some levelling
up. All its plans, all its economic development, all its new educational
and health and agricultural extension schemes must result in a certain amount of levelling up. They will, however, require years to take
noticeable effect.

Asian electorates demand something more spectacular. That means
levelling down. Therefore, there has been widespread land reform in

Japan, in India, in Burma, as well as in China, a land reform that has not merely abolished big landlords, but also what in Europe would be quite small farmers. Therefore, Japan and India and Pakistan have income taxation systems amongst the world's most severe. Therefore, Ceylon and Indonesia and increasingly Malaya tax their plantations to a level at which they run the risk of depriving them of the necessary capital for expansion. In Indonesia, indeed, the risk has already become an accomplished fact. Therefore, too, one of the major urges behind State initiative in industrialisation is to prevent too many large fortunes being built up in the private sector.

For Asia, nowadays, the ideal is the small man.

(1956)

Sources

1. The Old Testament, King James Version. (Excerpts from Genesis, Deuteronomy, Job, Proverbs, Isaiah, Jeremiah, Amos, Micah, Malachi.)

2. Herodotus, *The History*, Book II, 80 (Loeb Classical Library, Vol. 2, pp. 106-107); Book V, 78 (Vol. 3, p. 87). New York: G. P. Putnam's Sons, 1922. Reprinted by permission of Harvard University Press from Loeb Classical Library translation of *The History of Herodotus*, translated by A. D. Godley.

3. Euripides, *The Phoenician Maidens*, Vol. 3, pp. 387-388; *The Suppliants*, Vol. 3, pp. 535-537. New York: The Macmillan Company, 1912. Reprinted by permission of Harvard University Press from Loeb Classical Library translation of Euripides, translated by A. S. Way.

4. Thucydides, *History of the Peloponnesian War*. Excerpt from "Funeral Oration" of Pericles reprinted from *Fountainheads of Freedom*, by Irwin Edman and Herbert W. Schneider, pp. 204-205. New York: Reynal & Hitchcock, 1941. Used by permission of Harcourt, Brace and Company, Inc., publishers.

5. Isocrates, *Areopagiticus*, Vol. 2, pp. 115-117, 143. New York: G. P. Putnam's Sons, 1929. Reprinted by permission of Harvard University Press from Loeb Classical Library translation of Isocrates, translated by George Norlin.

6. Plato, *The Republic*, Book V. Jowett translation, pp. 142-150. Oxford: The Clarendon Press, 1888.

7. Aristotle, *The Politics*, Bk. V, ch. 1; Bk. VI, chs. 2, 3; Bk. VII, ch. 14. Modern Library Edition, pp. 209-212, 260-263, 307-308. New York: Random House, Inc., 1943. Jowett translation used by permission of Oxford University Press, Inc.

8. Cicero, *De Re Publica, De Legibus*, Bk. III, XXII, and Bk. I, X-XIII. New York: G. P. Putnam's Sons, 1928. Reprinted by permission of Harvard University Press from Loeb Classical Library translation of Cicero, *The Republic* (p. 211) and *Laws* (pp. 329-337), translated by C. W. Keyes.

9. Seneca, "On Benefits," Book III, 18, 20, 28. In Seneca's *Moral Essays*, Vol. 3, pp. 161, 165, 177-179. Cambridge: Harvard University Press, 1935. Reprinted by permission of the publishers from Loeb Classical Library translation of Seneca, *Moral Essays*, translated by John W. Bassore.

10. The New Testament, King James Version. (Excerpts from Matthew, Acts, Romans, First Corinthians, Galatians, Colossians, James, First Epistle of John.) Revised Standard Version of James 2:1-9, copyright 1946 by Division of Christian Education of the National Council of the Churches of Christ in the United States of America.

11. "Wisdom from the Gemara," in *The Wisdom of Israel*, edited by Lewis Browne, Modern Library Edition, pp. 190-191. Random House, Inc., 1945, 1956. Used by permission of Rabbi Louis I. Newman, co-compiler with Samuel Spitz of *The Talmudic Anthology*, published by Behrman's Jewish Book House, New York, 1946.

12. Cyprian, "On Works and Alms" (Treatise VIII), in *The Ante-Nicene Fathers*, edited by A. Roberts and J. Donaldson, Vol. 5, p. 483. New York: Charles Scribner's Sons, 1899. By permission.
Cyprian, "Ad Demetrianum," in *On the Government of God*, edited by E. M.

Sanford, p. 87. New York: Columbia University Press, 1930. Reprinted by permission of the publishers.

13. Lactantius, *The Divine Institutes*, in *Works of Lactantius*, translated by William Fletcher, Vol. VII, Bk. V, pp. 150-151. New York: The Christian Literature Company, 1886; Charles Scribner's Sons, 1925. By permission.

14. St. Benedict of Nursia, *The Rule of St. Benedict*, in *Documents of the Christian Church*, edited by Henry Bettenson, pp. 169-170. New York and London: Oxford University Press, 1943, 1956. Used by permission.

15. St. Gregory the Great, *The Book of Pastoral Rule*, Part III, Ch. V, in *Nicene and Post-Nicene Fathers of the Christian Church*, edited by Schaff and Wace, Second Series, Vol. XII, pp. 27-28. Oxford and London: Parker & Company, 1895; Grand Rapids: Wm. B. Eerdmans Publishing Co., 1956. Used by permission.

16. Thomas Aquinas, *The Summa Contra Gentiles*, Book III, Part II, Ch. CXVII. London: Burns, Oates & Washbourne, Ltd., 1929. Reprinted by permission.

17. Walther von der Vogelweide, "My Brother Man" in *I Saw the World*, translated by Ian G. Colvin. London: Edward Arnold (Publishers), Ltd., 1938. Quoted in *The Portable Medieval Reader*, edited by J. B. Ross and M. M. McLaughlin. New York: The Viking Press, Inc., 1949. Reprinted by permission of Edward Arnold, Ltd.

18. William Langland, "Piers Plowman's Protest." From *The Vision of Piers Plowman*, in the modern English version of Henry M. Wells (pp. 98, 114, 141, 211, 269-270, 199-201). Published by Sheed and Ward, Inc., New York, 1935. Reprinted by permission.

19. Marsilius of Padua, *The Defender of Peace*, Vol. II, translated by Alan Gewirth, pp. 47-48. New York: Columbia University Press, 1956. Reprinted by permission of the publishers.

20. Nicholas of Cusa, *De Concordantia Catholica*, Book II, Ch. 14. From Ewart Lewis, *Medieval Political Ideas*, Vol. I, p. 192. (Translated from Schard, *De Jurisdictione . . . ,* pp. 465-676.) New York: Alfred A. Knopf, Inc., 1954. Used by permission.

21. Desiderius Erasmus, *The Education of a Christian Prince*, translated by Lester K. Born, pp. 177-178. New York: Columbia University Press, 1936. Reprinted by permission of the publishers.

22. Martin Luther, *A Treatise Concerning the Blessed Sacrament*, in *Works of Martin Luther*, The Philadelphia Edition, Vol. II, pp. 10-17. Philadelphia: Muhlenberg Press, 1943. Used by permission.

23. Francisco Suarez, "On Laws and God the Lawgiver," in *The Classics of International Law*, No. 20, edited by James Brown Scott, Vol. II, p. 117. Oxford: The Clarendon Press, 1944. Used by permission of Carnegie Endowment for International Peace.

24. Samuel Rutherford, *Lex, Rex*, in *Puritanism and Liberty*, edited by A. S. P. Woodhouse, pp. 200-203, 205-207. London: J. M. Dent & Sons, Ltd., 1938, 1950. Used by permission of The University of Chicago Press.

25. John Lilburne, *The Free-man's Freedom Vindicated*, in *Puritanism and Liberty*, edited by A. S. P. Woodhouse, pp. 317-318. London: J. M. Dent & Sons, Ltd., 1938, 1950. Used by permission of The University of Chicago Press.

26. "An Agreement of the People, for a firm and present Peace, upon grounds of Common-Right," in *Leveller Manifestoes of the Puritan Revolution*, edited by

Don M. Wolfe, pp. 226-228. New York: Thomas Nelson and Sons, 1944. Used by permission.

27. From *The Putney Debates,* in *Puritanism and Liberty,* edited by A. S. P. Woodhouse, pp. 52-72. London: J. M. Dent & Sons, Ltd., 1938, 1950. Reprinted by permission of The University of Chicago Press.

28. From "The Humble Petition of Divers Well-Affected Women of the Cities of London and Westminster, the Borough of Southwark, Hamblets and Parts Adjacent." Reprinted in *Puritanism and Liberty,* edited by A. S. P. Woodhouse, pp. 367-369, 490(a). London: J. M. Dent & Sons, Ltd., 1938, 1950. Used by permission of The University of Chicago Press.

29. Anonymous, "More Light Shining in Buckingham-shire," as reprinted in the appendix of *The Works of Gerrard Winstanley,* edited by George H. Sabine, pp. 627-628, 633-634, 638-639. Ithaca: Cornell University Press, 1941. By permission.

30. Thomas Hobbes, *Leviathan,* Part I, Ch. XIII, p. 94. Reprinted from the Edition of 1651. Oxford: The Clarendon Press, 1909, 1947. Used by permission.

31. Gerrard Winstanley, *The Law of Freedom in a Platform* in *The Works of Gerrard Winstanley,* edited by George H. Sabine, pp. 506-512 (from the Dedicatory Epistle to Oliver Cromwell). Ithaca: Cornell University Press, 1941. By permission.

32. George Fox, "To The Protector and Parliament of England," pp. 14-15. Copied from the original pamphlet in the McAlpin Collection, Union Theological Seminary in New York.

33. John Locke, *The Second Treatise on Civil Government,* Sections 4-8, 54-55, 87-89, 95-97, 123. Oxford: Basil Blackwell, Publishers, 1946. Used by permission.

34. John Wise, "A Vindication of the Government of New England Churches," in Bernard Smith, *The Democratic Spirit,* Second Edition, revised, pp. 20-26. New York: Alfred A. Knopf, Inc., 1943. By permission.

35. John Woolman, *The Journal of John Woolman,* edited by Thomas S. Kepler, pp. 54-57. New York: The World Publishing Company, 1954. Used by permission.

36. Thomas Jefferson (et al.), "The Declaration of Independence" (as adopted by Congress July 4, 1776), in *The Papers of Thomas Jefferson,* edited by Julian P. Boyd, Vol. I (1760-1776), pp. 429-432. Princeton, N. J.: Princeton University Press, 1950. Used by permission.

37. Thomas Jefferson, "A Letter to Rev. James Madison," in *The Papers of Thomas Jefferson,* edited by Julian P. Boyd, Vol. 8 (25 February to 31 October 1785), pp. 681-682. Princeton, N. J.: Princeton University Press, 1953. Used by permission.

38. Immanuel Kant, *The Fundamental Principles of the Metaphysics of Morals,* found in Irwin Edman and Herbert W. Schneider, *Fountainheads of Freedom,* Part Two, pp. 401-403. New York: Reynal & Hitchcock, Inc., 1941. Used by permission of Harcourt, Brace and Company, Inc., publishers.

39. "Declaration of the Rights of Man and of the Citizen," in Edman and Schneider, *Fountainheads of Freedom,* Part Two, pp. 404-406. New York: Reynal & Hitchcock, Inc., 1941. Used by permission of Harcourt, Brace and Company, Inc., publishers.

40. John Adams, "A Letter to Thomas Brand-Hollis," in *The Works of John Adams,* edited by Charles Francis Adams, Vol. IX, pp. 569-571. Boston: Little, Brown and Company, 1854.

41. Thomas Paine, *The Rights of Man,* in *The Writings of Thomas Paine,* edited

by M. D. Conway, Vol. II, pp. 304-307. New York: G. P. Putnam's Sons, 1892. Used by permission of the publisher.

42. Georg Wilhelm Friedrich Hegel, "The Positivity of the Christian Religion," in G. W. F. Hegel, *Early Theological Writings,* translated by T. M. Knox, pp. 88-89. Chicago: University of Chicago Press, 1948. Copyright 1948 by the University of Chicago. Used by permission.

43. Jeremy Bentham, "Principles of the Civil Code," in *The Theory of Legislation,* edited by C. K. Ogden, pp. 103-109. London: Routledge & Kegan Paul, Ltd., 1931, 1950. Used by permission.

44. Thomas Skidmore, *The Rights of Man to Property, Being a Proposition to Make It Equal Among the Adults of the Present Generation.* Excerpt taken from *The Making of American Democracy,* Readings and Documents, edited by Ray A. Billington, B. J. Loewenberg, and S. H. Brockunier, Vol. I, pp. 249-251. New York: Rinehart and Company, Inc., 1950. By permission.

45. William Ellery Channing, "Honor Due to All Men," in *The Democratic Spirit,* edited by Bernard Smith, pp. 239-243. New York: Alfred A. Knopf, Inc., 1941. By permission.

46. Alexis de Tocqueville, *Democracy in America,* the Henry Reeve text, edited by Phillips Bradley, Vol. II, pp. 94-97, 138-139, 181-182. (Available also in the Vintage Edition.) New York: Alfred A. Knopf, Inc., 1945. By permission.

47. "The Seneca Falls Declaration of Sentiments," in *History of Woman Suffrage,* edited by Elizabeth Cady Stanton, Susan B. Anthony, and Matilda Joslyn Gage, pp. 70-71. Reprinted from T. V. Smith, *The American Philosophy of Equality,* Appendix A, pp. 327-331, by permission of The University of Chicago Press. Copyright 1927 by The University of Chicago Press, Chicago, Ill.

48. Abraham Lincoln, from speeches in *The Life and Writings of Abraham Lincoln,* edited by Philip Van Doren Stern, Modern Library Edition, pp. 422-423 (address delivered at Springfield, June 26, 1857); 463-464 (debate with Douglas, August 21, 1858); 592 (address delivered at New Haven, March 6, 1860). New York: Random House, Inc., 1942. By permission.

49. Henry J. S. Maine, *Ancient Law,* pp. 88-92. New York: Henry Holt and Company, 1864, 1875.

50. John Stuart Mill, *Utilitarianism,* in Edwin A. Burtt, *The English Philosophers from Bacon to Mill,* Modern Library Edition, pp. 932-933, 945-947. New York: Random House, Inc., 1939. By permission.

51. Karl Marx, "Criticism of the Gotha Program," in *Capital and Other Writings,* edited by Max Eastman, Modern Library Edition, pp. 3, 5-7. New York: Random House, Inc., 1932. Used by permission.

52. Friedrich Engels, *Anti-Dühring,* in E. Burns, *Handbook of Marxism,* pp. 249-254. New York: Random House, Inc., 1935. Used by permission of International Publishers, New York.

53. Henry George, *Progress and Poverty,* pp. 475-478, 479, 489-490. New York: D. Appleton and Company, 1883.

54. Franz Boas, *The Mind of Primitive Man,* pp. 17-29, 268-278. New York: The Macmillan Company, 1911. Used by permission.

55. Louis D. Brandeis, "On Industrial Relations," in Brandeis, *The Curse of Bigness,* pp. 72-74, 78-79. New York: The Viking Press, Inc., 1934. By permission.

56. Harold J. Laski, *A Grammar of Politics,* pp. 152-160, 161-164. New Haven: Yale University Press, 1925. Used by permission.

57. R. H. Tawney, *Equality*, excerpts from pp. 40-56, 61-62. London: George Allen & Unwin, Ltd., 1931. Used by permission.

58. E. F. Carritt, *Morals and Politics*, Ch. XIII, pp. 198-201. London: Oxford University Press, 1935. Used by permission.

59. Otto Klineberg, *Race Differences*, pp. 152-155, 162-164, 174-176, 182-189. New York: Harper & Brothers, 1935. Reprinted by permission of author and publisher.

60. *Norris* v. *Alabama,* in U. S. Reports, Vol. 294, *Cases Adjudged in the Supreme Court,* pp. 588-599 (capitalization changed slightly). Washington: U. S. Government Printing Office, 1935. (Available also in MacDonald, Webb, Lewis and Strauss, *Outside Readings in American Government,* pp. 139-143. Crowell, 1949.)

61. John Dewey, "Democracy and Educational Administration," in *School and Society,* Vol. 45 (April 3, 1937), pp. 458-459. By permission of *School and Society.*

62. Walter T. Stace, *The Concept of Morals*, pp. 176-179. New York: The Macmillan Company, 1937. Reprinted by permission of Walter T. Stace.

63. *Missouri ex rel. Gaines* v. *Canada, Registrar of the University of Missouri, et al.,* in U. S. Reports, Vol. 305, *Cases Adjudged in the Supreme Court,* pp. 342-352. Washington: U. S. Government Printing Office, 1939.

64. Jacques Maritain, *Ransoming the Time*, pp. 17-31. From *Ransoming the Time* by Jacques Maritain, copyright 1941 by Charles Scribner's Sons. Reprinted by permission of the publisher. Acknowledgment is also made to Geoffrey Bles Ltd., London, publishers of the volume under the title *Redeeming the Time*.

65. Ralph Barton Perry, *Puritanism and Democracy,* pp. 551-556, 572-575. Reprinted by permission of the publishers, The Vanguard Press, from *Puritanism and Democracy* by Ralph Barton Perry. Copyright, 1944, by Ralph Barton Perry.

66. Gunnar Myrdal, *An American Dilemma*, Vol. I, pp. 578-582. New York: Harper & Brothers, 1944. Reprinted by permission of the publisher.

67. Robert Redfield, "Race and Religion in Selective Admission," in *Journal of the American Association of Collegiate Registrars* (now *College & University*), Vol. 21 (July, 1946), pp. 527-540. Reprinted by permission of *College & University.*

68. Emil Brunner, *Christianity and Civilization*, pp. 116-121. From *Christianity and Civilization* by Emil Brunner, copyright 1948 by Charles Scribner's Sons. Reprinted by permission of the publisher. World rights, except in America, by courtesy of James Nisbet and Company, Ltd., Hertfordshire, England.

69. Harry S. Truman, "Message on Civil Rights" in New York *Times,* February 3, 1948. (Available also in MacDonald, Webb, Lewis and Strauss, *Outside Readings in American Government,* pp. 147-155. Crowell, 1949.)

70. "Universal Declaration of Human Rights," approved December 7, 1948, by the Social Committee of the United Nations General Assembly. L. Garvin, *A Modern Introduction to Ethics,* pp. 555-560. Boston: Houghton Mifflin Co., 1953.

71. Reinhold Niebuhr, *Faith and History*, pp. 189-195. From *Faith and History* by Reinhold Niebuhr, copyright 1949 by Charles Scribner's Sons. Reprinted by permission of the publisher. World rights, except in America, by courtesy of James Nisbet and Company, Ltd., Hertfordshire, England.

72. *Brown et al.* v. *Board of Education et al.,* in U. S. Reports, Vol. 347, *Cases Adjudged in the Supreme Court,* pp. 483-496. Washington: U. S. Government Printing Office, 1954.

73. Barrington Moore, Jr., "Notes on the Process of Acquiring Power," in *World Politics,* Vol. VIII, No. 1 (October, 1955), pp. 8-10. By permission of *World Politics.*

74. Maurice Zinkin, *Development for Free Asia*, pp. 183-191. London: Chatto & Windus, Ltd., 1956. Reprinted by permission of Essential Books, Inc., New York.

Index